Who Wrote the Bible?

Richard Elliott Friedman

HarperSanFrancisco
An Imprint of HarperCollins*Publishers*

First PERENNIAL LIBRARY edition published in 1989.

Maps by Ozzie Grief

HarperCollins Web Site: http://www.harpercollins.com
HarperCollins®, ▆®, and HarperSanFrancisco™ are trademarks of HarperCollins Publishers Inc.

Library of Congress Cataloging-in-Publication Data

Friedman, Richard Elliott.
    Who wrote the Bible? / Richard Elliott Friedman.
    Bibliography: p.
    Includes index.
    ISBN 0–06–063035–3 (pbk.)
    1. Bible. O.T. Pentateuch—Authorship. 2. Bible. O.T. Historical books—
Authorship. 3. Bible. O.T. Pentateuch—Criticism, interpretation, etc. 4. Bible.
O.T. Historical books—Criticism, interpretation, etc. 5. Documentary hypothesis
(Pentateuchal criticism) I. Title.
[BS1225.2.F75   1989]
222'.1066—dc19   88-45648

97 98 99 00 01 RRD/H 10 9 8 7 6 5 4 3 2 1

This book is dedicated to
Reva A. Friedman and Laraine Friedman Linn,
with love.

Contents

PREFACE TO THE SECOND EDITION   9

PREFACE   13

INTRODUCTION: *Who Wrote the Bible?*   15

CHAPTER 1
The World That Produced the Bible: 1200–722 B.C.   33

CHAPTER 2
J and E   50

CHAPTER 3
Two Kingdoms, Two Writers   70

CHAPTER 4
The World That Produced the Bible: 722–587 B.C.   89

CHAPTER 5
In the Court of King Josiah   101

CHAPTER 6
D   117

CHAPTER 7
A Priest in Exile   136

CHAPTER 8
The World That Produced the Bible: 587–400 B.C.   150

CHAPTER 9
A Brilliant Mistake   161

CHAPTER 10
The Sacred Text   174

8 *Contents*

CHAPTER 11
The Sacred Text   188

CHAPTER 12
In the Court of King Hezekiah   207

CHAPTER 13
The Great Irony   217

CHAPTER 14
The World That the Bible Produced   234

APPENDIX
Identification of Authors of the Five Books of Moses   246
Notes on Identification of Authors   256

NOTES   261

SELECTED BIBLIOGRAPHY   277

ACKNOWLEDGMENTS   284

INDEX   287

MAPS   301

Preface to the Second Edition

IT HAS BEEN ten years since I finished this book. Some interesting developments have occurred since then, and it is also interesting to observe some things that did *not* happen. Notably, I had feared that many of my colleagues in the field of biblical scholarship might dismiss the book as "popular"—the ultimate condemnation in the academic world. But that has generally not been the case. It has been cited and quoted, it is assigned in classes at universities and seminaries, and colleagues have been extremely complimentary and encouraging in comments and letters. In this second edition, I want to express my gratitude to my colleagues for the treatment they have accorded this book. As I indicated in the original preface ten years ago, I believe that this knowledge is important to a much larger community than just scholars and clergy. My aim was not to write a "popular" book but rather an *accessible* one, to open this knowledge up to anyone who wanted to learn about it, and to show why it is so valuable and interesting. The original American and British editions carried on their covers endorsements from scholars at major universities and Christian and Jewish seminaries in order to convey to both scholars and laypersons that this was in fact accessible scholarship on the Bible and not a watered-down popularization of fringe theories.

There have been exceptions, of course. For those colleagues who have felt free to dismiss this presentation, my ego can take it if they choose not to cite this book because of its style. But it would be a shame if they failed to come to terms with the evidence and the arguments that are contained here. For those who do not feel obligated to address works that are "popular," there are my more "academic" publications, and I have now assembled the data in the traditional, unembellished manner of scholarship in my entries in the *Anchor Bible Dictionary*. The entry on "Torah," in particular, is meant to be the largest collection of evidence to date in support of the hypothesis.

Another development had been anticipated but did not occur: there has been surprisingly little polemic. A very positive article on the front page of the *Wall Street Journal* spoke of how this book was bringing the scholarly debate into the public arena and foresaw considerable controversy. A story in *U.S. News and World Report* said that this book "promises to rekindle heated debate about the Good Book's origins." And a rather more inflammatory article in the London *Sunday Times* predicted, "The religious world is about to be rocked." But the response on the whole has been much kinder than expected—again with a few exceptions. Though this book presents the results of critical biblical scholarship, which challenge traditional beliefs about the Bible's authorship, many pious fundamentalist Christians and orthodox Jews have shown great courtesy and have behaved graciously. I hope that this is because I do not present these things as an attack or a breaking-down, nor does this book reflect a lack of appreciation and reverence for the Bible. Anyone who cites this book in order to support such an attack is abusing the book and missing the point. The first and last pages of this book recognize the greatness of the Bible, its beauty and its power. What comes in between is a picture of how critical biblical scholarship accounts for this greatness. Years ago I studied in a class that was taught by an extremely pious orthodox rabbi, a gentle soul who came to teach people who were not orthodox like himself. When a student in the class declared, "I disagree," the rabbi said, "That's what I learned in this place: that I can sit with people with whom I disagree and study together." We can all learn from him that people can disagree strongly in matters of religion and still not be enemies.

One point in this book that did give birth to some controversy was the suggestion I made that one of the biblical writers in particular (the author of the text known among scholars as "J") may have been a woman. This became a subject of much debate as other scholars, drawing on my research, latched onto this idea. I would just warn that I proposed this tentatively and cautiously. I thought, and still think, that biblical scholars had made an error in too easily assuming that the authors of these biblical books were male. Determining, if possible, if the writer was male or female seems to me to be at least as important as determining whether the author was a priest or layperson, upper or lower class, or from the eighth century B.C. or the fifth. Nonetheless, I was saying only that we must fairly recognize this possibility. Those who borrowed this idea and blew it up from a possibility into a major conclusion have enjoyed the fruits of temporary publicity but have not helped us to advance our knowledge of the subject.

I must acknowledge that, since the time when I began this research, some of the unanimity of the field has broken down. The model of biblical authorship that has dominated this field for the past hundred years has been challenged by scholars—especially in Germany; to a lesser extent in the United States—who date the biblical authors later and later. They claim to have thrown the field into disarray. Now, I am open to challenging dominant models. I myself oppose the majority view regarding much of the Five Books of Moses in the last chapters of this book. But I have debated the leading proponents of these new challenges from the United States and Germany in print and in a public session. Besides my criticism of their arguments, my main point in our public debate and to this day is that they have never come to terms with all the evidence that made this the dominant model in the first place. The most powerful categories of this evidence that are described in this book are (1) the convergence of many different lines of evidence, (2) linguistic evidence for the dates of texts, (3) the narrative continuity of texts that are ascribed to particular authors, and (4) how well the texts match the history of the periods from which they come. As of the time that I am writing this, these scholars have rarely even mentioned these categories, much less confronted them. I shall deal with their cases further in a coming book, but for now I just want to note that they cannot be said to have presented a compelling challenge to classical biblical scholarship so long as they fail to respond to the core of the case for it.

In this period there has also been a load of less helpful publications, including some absurd computer studies, that most biblical scholars have considered not to be worth responding to. I have nonetheless dealt with some of them because I think that it is healthy to air these things and because I think that it is ironic that such ill-conceived analyses persist at the same time that advanced linguistic, literary, and historical research is going on. Those who are interested in such cases after reading this book can now turn to my treatment of them in a recent article.[1]

I should add that I have received many letters from readers whose curiosity was aroused on hundreds of points after reading this, and I was not able to answer so many inquiries. One important development since the first publication of this book is the appearance of the six-volume *Anchor Bible Dictionary*, edited by my distinguished colleague, David Noel Freedman. It is a splendid new resource, containing entries by scholars from many religious backgrounds and points of view. Of course some entries are more helpful than others, and one must read them critically, but the overall quality of the articles is high, and each entry includes a bibliography so that readers who are still not satisfied have some clues as to where to look next. So I am happy to have a new source of information to recommend to those whose reading of this book inspires new ideas and questions.

English translations of the Bible in this book are my own.

The most prominent (dramatic) change here from the first edition of this book is a major shift in my thinking about one of the writers of the Bible. Those who have read the first edition are likely to be surprised at the change I have made in my identification of this person in chapter 7.[2] I am avoiding saying the name here so as not to spoil the mystery for those who are reading this for the first time. To some the change may come as a disappointment, because the person whom I had originally identified is a prominent person in the Bible, but on the positive side this means that I am now more certain than before about the person whom I do think is the author—and the person whom I identified in the first edition is still very much in the picture, as you will see.

I have also made some changes in the identification of the authors of the Five Books of Moses that appears in the appendix at the end of the book. These changes are at least partly the result of my continuing to work through the text with my students and my superb colleagues at the University of California, and I acknowledge my debt to them.

These changes constitute refinements in a theory, which I believe make the theory stronger. If there are two things that scholars hate to say, they are "I was wrong" and "I don't know." Well, I was wrong about those particular identifications, and there are still parts of this mystery whose answer I don't know. But I find the theory to be sound, and I continue to delight in the process of refinement and new discoveries.

Above all, this book is meant to enhance people's appreciation of the Bible: to understand better the world in which it was born and how inextricably connected it was to that world; to appreciate the wonder of how it came together; to appreciate that literary study and historical study of the Bible are not enemies, or even alternatives to one another. Rather, they enrich one another. Whether one is a Christian or a Jew or from another religion or no religion, whether one is religious or not, the more one knows of the Bible the more one stands in awe of it.

Richard Elliott Friedman, 1996

1. "Some Recent Non-Arguments Concerning the Documentary Hypothesis," in Michael Fox et al., eds., *Texts, Temples, and Traditions*, Menahem Haran *Festschrift* (Winona Lake, IN: Eisenbrauns, 1996), pp. 87–101.

2. The detailed treatment of this appears in a recent article, "The Deuteronomistic School," in Astrid Beck et al., eds., *Fortunate the Eyes That See*, David Noel Freedman *Festschrift* (Grand Rapids, MI: Eerdmans, 1995), pp. 70–80.

Preface

THIS is a synthesis of the research that I have done during the past ten years. I have published individual components of this research in the academic journals and series publications within the field of biblical studies, but I have chosen to publish some of the more recent findings and the synthesis of the parts here in a mode that is more accessible to readers who are not specialists in the Bible. I have tried to avoid technical jargon and elaborate footnotes, and I have provided background explanations for readers who are new to this subject.

I chose to write in this mode simply because I sincerely believe that this subject is important to a wider circle of readers than just my colleagues in the field of biblical scholarship. The analysis of biblical authorship is referred to in almost any standard introduction to the Old or New Testament, in hundreds of commentaries on the Bible, and in most college and seminary courses on the Bible. But it still is not widely known or understood. This is all the more remarkable because this analysis is at least as relevant as issues of evolution and geological evidence for the age of the earth; yet every schoolchild has heard of these matters, while the discoveries regarding no less a matter than who wrote the Bible go unknown outside scholarly circles.

In part, this may be because these were not extraordinary individual discoveries like the Dead Sea Scrolls or Darwin's finds in the Galapagos. They were rather part of a long, painstaking search, assembling small pieces of an enormous puzzle over centuries. Few of these pieces were news in their day. But I think that we have finally completed enough of the puzzle to provide a picture of the writers of the Bible that will interest general readers and which I believe it is important to share with them.

INTRODUCTION

Who Wrote the Bible?

PEOPLE have been reading the Bible for nearly two thousand years. They have taken it literally, figuratively, or symbolically. They have regarded it as divinely dictated, revealed, or inspired, or as a human creation. They have acquired more copies of it than of any other book. It is quoted (and misquoted) more often than other books. It is translated (and mistranslated) more than the others as well. It is called a great work of literature, the first work of history. It is at the heart of Christianity and Judaism. Ministers, priests, and rabbis preach it. Scholars spend their lives studying and teaching it in universities and seminaries. People read it, study it, admire it, disdain it, write about it, argue about it, and love it. People have lived by it and died for it. And we do not know who wrote it.

It is a strange fact that we have never known with certainty who produced the book that has played such a central role in our civilization. There are traditions concerning who wrote each of the biblical books—the Five Books of Moses are supposed to be by Moses, the book of Lamentations by the prophet Jeremiah, half of the Psalms by King David—but how is one to know if these traditional ascriptions are correct?

Investigators have been working on the solution to this mystery for nearly a thousand years, and particularly in the last two centuries they have made extraordinary discoveries. Some of these discoveries challenge traditional beliefs. Still, this investigation did not develop as a controversy of religion versus science or religion versus the secular. On the contrary, most of the investigators were trained in religious traditions and knew the Bible as well as those who accepted only the traditional answers. Indeed, from the outset to the present day, a significant proportion of critical biblical scholars, perhaps the majority, have been, at the same time, members of the clergy. Rather, the effort to discover who wrote the Bible began and con-

15

tinued because the answer had significant implications for both the traditional and the critical study of the Bible.

It was the Bible, after all. Its influence on Western civilization—and subsequently on Eastern civilization—has been so pervasive that it has hardly been possible to recognize its impact, much less to accept its authority, without caring from where it came. If we think that the Bible is a great work of literature, then who were the artists? If we think of it as a source to be examined in the study of history, then whose reports are we examining? Who wrote its laws? Who fashioned the book out of a diverse collection of stories, poetry, and laws into a single work? If we encounter an author when we read a work, to whatever degree and be it fiction or nonfiction, then whom do we encounter when we read the Bible?

For most readers, it makes a difference, whether their interest in the book is religious, moral, literary, or historical. When a book is studied in a high school or university class, one usually learns something of the author's life, and generally this contributes to the understanding of the book. Apart from fairly advanced theoretical literary considerations, most readers seem to find it significant to be able to see connections between the author's life and the world that the author depicts in his or her work. In the case of fiction, most would find it relevant that Dostoyevsky was Russian, was of the nineteenth century, was an orthodox Christian of originally revolutionary opinions, and was epileptic and that epilepsy figures in important ways in *The Idiot* and in *The Brothers Karamazov*; or that Dashiell Hammett was a detective; or that George Eliot was a woman. Similarly in nonfiction, there appears to be no limit to the fascination people have with Freud the man and the degree to which his own experience is reflected in his writings; or with Nietzsche, where everything from his insanity to his relationship with Lou Salomé to his sometimes uncanny bond with Dostoyevsky figures in readings of his works.

The more obvious this seems, the more striking is the fact that this information has been largely lacking in the case of the Bible. Often the text cannot be understood without it. Did the author of a particular biblical story live in the eighth century B.C. or the fifth? —and thus when the author uses a particular expression do we understand it according to what it meant in the eighth century or the fifth? Did the author witness the events in the story? If not, how did the author come to have an idea of what happened? Was it through written sources, old family stories, divine revelation, completely fictional composition, or some other means? How much did the events of the author's own day affect the way in which the author told the story? Did the author write the work with the intent that it should become a sacred, authoritative text?

Such questions are important to understanding what the text meant in the biblical world itself. But they also offer an opportunity for producing a new and richer understanding of the book today, for both the religious and the nonreligious reader, once we come to know the persons and forces that produced it.

The Five Books of Moses

It is one of the oldest puzzles in the world. Investigators have been wrestling with it practically since the Bible was completed. As it happens, it did not start as an investigation into the authorship of the Bible. It simply began with individuals raising questions about problems that they observed in the biblical text itself. It proceeded like a detective story spread across centuries, with investigators uncovering clues to the Bible's origin one by one.

It began with questions about the first five books of the Bible: Genesis, Exodus, Leviticus, Numbers, and Deuteronomy. These books are known as the Pentateuch (from Greek, meaning "five scrolls") or the Torah (from Hebrew, meaning "instruction"). They are also known as the Five Books of Moses. Moses is the major figure through most of these books, and early Jewish and Christian tradition held that Moses himself wrote them, though nowhere in the Five Books of Moses themselves does the text say that he was the author.[1] But the tradition that one person, Moses, alone wrote these books presented problems. People observed contradictions in the text. It would report events in a particular order, and later it would say that those same events happened in a different order. It would say that there were two of something, and elsewhere it would say that there were fourteen of that same thing. It would say that the Moabites did something, and later it would say that it was the Midianites who did it. It would describe Moses as going to a Tabernacle in a chapter before Moses builds the Tabernacle.

People also noticed that the Five Books of Moses included things that Moses could not have known or was not likely to have said. The text, after all, gave an account of Moses' death. It also said that Moses was the humblest man on earth; and normally one would not expect the humblest man on earth to point out that he is the humblest man on earth.

At first the arguments of those who questioned Mosaic authorship were rejected. In the third century A.D. the Christian scholar Origen responded to those who raised objections to the unity and Mosaic authorship of the Pentateuch. The rabbis of the centuries that followed the completion of the Hebrew Bible (also known as the Old Testament or the Holy Scriptures) likewise explained the problems and contradictions within the boundaries of the tradition: contradictions were only apparent contradictions. They could be explained through interpretation—often very elaborate interpretation—or through the introduction of additional narrative details that did not appear in the biblical text. As for Moses' references to things that should have been unknown to him, they were explained as owing to the fact that Moses was a prophet. These tradition-oriented responses to the problems in the text prevailed into medieval times. The medieval biblical commentators, such as Rashi in France and Nachmanides in Spain, were especially skillful at seeking explanations to reconcile each of the contradictions. But, also in the medieval period, investigators began to give a new kind of answer to the old questions.

Six Hundred Years of Investigation

At the first stage, investigators still accepted the tradition that Moses wrote the Five Books, but they suggested that a few lines were added here or there. In the eleventh century, Isaac ibn Yashush, a Jewish court physician of a ruler in Muslim Spain, pointed out that a list of Edomite kings that appears in Genesis 36 named kings who lived long after Moses was dead. Ibn Yashush suggested that the list was written by someone who lived after Moses. The response to his conclusion was that he was called "Isaac the blunderer."

The man who labeled him Isaac the blunderer was Abraham ibn Ezra, a twelfth-century Spanish rabbi. Ibn Ezra added, "His book deserves to be burned." But, ironically, ibn Ezra himself included several enigmatic comments in his own writings that hint that he had doubts of his own. He alluded to several biblical passages that appeared not to be from Moses' own hand: passages that referred to Moses in the third person, used terms that Moses would not have known, described places where Moses had never been, and used language that reflected another time and locale from those of Moses. Nonetheless, ibn Ezra apparently was not willing to say outright that Moses was not the author of the Five Books. He simply wrote, "And if you understand, then you will recognize the truth." And in another reference to one of these contradictory passages, he wrote, "And he who understands will keep silent."

In the fourteenth century, in Damascus, the scholar Bonfils accepted ibn Ezra's evidence but not his advice to keep silent. Referring to the difficult passages, Bonfils wrote explicitly, "And this is evidence that this verse was written in the Torah later, and Moses did not write it; rather one of the later prophets wrote it." Bonfils was not denying the revealed character of the text. He still thought that the passages in question were written by "one of the later prophets." He was only concluding that they were not written by Moses. Still, three and a half centuries later, his work was reprinted with the references to this subject deleted.

In the fifteenth century, Tostatus, bishop of Avila, also stated that certain passages, notably the account of Moses' death, could not have been written by Moses. There was an old tradition that Moses' successor Joshua wrote this account. But in the sixteenth century, Carlstadt, a contemporary of Luther, commented that the account of Moses' death is written in the same style as texts that precede it. This makes it difficult to claim that Joshua or anyone else merely added a few lines to an otherwise Mosaic manuscript. It also raises further questions about what exactly was Mosaic and what was added by someone else.

In a second stage of the process, investigators suggested that Moses wrote the Five Books but that editors went over them later, adding an occasional word or phrase of their own. In the sixteenth century, Andreas van Maes, who was a Flemish Catholic, and two

Jesuit scholars, Benedict Pereira and Jacques Bonfrere, thus pictured an original text from the hand of Moses upon which later writers expanded. Van Maes suggested that a later editor inserted phrases or changed the name of a place to its more current name so that readers would understand it better. Van Maes' book was placed on the Catholic Index of Prohibited Books.

In the third stage of the investigation, investigators concluded outright that Moses did not write the majority of the Pentateuch. The first to say it was the British philosopher Thomas Hobbes in the seventeenth century. Hobbes collected numerous cases of facts and statements through the course of the Five Books that were inconsistent with Mosaic authorship. For example, the text sometimes states that something is the case "to this day." "To this day" is not the phrase of someone describing a contemporary situation. It is rather the phrase of a later writer who is describing something that has endured.

Four years later, Isaac de la Peyrère, a French Calvinist, also wrote explicitly that Moses was not the author of the first books of the Bible. He, too, noted problems running through the text, including, for example, the words "across the Jordan" in the first verse of Deuteronomy. That verse says, "These are the words that Moses spoke to the children of Israel across the Jordan...." The problem with the phrase "across the Jordan" is that it refers to someone who is on the other side of the Jordan river from the writer. The verse thus appears to be the words of someone in Israel, west of the Jordan, referring to what Moses did on the east side of the Jordan. But Moses himself was never supposed to have been in Israel in his life. De la Peyrère's book was banned and burned. He was arrested and informed that in order to be released he would have to become Catholic and recant his views to the Pope. He did.

About the same time, in Holland, the philosopher Spinoza published a unified critical analysis, likewise demonstrating that the problematic passages were not a few isolated cases that could be explained away one by one. Rather, they were pervasive through the entire Five Books of Moses. There were the third-person accounts of Moses, the statements that Moses was unlikely to have made (e.g., "humblest man on earth"), the report of Moses' death, the expression "to this day," the references to geographical locales by names that they acquired after Moses' lifetime, the treatment of matters that were subsequent to Moses (e.g., the list of Edomite kings), and various contradictions and problems in the text of the sort that earlier investigators had observed. He also noted that the text says in Deuteronomy 34, "There never arose another prophet in Israel like Moses. ..." Spinoza remarked that these sound like the words of someone who lived a a long time after Moses and had the opportunity to see other prophets and thus make the comparison. (They also do not sound like the words of the humblest man on earth.) Spinoza wrote, "It is ... clearer than the sun at noon that the Pentateuch was not written by Moses, but by someone who lived long after Moses." Spinoza had been excommunicated from Judaism. Now his work was condemned by Catholics and Protestants as well. His book was placed on the Catholic Index, within six years thirty-seven edicts were issued against it, and an attempt was made on his life.

A short time later, in France, Richard Simon, a convert from Protestantism who had become a Catholic priest, wrote a work that he intended to be critical of Spinoza. He said that the core of the Pentateuch (the laws) was Mosaic but that there were some additions. The additions, he said, were by scribes who collected, arranged, and elaborated upon the old texts. These scribes, according to Simon, were prophets, guided by the divine spirit, and so he regarded his work as a defense of the sanctity of the biblical text. His contemporaries, however, apparently were not ready for a work that said that any part of the Five Books was not Mosaic. Simon was attacked by other Catholic clergy and expelled from his order. His books were placed on the Index. Forty refutations of his work were written by Protestants. Of the thirteen hundred copies printed of his book, all but six were burned. An English version of the book came out, translated by John Hampden, but Hampden later recanted. The understated report by the scholar Edward Gray in his account of the events tells it best: Hampden "repudiated the opinions he had held in common with Simon ... in 1688, probably shortly before his release from the tower."

The Sources

Simon's idea that the biblical writers had assembled their narrative out of old sources at their disposal was an important step on the way to discovering who wrote the Bible. Any competent historian knows the importance of sources in writing an ongoing narrative of events. The hypothesis that the Five Books of Moses were the result of such a combining of several older sources by different authors was exceptionally important because it prepared the way to deal with a new item of evidence that was developed by three investigators in the following century: the doublet.

A doublet is a case of the same story being told twice. Even in translation it is easy to observe that biblical stories often appear with variations of detail in two different places in the Bible. There are two different stories of the creation of the world. There are two stories of the covenant between God and the patriarch Abraham, two stories of the naming of Abraham's son Isaac, two stories of Abraham's claiming to a foreign king that his wife Sarah is his sister, two stories of Isaac's son Jacob making a journey to Mesopotamia, two stories of a revelation to Jacob at Beth-El, two stories of God's changing Jacob's name to Israel, two stories of Moses' getting water from a rock at a place called Meribah, and more.

Those who defended the traditional belief in Mosaic authorship argued that the doublets were always complementary, not repetitive, and that they did not contradict each other, but came to teach us a lesson by their "apparent" contradiction. But another clue was discovered that undermined this traditional response. Investigators found that in most cases one of the two versions of a doublet story would refer to the deity by the divine name, Yahweh (formerly mispronounced Jehovah), and the other version of the story would refer to the deity simply as "God." That is, the doublets lined up into two groups of parallel versions of stories. Each group was almost always consistent about the name of the deity that it used. Moreover, the investigators found that it was not only the names of the deity that lined up. They found various other terms and characteristics that regularly appeared in one or the other group. This tended to support the hypothesis that someone had taken two different old source documents, cut them up, and woven them together to form the continuous story in the Five Books of Moses.

And so the next stage of the investigation was the process of separating the strands of the two old source documents. In the eighteenth century, three independent investigators arrived at similar conclusions based on such studies: a German minister (H. B. Witter), a French medical doctor (Jean Astruc), and a German professor (J. G. Eichhorn). At first it was thought that one of the two versions of the stories in the book of Genesis was an ancient text that Moses used as a source and that the other version of the stories was Moses' own writing, describing these things in his own words. Later, it was thought that both versions of the stories were old source documents that Moses had used in fashioning his work. But ultimately it was concluded that both of the two sources had to be from writers who lived after Moses. Each step of the process was attributing less and less to Moses himself.

By the beginning of the nineteenth century, the two-source hypothesis was expanded. Scholars found evidence that there were not two major source documents in the Pentateuch after all—there were four! Two scholars found that in the first four books of the Bible there were not only doublets, but a number of triplets of stories. This converged with other evidence, involving contradictions and characteristic language, that persuaded them that they had found another source within the Pentateuch. And then a young German scholar, W. M. L. De Wette, observed in his doctoral dissertation that the fifth of the Five Books of Moses, the book of Deuteronomy, was strikingly different in its language from the four books that preceded it. None of the three old source documents appeared to continue into this book. De Wette hypothesized that Deuteronomy was a separate, fourth source.

Thus from the work of a great many persons, and at personal cost for some of them, the mystery of the Bible's origins had come to be addressed openly, and a working hypothesis had been formed. It was a remarkable stage in the Bible's history. Scholars could open the book of Genesis and identify the writing of two or even three authors on the same page. And there was also the work of the editor, the person who had cut up and combined the source documents into a single story; and so as many as four different persons could have contributed to producing a single page of the Bible. Investigators were now able to see that a puzzle existed and what the basic character of the puzzle was. But they still did not know who the authors of any of the four old source documents were, when they lived, or why they wrote. And they had no idea who the mysterious editor was who had combined them, nor did they have any idea why this person had combined them in this complex way.

The Hypothesis

To state it as succinctly as possible, the puzzle was as follows:

There was evidence that the Five Books of Moses had been composed by combining four different source documents into one continuous history. For working purposes, the four documents were identified by alphabetic symbols. The document that was associated with the divine name Yahweh/Jehovah was called J. The document that was identified as referring to the deity as God (in Hebrew, Elohim) was called E. The third document, by far the largest, included most of the legal sections and concentrated a great deal on matters having to do with priests, and so it was called P. And the source that was found only in the book of Deuteronomy was called D. The question was how to uncover the history of these four documents— not only who wrote them, but why four different versions of the story were written, what their relationship to each other was, whether any of the authors were aware of the existence of the others' texts, when in history each was produced, how they were preserved and combined, and a host of other questions.

The first step was to try to determine the relative order in which they were written. The idea was to try to see if each version reflected a particular stage in the development of religion in biblical Israel. This approach reflected the influence in nineteenth-century Germany of Hegelian notions of historical development of civilization. Two nineteenth-century figures stand out. They approached the problem in very different ways, but they arrived at complementary findings. One of them, Karl Heinrich Graf, worked on deducing from references in the various biblical texts which of the texts logically must have preceded or followed others. The other investigator, Wilhelm Vatke, sought to trace the history of the development of ancient Israelite religion by examining texts for clues as to whether they reflected early or late stages of the religion.

Graf concluded that the J and E documents were the oldest versions of the biblical stories, for they (and other early biblical writings) were unaware of matters that were treated in other documents. D was later than J and E, for it showed acquaintance with developments in a later period of history. And P, the priestly version of the story, was the latest of all, for it referred to a variety of matters that were unknown in all of the earlier portions of the Bible such as the books of the prophets. Vatke meanwhile concluded that J and E reflected a very early stage in the development of Israelite religion, when it was essentially a nature/fertility religion. He concluded that D reflected a middle stage of religious development, when the faith of Israel was a spiritual/ethical religion; in short, the age of the great Israelite prophets. And he regarded the P document as reflecting the latest stage of Israelite religion, the stage of priestly religion, based on priests, sacrifices, ritual, and law.

Vatke's attempt to reconstruct the development of the religion of Israel and Graf's attempt to reconstruct the development of the sources of the Pentateuch pointed in the same direction. Namely, the great majority of the laws and much of the narrative of the Pentateuch were not a part of life in the days of Moses—much less were they written by Moses—nor even of life in the days of the kings and prophets of Israel. Rather, they were written by someone who lived toward the end of the biblical period.

There were a variety of responses to this idea. The negative responses came from both traditional and critical scholars. Even De Wette, who had identified the D source, would not accept the idea that so much of the law was so late. He said that this view "suspended the beginnings of Hebrew history not upon the grand creations of Moses, but upon airy nothings." And traditional scholars pointed out that this view pictured biblical Israel as a nation not governed by law for its first six centuries. Graf's and Vatke's ideas, nonetheless, came to dominate the field of biblical studies for a hundred years primarily because of the work of one man: Wellhausen.

Julius Wellhausen (1844–1918) stands out as a powerful figure in the investigation into the authorship of the Bible and in the history of biblical scholarship in general. It is difficult to pinpoint any one person as the "founder," "father," or "first to" of this enterprise, because a number of persons made contributions that brought the search to some new stage. Indeed, books and articles on the field of biblical scholarship attribute these titles variously to Hobbes, Spinoza, Simon, Astruc, Eichhorn, Graf, or Wellhausen. Wellhausen himself applies such a term to De Wette. But Wellhausen occupies a special place in the history of this enterprise. His contribution does not so much constitute a beginning as a culmination in that history. Much of what Wellhausen had to say was taken from those who preceded him, but Wellhausen's contribution was to bring all of these components together, along with considerable research and argumentation of his own, into a clear, organized synthesis.

Wellhausen accepted Vatke's picture of the religion of Israel as having developed in three stages, and he accepted Graf's picture of the documents as having been written in three distinct periods. He then simply put the two pictures together. He examined the biblical stories and laws that appear in J and E, and he argued that they reflected the way of life of the nature/fertility stage of religion. He argued that the stories and laws of Deuteronomy (D) reflected the life of the spiritual/ethical stage. And he argued that P derived from the priestly/legal stage. He traced the characteristics of each stage and period meticulously through the text of each document, examining the way in which the document reflected each of several fundamental aspects of religion: the character of the clergy, the types of sacrifices, the places of worship, and the religious holidays. He drew on both the legal and the narrative sections, through all five books of the Pentateuch, and through other historical and prophetic books of the Bible. His presentation was sensible, articulate, and extremely influential. His was a powerful construction, above all, because it did more than just divide the sources by the usual criteria (doublets, contradictions, etc.). It tied the source documents to history. It provided a believable framework in which they could have developed. Thus the Wellhausen model began to answer the question of why the different sources existed. The first real acceptance of this field of study, then, came when historical and literary analyses were first successfully merged. This model of the combination of the source documents came to be known as the Documentary Hypothesis. It has dominated the field ever since. To this day, if you want to disagree, you disagree with Wellhausen. If you want to pose a new model, you compare its merits with those of Wellhausen's model.

The Present State

Religious opposition to the new investigation persisted during the nineteenth century. The Documentary Hypothesis became known in English-speaking countries in large part because of the work of William Robertson Smith, a professor of Old Testament in the Free Church of Scotland college at Aberdeen and editor of the *Encyclopaedia Britannica*. He wrote articles in the encyclopedia and published articles by Wellhausen there as well. He was put on trial before the church. Though he was cleared of the charge of heresy, he was expelled from his chair. Also in the nineteenth century, in South Africa, John Colenso, an Anglican bishop, published similar conclusions, and within twenty years three hundred responses were written. He was called "the wicked bishop."

Things began to change, though, in the twentieth century. There had been considerable opposition to this investigation in the Catholic Church for centuries, but a major turning point was the encyclical *Divino Afflante Spiritu* of Pope Pius XII in 1943. It has been called "a Magna Carta for biblical progress." The Pope encouraged scholars to pursue knowledge about the biblical writers, for those writers were "the living and reasonable instrument of the Holy Spirit..." He concluded:

> Let the interpreter then, with all care and without neglecting any light derived from recent research endeavor to determine the peculiar character and circumstances of the sacred writer, the age in which he lived, the sources written or oral to which he had recourse and the forms of expression he employed.

As to the results of the Pope's encouragement, the Catholic *Jerome Biblical Commentary*, which appeared in 1968, began with this statement by the editors:

It is no secret that the last fifteen or twenty years have seen almost a revolution in Catholic biblical studies—a revolution encouraged by authority, for its Magna Carta was the encyclical *Divino Afflante Spiritu* of Pope Pius XII. The principles of literary and historical criticism, so long regarded with suspicion, are now, at last, accepted and applied by Catholic exegetes. The results have been many: a new and vital interest in the Bible throughout the Church; a greater contribution of biblical studies to modern theology; a community of effort and understanding among Catholic and non-Catholic scholars.

Opposition to the critical examination of the Bible has also diminished among Protestants. The Bible has come to be studied and taught by critical scholars, in leading Protestant institutions of Europe and Great Britain. In the United States as well, critical scholars teach at major Protestant institutions such as Harvard Divinity School, Yale Divinity School, Princeton Theological Seminary, Union Theological Seminary, and a great many others. Critical examination of the text and its authors also has become accepted at leading Jewish institutions, particularly Hebrew Union College, which is the Reform rabbinical school, and the Jewish Theological Seminary, the Conservative rabbinical school. It is also taught at major universities around the world.

Until the past generation there were orthodox Christian and Jewish scholars who contested the Documentary Hypothesis in scholarly circles. At present, however, there is hardly a biblical scholar in the world actively working on the problem who would claim that the Five Books of Moses were written by Moses—or by any one person.[2] Scholars argue about the number of different authors who wrote any given biblical book. They argue about when the various documents were written and about whether a particular verse belongs to this or that document. They express varying degrees of satisfaction or dissatisfaction with the usefulness of the hypothesis for literary or historical purposes. But the hypothesis itself continues to be the starting point of research, no serious student of the Bible can fail to study it, and no other explanation of the evidence has come close to challenging it.

The critical analysis of authorship has also extended beyond the Five Books of Moses and has touched every book of the Bible. For example, the book of Isaiah was traditionally ascribed to the prophet Isaiah, who lived in the eighth century B.C. Most of the first half of the book fits with such a tradition. But chapters 40 through 66 of the book of Isaiah appear to be by someone living about two centuries later. Even the book of Obadiah, which is only one page long, has been thought to be a combination of pieces by two authors.

In our own day, new tools and new methods have produced important contributions. New methods of linguistic analysis, developed largely within the last fifteen years, have made it possible to establish relative chronology of portions of the Bible and to measure and describe characteristics of biblical Hebrew in various periods. In the simplest terms, Moses was further from the language of much of the Five Books than Shakespeare was from modern English. Also since Wellhausen's days there has been an archeological revolution, which has yielded important discoveries that must now figure in any research into the Bible's authors. I shall discuss the relevant archeological finds in the course of this book.

Still, the simple fact is that, in large part, the puzzle remains unsolved. And the elusiveness of the solution continues to frustrate our work on a variety of other questions about the Bible. My own experience is a case in point. When I was introduced to this area of biblical studies in my college years, I responded that it just did not matter very much to me, that my interest was in what the text said and what its relevance was today—not in who wrote it. But as I worked more and more with the text through my graduate years, I found that, no matter what question I addressed, it always came back to this problem.

If I worked on a literary question, I wanted to know why the text told the story this way and not another way. For example, consider the story of the golden calf. In the book of Exodus, God speaks the Ten Commandments out loud to the Israelites from the heavens over the mountain of God. Moses then climbs the mountain alone to receive a carved set of the commandments on stone tablets. When Moses delays to return, the people make a golden calf and sacrifice in front of it. Their leader, the man who personally makes the golden calf, is Moses' own spokesman, Aaron. When Moses returns and sees the calf, he throws down and smashes the tablets in his anger. He destroys the golden calf. He asks Aaron, "What did this people do to you that you brought a great sin on them?" Aaron answers that the people asked him to make gods, that he threw their gold into the fire, "and out came this calf!"

The question was, what would make someone write a story like this? What was happening in this writer's world that would make him[3] tell a story in which his own people commit heresy only forty days after hearing God speak from the sky? Why did he picture a golden calf, and not a bronze sheep, a silver snake, or anything else? Why did he picture Aaron, traditionally the first high priest of Israel, as a leader of a heresy? Is it simply that it happened that way, and the writer was just telling the story as he knew it? Or were there other issues and events happening in the writer's world that motivated him when he was fashioning the story?

If I worked on a moral question, I wanted to know why the text said, "Behave this way and not that way." For example, there are laws of war in the book of Deuteronomy that have important moral implications. One law exempts from military conscription any man who is afraid. Another law forbids the rape of a captured woman. The women of the group that has been defeated must be given time to mourn any lost family members, and then they may be taken as wives, or else they must be set free. In this case it seemed important to me to understand what gave birth to such laws. How did the biblical standard of conduct come to include these particular practices and prohibitions? What was happening in the biblical world that prompted someone to conceive of such laws and that led a community to adopt them?

If it was a theological question, I wanted to know why the text pictured the deity as it does. For example, the Bible often pictures the deity as torn between divine justice and divine mercy. There is a recurring tension through the Bible between the forces that say "punish" and the forces that say "forgive." What events and what different conceptions of the character of God at various times and places in the biblical world played a part in forging this powerful and bewildering notion of divine-human relations?

Perhaps most serious were historical questions. If one is interested in the historicity of the biblical accounts, then one must inquire into when the writer lived. Was the writer a witness to the events he described? If not, what were his sources? What were his interests? Was the writer a priest or a lay person, a man or a woman, someone associated with the court or a commoner? Whom did he favor, whom did he oppose, from where did he come? And so on.

My teacher was Professor Frank Moore Cross at Harvard University. In my second year of studies there, there was a discussion in a seminar of the Department of Near Eastern languages and Civilizations one day in which Professor Cross referred to another seminar in which he had participated many years earlier. In that earlier seminar, the participants had decided to work through the text of the Pentateuch from the beginning, without assuming the validity of the Documentary Hypothesis or any other hypothesis, to see, through fresh, careful study of the text themselves, where the evidence would take them. Later that day I had an appointment with Professor Cross at which I asked him for a supervised study course under his direction. He proposed that we do what his seminar had done years earlier, and so I found myself at last taking on the ever-present problem of the formation of the biblical text. We started from the beginning, working through the text of the Pentateuch, not assuming the correctness of the hypothesis, but weighing the evidence as we went. I have been intrigued by the problem ever since.

I hope to advance the process of solution with my contributions here. To a large extent, I defend the model that has developed as the consensus of investigators in the last few centuries. I shall present new evidence that I believe supports the model. Where I differ with past scholars, including, occasionally, my own teachers, I shall make that clear and give my evidence. Specifically, what is new here is:

—I mean to be more specific about who the writers of the Bible were: not only when they lived, but where they resided, the groups to which they belonged, their relationships to major persons and events of their historical moment, whom they liked, whom they opposed, and their political and religious purposes in writing their works.

—I mean to shed light on the relationship among the various authors. Did any of them know any of the others' works? As it happens, they did. And this, in some unexpected ways, affected the way in which the Bible came out.

—I mean to shed more light on the chain of events that brought all of the documents together into one work. This will also reveal something about how that work came to be accepted as the Bible.

—In at least one case, I mean to challenge the majority view of who one of the authors of the Bible was, when he lived, and why he wrote.

—When dealing with biblical stories, I mean to show why each story came out in the particular way it did and what its relationship was to the history of the period in which it was written.

It is, of course, impossible to cover all of the books of the Bible in this one volume. I shall deal with the books that tell the core story out of which the rest of the Bible grew (eleven books) and refer to many of the other books, and I shall discuss the implications of these discoveries for the Bible as a whole.

The way to begin, it seems to me, is to reconstruct a picture of the biblical world to the best extent possible based on archeological evidence and the most cautious possible reading of the historical books of the Bible, aiming to identify what portions of the biblical report are historically trustworthy for each period. The next step is to locate the biblical authors who wrote in each respective period and to see to what extent the persons and events of that moment in history affected the way in which the Bible came out. In the end we can turn back to what mattered to me so much in the first place: the implications of these findings for the way in which people understand, value, and use the Bible today.

CHAPTER 1

The World That Produced the Bible: 1200–722 B.C.

The Setting

THE land in which the Bible was born was about the size of a large North American county. It was located along the eastern coast of the Mediterranean Sea, a natural meeting point of Africa, Asia, and Europe. It had a fabulous variety of climate, flora and fauna, and topographic characteristics. In the northeast was a beautiful fresh-water lake, the Sea of Galilee. It flowed into the Jordan River to the south. The river flowed in a straight line south and emptied into the Dead Sea, which was as unlike the Galilee as two bodies of water can possibly be. It was thick with salt. It was surrounded by hot wilderness. According to the traditions of that region the Dead Sea area had once been a pleasant, fertile place, but the people who lived there were so corrupt that God rained brimstone and fire on the place until it was left hardly fit for occupation.

The northern part of the country was fertile, with plains, small hills and valleys. The center of the country had beaches and low-lands along the Mediterranean coast on the west, and hills and mountains on the east. The southern part of the country was largely desert. It was hot and humid along the coast, especially in summer. It was drier in the hills, still drier in the desert. It was cold enough to snow occasionally on the hills in winter. It was beautiful. The people could see the beauty of the sea, the beauty of lake, flowers, and fields, and the beauty of desert all within a few miles of each other.

As striking as the variety of the land itself was the variety of its people. The Bible refers to peoples from numerous backgrounds who mixed there: Canaanites, Hittites, Amorites, Perizzites, Hivites, Girgashites, Jebusites. There were also the Philistines, who stood out as different from the others, apparently having come across the Mediterranean from the Greek islands. There was also a circle of people around the borders of the land. To the north were the Phoenicians, who are usually credited with having introduced writing in that region. Along the eastern borders were Syria in the north, then Ammon, then Moab, then Edom to the south. Then of course there were the Israelites, the most numerous people within the boundaries of the land from the twelfth century B.C. on, the people about whom most of the biblical stories are told. The land lay along the route of travel between Africa and Asia, and so there were the influences—and interests—of Egypt and Mesopotamia in the region as well.

The population was both urban and rural; it is difficult to say in what proportion. Certainly the percentage of city residents was large. There were times of considerable economic prosperity and times of hardship. There were times of great political strength and influence, and there were periods of domination by foreign powers. And, of course, there were times of peace and times of war.

The dominant religion across the ancient Near East was pagan religion. Pagan religion was not idol worship, as formerly it was thought to be. The archeological revolution of the past hundred years has opened up that world to us and given us, among other revelations, a new understanding and appreciation of the pagan religious worldview. At Nineveh alone—the greatest archeological discovery of all time—were found fifty thousand tablets, the library of the emperor of Assyria. At the Canaanite city of Ugarit, three thousand more tablets were found. We can read the pagan hymns, prayers, and myths; we can see the places where they worshiped; and we can see how they depicted their gods in art.

Pagan religion was close to nature. People worshiped the most powerful forces in the universe: the sky, the storm wind, the sun, the sea, fertility, death. The statues that they erected were like the icons in a church. The statues depicted the god or goddess, reminded the worshiper of the deity's presence, showed the humans' respect for their gods, and perhaps made the humans feel closer to their gods. But, as a Babylonian text points out, the statue was not the god.

The chief pagan god in the region that was to become Israel was El. El was male, patriarchal, a ruler. Unlike the other major god of the region, Haddu (the storm wind[1]), El was not identified with any particular force in nature. He sat at the head of the council of the gods and pronounced the council's decisions.

The God of Israel was Yahweh.[2] He, too, was male, patriarchal, a ruler, and not identified with any one force in nature. Rather than describing him in terms of nature or myths, the people of Israel spoke of Yahweh in terms of his acts in history—as we shall see.

The people of Israel spoke Hebrew. Other languages of the area were similar to Hebrew: Phoenician, Canaanite (Ugaritic), Aramaic, and Moabite are all in the Semitic family of languages. Hebrew and these other languages each had an alphabet. People wrote documents on papyrus and sealed them with stamps pressed in wet clay. They also wrote texts on leather and on clay tablets and occasionally carved them in stone or wrote them on plaster. They wrote shorter notes on pieces of broken pottery.

People lived in one- and two-story homes, mostly of stone. In cities the houses were built close together. Some of the cities had impressive water systems, including long underground tunnels and huge cisterns. Some houses had indoor plumbing. Cities were surrounded by walls. People ate beef, lamb, fowl, bread, vegetables, fruits, and dairy products. They made wine and beer. They made pots and jars of all sizes out of clay. Their metals were bronze, iron, silver, and gold. They had wind, string, and percussion musical instruments. Contrary to every Bible movie ever made, they did not wear kaffiyehs (Arab headdress).

There are traditions about the prehistory of the Israelites: their patriarchs, their experiences as slaves in Egypt, and their wandering in the Sinai wilderness. Unfortunately, we have little historical information about this from archeology or other ancient sources. The first point at which we actually have sufficient evidence to begin to picture the life of the biblical community is the twelfth century

B.C., the period when the Israelites became established in this region.

The Israelites' political life in their early years was organized around tribes. According to biblical tradition there were thirteen tribes, with considerable differences in size and population from the smallest to the largest. Twelve of the tribes each had a distinct geographical territory. The thirteenth, the tribe of Levi, was identified as a priestly group. Its members lived in cities in the other tribes' territories. Each tribe had its own chosen leaders. (See the map, p. 9.)

There were also individuals who acquired authority in individual tribes or over groups of tribes by virtue of their position in society or their personal qualities. These persons were either judges or priests. The office of judge did not involve only hearing legal cases. It included military leadership. In times of military threat to a tribe or group of tribes, therefore, a judge could acquire considerable power and authority. A judge could be male or female. Priests had to be male. Usually priests had to be from Levi. Their office was hereditary. They served at religious sites, presiding over religious ceremonies, which meant, above all, performing sacrifices. In return for their services, they received a portion of the sacrificed animal or produce.

One other type of person figured in a special way in the leadership of the community: the prophet. Being a prophet was not an office or profession like judge or priest. A person from any occupation could come to be a prophet. The prophet Ezekiel was a priest; the prophet Amos was a cowboy. The word in Hebrew for prophet is *nābî'*, which is understood to mean "called." The Israelite prophets were men or women who were regarded as having been called by the deity to perform a special task with regard to the people. The task might be to encourage or to criticize. It might be in the realm of politics, ethics, or ritual. The prophet generally would deliver his or her message in poetry or in a combination of poetry and prose.

The Rise of the Monarchy

The age of the judges' leadership culminated in Samuel, a man who was all three: a judge, a priest, and a prophet. The last of the judges, he wielded much political and religious authority. He lived at Shiloh, a city in the northern part of the land, which was a major religious center at the time. A tabernacle was located there which, according to a biblical account, housed the ark containing the tablets of the Ten Commandments; and a distinguished priestly family functioned there, a family which some scholars identify as descendants of Moses.

When the Philistines' domination in the area became too strong for any one or two tribes to oppose, the people sought a leader who could unite and lead all of the tribes. In other words, they wanted a king. It was Samuel who, somewhat reluctantly, anointed the first king of Israel, King Saul. That was the end of the period of the judges and the beginning of the period of the monarchy. Though there were to be no more judges, there still continued to be priests and prophets. And so Israel developed a political structure in which the king was by no means an absolute ruler. On the contrary, the king's power was checked and balanced by the powers of the tribal leaders, the chief priests, and, above all, the prophets.

This had a profound effect on both the political and the religious life of Israel. In order to become king and to maintain a stable rule, a man had to have the tribal leaders' acceptance, and he had to be designated by a prophet. He also needed a supportive priesthood. This was partly because the priests, prophets, and tribal leaders held well-established positions by the time of the creation of the monarchy, and it was partly because of ongoing political realities. The king needed the tribes because the tribal musters of troops provided the king with his army, without which he was virtually powerless. The king needed prophetic designation and priestly support because religion not only was not separated from state in that world, it was hardly separated from anything. As introductions to the Bible often point out, there was no word in the Hebrew language of that period for "*religion.*" Religion was not a separate, identifiable category of beliefs and activities. It was an *in*separable, pervasive part of life. A king could not have political legitimacy without religious legitimacy. A king who lost the support of his prophets and priests was in for trouble. And that is what happened to Saul.

Saul had a falling-out with Samuel, the priest-prophet who had designated him as king. The book of 1 Samuel gives two different accounts of the events that precipitated the break (from two different authors?), but the common element of the two stories is that both portray Saul as stepping over the boundary of his powers into the prerogatives of the priesthood. Samuel's response, apparently, was to designate another king: David.

The Rise of David

David was a well-known hero from the tribe of Judah. For a while he was a member of Saul's retinue, and he married one of Saul's daughters. Saul came to perceive David as a threat to his throne—quite correctly—and they became rivals. When David received the support of the priests of Shiloh,[3] Saul had them all massacred—*except one who escaped.*

Saul reigned until his death in battle against the Philistines. After his death the kingdom was split between his son Ishbaal and David. Ishbaal ruled in the northern portion of the country; David ruled in his own tribe, Judah, which was the largest of the tribes, almost the size of all the other tribes together, encompassing the southern portion of the country. Ishbaal was assassinated, and then David became king over the entire country, north and south.

Already at this early stage of Israelite history, then, we can see conflicts between king and priest, and between king and king. These political dynamics would one day play a decisive role in the formation of the Bible.

David stands out as a major figure in the Hebrew Bible, really the only one who comes close to the level of Moses in impact. There are several reasons for this. First, we simply have a larger amount of source material on him in the Bible than on other figures. We have the lengthy text known as the Court History of David (in the book of 2 Samuel), a work which is both beautifully written and a remarkable example of history-writing, remarkable because it openly criticizes its heroes, a practice that is all but unknown among ancient Near Eastern kings.

Second, David stands out because if even half of what the Bible says about him is true he lived an extraordinary life—by which I mean both his personal life and his political life. (The two are hardly separable in any case.)

The third reason for the singular place that David holds among biblical figures is that David established an enduring line of kings descended from him. The Davidic dynasty was in fact one of the longest-lasting ruling families of any country in the history of the world. Hence the powerful endurance of the messiah tradition in Judaism and Christianity—the trust that there would always be a descendant of David at hand in an hour of distress.

David's Empire

One of the things that may have made Saul an attractive candidate to be the first king of Israel was that he came from the tribe of Benjamin, which was a geographically small tribe. There was therefore little threat that he and his tribe would be able to dominate the other tribes through his position. David, on the other hand, coming from Judah, the largest tribe, epitomized that danger. David was a sensible and able politician, though, and he took a series of actions that enhanced his kingdom's unity.

First, he moved his capital from Hebron, which was the principal city of Judah, to Jerusalem. Jerusalem had been a Jebusite city, but David captured it, perhaps by a stratagem in which some of his men climbed the nearly vertical shaft of a water tunnel under the city. The tunnel, now known as Warren's Shaft, was cleared in the City of David excavations of biblical Jerusalem and opened to the public in 1985. Since Jerusalem had been occupied by the Jebusites prior to David's capture of it, it was not affiliated with any one of the tribes of Israel. David's selection of Jerusalem as the capital therefore offended no tribe and minimized any impression that he intended to favor Judah—much in the same way that Washington, D.C., was attractive as the capital of the United States because it was carved out and no longer regarded as part of any one of the states. Jerusalem, further, was fairly centrally located between the north and south of the country.

David's second action that facilitated the representation of both north and south in his new united kingdom was to appoint two chief priests in Jerusalem, one from the north and one from the south. Not unlike the presence of two chief rabbis in modern Israel, one from the Sephardic and one from the Ashkenazic community, David's two chief priests were a means of satisfying two formerly separate, now united, constituencies. David's northern priest was Abiathar, who was the one priest who had escaped Saul's massacre of the priests of Shiloh. David's southern priest was Zadok, who came from David's former capital in Judah, the city of Hebron. Zadok and the priests of Hebron apparently were regarded as descendants of Aaron, the first high priest of Israel. David's dual chief priesthood may therefore have been not only a compromise with respect to north and south. It may also have been a compromise with respect to two old, distinguished, and politically important priestly families: the family of Moses and the family of Aaron.

As strong as any other cement for holding the kingdom together was David's record of marriages. He married women who came from several regions of political importance, which could only strengthen the social bond between each of those regions and the royal family.

Most practical of David's policies was his establishment of a standing professional army. This military force included foreigners (Cheretites, Peletites, Hittites) and was responsible to David and his personally appointed general. David was therefore no longer dependent on the individual tribes to muster (i.e., draft) their men into service in times of crisis. David had solved the main part of the problem of dependence on the tribes.

By one military success after another, David brought Edom, Moab, Ammon, Syria, and perhaps Phoenicia under his dominion. He built an empire that extended from the river of Egypt (the wadi El Arish, not the Nile) to the Euphrates River in Mesopotamia. He made Jerusalem both the religious and the political center of his empire, bringing the most sacred object, the ark, there and establishing both of his chief priests there. It was a politically significant empire in that world.

The Royal Family

In order to see how the life, events, and individual persons of that world produced the Bible, one must also look into the story of the royal family. Their relationships, conflicts, and political alignments affected the course of history and, with that, the character of the Bible.

David's having many wives meant that he also had very many children who were half brothers and half sisters to each other. David's oldest son and likely heir was Amnon. According to the Court History of David, in one of the classically male-sexist depictions of all time, Amnon first raped and then rejected his half sister Tamar. Tamar was the daughter of David and a Geshurite princess. Tamar's full brother Absalom killed Amnon in revenge. The elimination of Amnon accomplished more for Absalom, though, than revenge for his wronged sister—it also placed him in contention for the throne. So it is in monarchic politics: family relations and political relations are inseparable. Absalom later rebelled against his father. The tribal musters of troops supported Absalom, the professional army was with David. The professionals won. Absalom was killed.

In David's old age, two more of his sons contended for the succession to his throne: Adonijah, who was one of the oldest sons, and Solomon, who was the son of David's favorite wife, Bathsheba. Each son had his party of supporters in the palace. Adonijah apparently had the support of the other princes. He also had the general who was over the tribal musters. Solomon had the support of the prophet Nathan and of his mother, Bathsheba, both of whom were extremely influential with David, and Solomon also had the general of the professional army.

Two other men took sides in these palace alignments, and their participation ultimately had crucial consequences for Israelite history and for the Bible. They were the two chief priests. Abiathar, the northern priest, from the old priesthood of Shiloh, and possibly a descendant of Moses, supported Adonijah. Zadok, the southern priest, from Hebron in the tribe of Judah, and possibly a descendant of Aaron, supported Solomon.

David chose Solomon. With the professional army behind him, Solomon won without an actual fight.

After David's death, Solomon ordered the execution of his half brother Adonijah and of Adonijah's general, Joab. Solomon could not so easily eliminate the priest Abiathar, however. The king could not just execute a chief priest. Still, he could not tolerate the continued presence in power of those who opposed his succession to the throne. Solomon therefore expelled Abiathar from the Jerusalem priesthood and from Jerusalem. He banished him to an estate in Anathoth, a small village located a few miles outside the capital.

Solomon's Empire

King Solomon is famous for his wisdom. The biblical picture of him is that he maintained a strong, prosperous kingdom and that he accomplished this through diplomatic and economic skill rather than on the battlefields as his father David had done. He outdid his father in marriage diplomacy. The biblical record asserts that he had seven hundred daughters of kings as wives (and three hundred concubines). Even if we take that as an exaggeration, it indicates that political marriages were a major part of his policy. He carried on trade in Africa and Asia, taking advantage of Israel's geographical location. He amassed enormous quantities of gold and silver. He built a Temple in Jerusalem, in which he placed the ark. This especially strengthened the image of Jerusalem as the nation's religious center as well as its capital.

The Temple was not impressive in size. It was only sixty cubits long and twenty cubits wide. A cubit is the length of a man's arm from the elbow to the second knuckle of the hand, about eighteen inches. Size was not really important, though, because no one was ever allowed to go inside the Israelite Temple except the priests. The ceremonies and sacrifices were performed in the courtyard at the entrance to the Temple. The impressive qualities of the Temple were rather its physical characteristics and its contents. Its walls were paneled in cedar. Its interior was divided into two rooms, an outer room called the Holy and an inner sanctum called the Holy of Holies.

The Holy of Holies was a perfect cube, twenty cubits long, wide, and high. In it were two tremendous statues, the cherubs. Cherubs in that world were not the angelic little boys of later art who shoot arrows and make people fall in love. A cherub was a sphinx, usually with the body of a four-legged animal, the head of a human, and the wings of a bird. The Temple cherubs were carved out of olive wood and plated with gold. They were not idols. They were rather the throne platform of Yahweh, who was invisibly enthroned on them. Under their wings, in the middle of the room, was Israel's most sacred object, the ark, the golden box containing the tablets of the Ten Commandments.

Besides the Temple, Solomon had numerous other building projects. He built a great palace for himself, which was bigger than the Temple. He also constructed military fortifications around the country.

Thus the Bible pictures King Solomon as a great monarch of the ancient Near East. To look into that world and especially to feel the political issues of life then, first one must have a good knowledge of the geography of the land. Then one must have a real sensitivity to political and economic forces. And then one must read carefully what most people would consider to be among the most boring passages in the Bible: lists of territories, building projects, and notations of political developments in neighboring countries. The best analysis of all of this, in my judgment, is by an American biblical scholar, Baruch Halpern. I reached some of my conclusions concerning who wrote the Bible on several important points by applying his insights into political history to the Bible. What is also impressive about Halpern's analysis of Solomon's political world is that he wrote it when he was only twenty years old and an undergraduate at Harvard in 1972. He demonstrated that Solomon's domestic and foreign policies threatened the country's unity.

From One Country to Two

We must keep in mind that the country had once been two separate kingdoms, one in the north and one in the south, and that the northern kingdom had itself been composed of individual tribes. The old tribal divisions had not ceased to exist under David and Solomon, nor had the memory of a once independent north. Many of Solomon's policies, nonetheless, alienated the northerners instead of encouraging their support.

For one thing, he had removed the northern community's chief priest, Abiathar. For another example, there were, of course, taxes to be paid by everyone, north and south, but, as Halpern pointed out, the record of Solomon's building projects shows that he spent the tax revenues disproportionately on military defenses in the south. He was providing his own tribe, Judah, with protection from the military threat of Egypt. But Syria had broken away from his empire during this period, yet Solomon did not give the northern tribes equal protection from the very real threat of Syria there. The people of the north were paying for the security of the south.

As another example of Solomon's policy toward northern Israel, Solomon received help in building the Temple and the palace from Hiram of Tyre, king of the Phoenicians, who was Solomon's father-in-law. (Actually, nearly every king in the ancient Near East must have been Solomon's father-in-law.) Hiram provided the cedars of Lebanon and 120 talents of gold. In return, Solomon ceded to the Phoenician king a tract of *northern* Israelite territory containing twenty cities. In this action, too, Solomon was building up his own capital solely at the expense of the north.

One of Solomon's policies in particular cut into the very structure of the tribal system. Solomon established twelve administrative districts, each of which was to provide food for the court in Jerusalem for one month of the year. The boundaries of these twelve new districts did not correspond to the existing boundaries of the twelve tribes. Solomon personally appointed the heads of each administrative district. This is like gerrymandering, squared. It would be as if the president of the United States established fifty new taxation districts which did not correspond to the existing fifty states and within which each would have a politically appointed administrator instead of its own elected governor and legislators. Solomon's redistricting, to make matters even worse, was only of the north. The twelve new districts did not include the territory of Judah.

If all of this did not convince the populace that their king meant to exercise powerful centralized control from Jerusalem, Solomon established one more economic policy that could leave no doubt. He instituted the *missîm*. The term *missîm* in Hebrew refers to a sort of tax, not of money but of physical labor. Citizens owed a month of required work to the government each year. Given that we are talking about Israel, a nation that had a tradition that they had once been slaves in Egypt and now were free, a law of required labor must have been a bitter pill to swallow.

We have two pieces of evidence of just how bitter it was. The first is that one of the writers of the book of Exodus later described the *Egyptian* supervisers of the Israelite slaves not by the usual term "taskmasters," but rather as "officers of *missîm*." I shall identify the man who wrote those words in the next chapter. He was no friend of the royal family.

The second piece of evidence is an incident that took place shortly after Solomon died. Despite any dissatisfaction that the northern tribes had felt over his policies, Solomon had been strong enough to hold the nation together, and the northern tribes did not secede during his reign. However, when Solomon died, his son, King Rehoboam, lacked whatever was needed to hold on to the united kingdom. Rehoboam went to Shechem, a major city in the north, for coronation. The northern leaders asked him there if he intended to continue his father's policies. Rehoboam said that he did. The northern tribes seceded. An indicator of what was bothering them is the incident to which I have referred: the first act of rebellion was their stoning one of Rehoboam's officials to death. The man they stoned was the chief of the *missîm*.

And so Rehoboam ruled only Judah (and Benjamin, which Judah dominated). The rest of Israel chose a man named Jeroboam as king. David's empire now became two countries: Israel in the north, and Judah in the south. We need to look into the life, especially the religious life, of the two kingdoms, and then we shall be ready to identify two of the writers of the Bible.

Israel and Judah

The similarity of the two kings' names, Rehoboam and Jeroboam, is no coincidence. Both names in Hebrew can mean that the people should become numerous or widespread. Each king apparently chose a throne name that suggested his interest in the expansion of his portion of the once-united nation. Rehoboam ruled from Jerusalem, the City of David. Jeroboam made Shechem the capital of the new northern kingdom.

The political division of the country into two had enormous implications for the religion. Religion was not separate from state. Jerusalem had been both the political capital and the religious center of the country. Jeroboam, king of Israel, therefore was in an extremely difficult position. Israel and Judah might have become two separate countries, but they still shared a common religion. Both worshiped the God Yahweh. Both held beliefs and traditions about the patriarchs, the slavery and exodus from Egypt, and experiences at a mountain in the Sinai wilderness. The Temple, the ark, and the chief priest of that religion were all located in Jerusalem. This meant that at least on holidays, and on various other occasions as well, masses of Jeroboam's population would cross the border into Judah, taking a sizable portion of the country's livestock and produce with them for sacrifices. They would go to the City of David, pray and sacrifice at the Temple of Solomon, and see King Rehoboam in the center of the activities. This scenario could hardly have filled Jeroboam's heart with feelings of stability.

Jeroboam could not just make up a new religion to keep the people from going to Jerusalem. He could, however, establish for his new kingdom its own national version of the common religion.

And so the kingdom of Israel, like the kingdom of Judah, continued to worship Yahweh, but Jeroboam established new religious centers, new holidays, new priests, and new symbols of the religion. The new religious centers that were to substitute for Jerusalem were the cities of Dan and Beth-El. Dan was the northernmost city in Israel, and Beth-El was one of the farthest south. Beth-El was in fact only a short distance north of Jerusalem on the Israel-Judah border, and so any Israelites who might have thought of worshiping in Jerusalem would be inclined to stop at Beth-El rather than make the additional travel—uphill—to Jerusalem.

Jeroboam's new national religious holiday was celebrated in the fall, one month after the major fall holiday of Judah. His new symbols of the religion, instead of the two golden cherubs in Jerusalem, were two molten golden calves. The word "calves," which appears in most translations, is, by the way, misleading. The word in the Hebrew text means a young bull, which is a symbol of strength, rather than the weaker images that the word "*calf*" usually connotes. The calf, or young bull, was often associated with the god El, the chief god of the Canaanites, who was in fact referred to as "Bull El." We therefore have some reason to believe that Jeroboam's version of the religion somehow identified Yahweh with El. The idea that Yahweh and El were one would have the added value of further uniting the Israelite population with the still large Canaanite population in Jeroboam's kingdom.

Jeroboam set up one of the golden calves in Beth-El and one in Dan. This was impressive because the calves, like the cherubs, were not statues of gods, but only the pedestal of the invisible God Yahweh. Thus God may have been pictured in Israel as enthroned over the entire kingdom, from the northern border to the southern, rather than as enthroned only in the Temple as in Judah.

King Jeroboam's Priests

Jeroboam's choice of priests for the new kingdom was crucial. The northern Levites had suffered badly under Solomon. Many had been residents of the twenty cities that Solomon gave to Hiram, the Phoenician king. Those who came from Shiloh suffered the most. In the days of the judges, Shiloh had been the location of the Tabernacle and ark, the people's central shrine. The priest-prophet-judge of Shiloh, Samuel, had designated and anointed the first two kings, Saul and David. Abiathar, from the priests of Shiloh, had been one of the two chief priests under David. Then Solomon expelled

Abiathar for supporting the losing brother in the fight for the succession, and the priests of Shiloh were out of power in Jerusalem. These members of the old priestly establishment of Israel had as much reason as anyone, or more, to feel betrayed and excluded by the royal house in Jerusalem. It is therefore interesting and hardly surprising that the prophet who instigated the secession and designated Jeroboam as king was a man called Ahijah of *Shiloh*.

The priests from Shiloh soon felt betrayed and excluded again. Jeroboam did not appoint them either at Dan or Beth-El. At Dan there was an old, established priesthood, founded by Moses' grandson according to the book of Judges. It probably continued to function there. At Beth-El, Jeroboam was appointing new faces, including individuals who were not Levites, to function at the altar of the golden calf. According to one biblical text, the new criterion for appointment to the priesthood under Jeroboam was not whether one was a Levite, but whether one would "fill his hand" with a young bull and seven rams.

The priests from Shiloh had no place in Jeroboam's new religious structure. They condemned the golden calves, which were the symbols of the religion, as heresy. Ahijah of Shiloh, the same prophet who is credited with having designated Jeroboam as king, is said later to have prophesied the fall of Jeroboam's family on account of the heresy. Since the tribe of Levi had no territory of its own as the other tribes had, the Levites of Shiloh and elsewhere in Israel had only two choices: they could move to Judah and try to find a place in the priestly hierarchy there, or they could remain in Israel and make whatever living they could, perhaps performing various religious services outside of the two major religious centers, perhaps depending on others' generosity. If the priests of Shiloh were indeed descendants of Moses, their present status, or lack of status, in both kingdoms must have been bitter for them. They had fallen from leadership of the nation to poor, landless dependency.

The Fall of Israel

The nation itself was now two nations, related but divided. They had a common language, a shared treasury of traditions, and similar but not identical forms of religious expression. The total area that the two kingdoms occupied was still quite small. The other areas that they controlled diminished considerably. Syria and Phoenicia had already broken free of the empire in Solomon's time. After the division of the kingdom, Judah controlled Edom, on its eastern border, for about a century, and then Edom rebelled and broke free. Israel controlled Moab for about the same length of time, and then Moab, too, rebelled and became independent. Israel and Judah were left as two small kingdoms, vulnerable to powerful nations like Egypt and Assyria. (See the map, p. 10.)

In Israel the monarchy was unstable. No family of kings ever held on to the throne for more than a few generations. The kingdom lasted two hundred years. Then the Assyrian empire conquered it in 722 B.C. and ended its existence as a nation. The population was dispersed. The Assyrians deported many Israelites into exile in various sections of the Assyrian empire. The exiled Israelites have come to be known as the ten lost tribes of Israel. Presumably there were also great numbers of refugees who fled from Israel south to Judah to escape the approaching Assyrian forces.

In Judah the monarchy was extremely stable, one of the longest-reigning dynasties in history. Judah survived for over a hundred years past the destruction of Israel.

During the two hundred years that these two kingdoms existed side by side, there lived two of the writers we are seeking. Each composed a version of the people's story. Both versions became part of the Bible. With this picture of the early years of the biblical world, we are now ready to identify these two of the writers of the Bible.

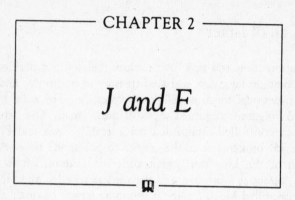

CHAPTER 2

J and E

Two Clues Converge

Two and a half thousand years after the events that I described in the last chapter took place, three investigators of who wrote the Bible each independently made the same discovery. One was a minister, one was a physician, and one was a professor. The discovery that they all made ultimately came down to the combination of two pieces of evidence: doublets and the names of God. They saw that there were apparently two versions each of a large number of biblical stories: two accounts of the creation, two accounts of each of several stories about the patriarchs Abraham and Jacob, and so on. Then they noticed that, quite often, one of the two versions of a story would refer to God by one name and the other version would refer to God by a different name.

In the case of the creation, for example, the first chapter of the Bible tells one version of how the world came to be created, and the second chapter of the Bible starts over with a different version of what happened.[1] In many ways they duplicate each other, and on several points they contradict each other. For example, they de-

scribe the same events in different order. In the first version, God
creates plants first, then animals, then man and woman. In the
second version, God creates *man* first. Then he creates plants.
Then, so that the man should not be alone, God creates animals.
And last, after the man does not find a satisfactory mate among the
animals, God creates woman. And so we have:

Genesis 1	Genesis 2
plants	man
animals	plants
man & woman	animals
	woman

   The two stories have two different pictures of what happened.
Now, the three investigators noticed that the first version of the
creation story always refers to the creator as God—thirty-five times.
The second version always refers to him by his name, *Yahweh God*—
eleven times. The first version never calls him Yahweh; the second
version never calls him God.

Later comes the story of the great flood and Noah's ark, and it,
too, can be separated into two complete versions that sometimes
duplicate each other and sometimes contradict each other.[2] And,
again, one version always calls the deity God, and the other version
always calls him Yahweh. There are two versions of the story of the
convenant between the deity and Abraham.[3] And, once again, in one
the deity introduces himself as Yahweh, and in one he introduces
himself as God. And so on. The investigators saw that they were not
simply dealing with a book that repeated itself a great deal, and they
were not dealing with a loose collection of somewhat similar stories.
They had discovered two separate works that *someone* had cut up
and combined into one.

The Discovery of the Sources

The first of the three persons who made this discovery was a German minister, Henning Bernhard Witter, in 1711. His book made very little impact and was in fact forgotten until it was rediscovered two centuries later, in 1924.

The second person to see it was Jean Astruc, a French professor of medicine and court physician to Louis XV. He published his findings at the age of seventy, anonymously in Brussels and secretly in Paris in 1753. His book, too, made very little impression on anyone. Some belittled it, perhaps partly because it was by a medical doctor and not by a scholar.

But when a third person, who was a scholar, made the same discovery and published it in 1780, the world could no longer ignore it. The third person was Johann Gottfried Eichhorn, a known and respected scholar in Germany and the son of a pastor. He called the group of biblical stories that referred to the deity as God "E," because the Hebrew word for God is El or Elohim. He called the group of stories that referred to the deity as Yahweh "J" (which in German is pronounced like English Y).

The idea that the Bible's early history was a combination of two originally separate works by two different people lasted only eighteen years. Practically before anyone had a chance to consider the implications of this idea for the Bible and religion, investigators discovered that the first five books of the Bible were not, in fact, even by *two* writers—they were by *four*.

They discovered that E was not one but two sources. The two had looked like only one because they both called the deity Elohim, not Yahweh. But the investigators now noticed that within the group of stories that called the deity Elohim there were still doublets. There were also differences of style, differences of language, and differences of interests. In short, the same kinds of evidence that had led to the discovery of J and E now led to the discovery of a third source that had been hidden within E. The differences of interests were intriguing. This third set of stories seemed to be particularly intersted in *priests*. It contained stories about priests, laws about priests, matters of ritual, sacrifice, incense-burning, and purity, and concern with dates, numbers, and measurements. This source therefore came to be known as the Priestly source—for short, P.

The sources J, E, and P were found to flow through the first four of the five Books of Moses: Genesis, Exodus, Leviticus, and Numbers. However, there was hardly a trace of them in the fifth book, Deuteronomy, except for a few lines in the last chapters. Deuteronomy is written in an entirely different style from those of the other four books. The differences are obvious even in translation. The vocabulary is different. There are different recurring expressions and favorite phrases. There are doublets of whole sections of the first four books. There are blatant contradictions of detail between it and the others. Even part of the wording of the Ten Commandments is different. Deuteronomy appeared to be independent, a fourth source. It was called D.

The discovery that the Torah of Moses was really four works that had once been separate was not necessarily a crisis in itself. After all, the New Testament also began with four Gospels—Matthew, Mark, Luke, and John—each of which told the story in its own way. Why then was there such a hostile reaction, among Christians and Jews, to the idea that the Old Testament (or Hebrew Bible) might begin with four "gospels" as well? The difference was that the Hebrew Bible's four sources had been combined so intricately and accepted as Moses' own writing for so long, about two thousand years; the new discoveries were flying in the face of an old, accepted, sacred tradition. The biblical investigators were unraveling a finely woven garment, and no one knew where these new investigations would lead.

The Story of Noah—Twice

These first books of the Bible had as extraordinary a manner of composition as any book on earth. Imagine assigning four different people to write a book on the same subject, then taking their four different versions and cutting them up and combining them into one long, continuous account, then claiming that the account was all by one person. Then imagine giving the book to detectives and leaving them to figure out (1) that the book was not by one person, (2) that it was by four, (3) who the four were, and (4) who combined them.

For those readers who want to get a better sense of how this looks, I have translated the biblical story of Noah's ark, as it appears in Genesis, with its two sources printed in two different kinds of type. The flood story is a combination of the J source and the P source. J is printed here in regular type, and P is printed in boldface capitals. If you read either source from beginning to end, and then go back and read the other one, you will be able to see for yourself two complete, continuous accounts, each with its own vocabulary and concerns:

The Flood—Genesis 6:5–8:22

(Priestly text in boldface capitals, J text in regular type)

GENESIS 6:

5   And Yahweh saw that the evil of humans was great in the earth, and all the inclination of the thoughts of their heart was only evil all the day.

6   And Yahweh regretted that he had made humans in the earth, and he was grieved to his heart.

7   And Yahweh said, "I shall wipe out the humans which I have created from the face of the earth, from human to beast to creeping thing to bird of the heavens, for I regret that I have made them."

8   But Noah found favor in Yahweh's eyes.

9   **THESE ARE THE GENERATIONS OF NOAH: NOAH WAS A RIGHTEOUS MAN, PERFECT IN HIS GENERATIONS. NOAH WALKED WITH GOD.**

10   **AND NOAH SIRED THREE SONS: SHEM, HAM, AND JAPHETH.**

11   **AND THE EARTH WAS CORRUPTED BEFORE GOD, AND THE EARTH WAS FILLED WITH VIOLENCE.**

12   **AND GOD SAW THE EARTH, AND HERE IT WAS CORRUPTED, FOR ALL FLESH HAD CORRUPTED ITS WAY ON THE EARTH.**

13 AND GOD SAID TO NOAH, "THE END OF ALL FLESH HAS COME BEFORE ME, FOR THE EARTH IS FILLED WITH VIOLENCE BECAUSE OF THEM, AND HERE I AM GOING TO DESTROY THEM WITH THE EARTH.

14 MAKE YOURSELF AN ARK OF GOPHER WOOD, MAKE ROOMS WITH THE ARK, AND PITCH IT OUTSIDE AND INSIDE WITH PITCH.

15 AND THIS IS HOW YOU SHALL MAKE IT: THREE HUNDRED CUBITS THE LENGTH OF THE ARK, FIFTY CUBITS ITS WIDTH, AND THIRTY CUBITS ITS HEIGHT.

16 YOU SHALL MAKE A WINDOW FOR THE ARK, AND YOU SHALL FINISH IT TO A CUBIT FROM THE TOP, AND YOU SHALL MAKE AN ENTRANCE TO THE ARK IN ITS SIDE. YOU SHALL MAKE LOWER, SECOND, AND THIRD STORIES FOR IT.

17 AND HERE I AM BRINGING THE FLOOD, WATER OVER THE EARTH, TO DESTROY ALL FLESH IN WHICH IS THE BREATH OF LIFE FROM UNDER THE HEAVENS. EVERYTHING WHICH IS ON THE LAND WILL DIE.

18 AND I SHALL ESTABLISH MY COVENANT WITH YOU. AND YOU SHALL COME TO THE ARK, YOU AND YOUR SONS AND YOUR WIFE AND YOUR SONS' WIVES WITH YOU.

19 AND OF ALL THE LIVING, OF ALL FLESH, YOU SHALL BRING TWO TO THE ARK TO KEEP ALIVE WITH YOU, THEY SHALL BE MALE AND FEMALE.

20 OF THE BIRDS ACCORDING TO THEIR KIND, AND OF THE BEASTS ACCORDING TO THEIR KIND, AND OF ALL THE CREEPING THINGS OF THE EARTH ACCORDING TO THEIR KIND, TWO OF EACH WILL COME TO YOU TO KEEP ALIVE.

21 AND YOU, TAKE FOR YOURSELF OF ALL FOOD WHICH WILL BE EATEN AND GATHER IT TO YOU, AND IT WILL BE FOR YOU AND FOR THEM FOR FOOD."

22 AND NOAH DID ACCORDING TO ALL THAT GOD COMMANDED HIM—SO HE DID.

GENESIS 7:

1 And Yahweh said to Noah, "Come, you and all your household, to the ark, for I have seen you as righteous before me in this generation.

2 Of all the clean beasts, take yourself seven pairs, man and his

woman; and of the beasts which are not clean, two, man and his woman.

3   Also of the birds of the heavens seven pairs, male and female, to keep alive seed on the face of the earth.

4   For in seven more days I shall rain on the earth forty days and forty nights, and I shall wipe out all the substance that I have made from upon the face of the earth."

5   And Noah did according to all that Yahweh had commanded him.

6   AND NOAH WAS SIX HUNDRED YEARS OLD, AND THE FLOOD WAS ON THE EARTH.

7   And Noah and his sons and his wife and his sons' wives with him came to the ark from before the waters of the flood.

8   OF THE CLEAN BEASTS AND OF THE BEASTS WHICH WERE NOT CLEAN, AND OF THE BIRDS AND OF ALL THOSE WHICH CREEP UPON THE EARTH,

9   TWO OF EACH CAME TO NOAH TO THE ARK, MALE AND FEMALE, AS GOD HAD COMMANDED NOAH.

10   And seven days later the waters of the flood were on the earth.

11   IN THE SIX HUNDREDTH YEAR OF NOAH'S LIFE, IN THE SECOND MONTH, IN THE SEVENTEENTH DAY OF THE MONTH, ON THIS DAY ALL THE FOUNTAINS OF THE GREAT DEEP WERE BROKEN UP, AND THE WINDOWS OF THE HEAVENS WERE OPENED.

12   And there was rain on the earth, forty days and forty nights.

13   IN THIS VERY DAY, NOAH AND SHEM, HAM, AND JAPHETH, THE SONS OF NOAH, AND NOAH'S WIFE AND HIS SONS' THREE WIVES WITH THEM CAME TO THE ARK,

14   THEY AND ALL THE LIVING THINGS ACCORDING TO THEIR KIND, AND ALL THE BEASTS ACCORDING TO THEIR KIND, AND ALL THE CREEPING THINGS THAT CREEP ON THE EARTH ACCORDING TO THEIR KIND, AND ALL THE BIRDS ACCORDING TO THEIR KIND, AND EVERY WINGED BIRD.

15   AND THEY CAME TO NOAH TO THE ARK, TWO OF EACH, OF ALL FLESH IN WHICH IS THE BREATH OF LIFE.

16   AND THOSE WHICH CAME WERE MALE AND FEMALE, SOME OF ALL FLESH CAME, AS GOD HAD COMMANDED HIM. And Yahweh closed it for him.

17 And the flood was on the earth for forty days and forty nights, and the waters multiplied and raised the ark, and it was lifted from the earth.

18 And the waters grew strong and multiplied greatly on the earth, and the ark went on the surface of the waters.

19 And the waters grew very very strong on the earth, and they covered all the high mountains that are under all the heavens.

20 Fifteen cubits above, the waters grew stronger, and they covered the mountains.

21 AND ALL FLESH, THOSE THAT CREEP ON THE EARTH, THE BIRDS, THE BEASTS, AND THE WILD ANIMALS, AND ALL THE SWARMING THINGS THAT SWARM ON THE EARTH, AND ALL THE HUMANS EXPIRED.

22 Everything that had the breathing spirit of life in its nostrils, everything that was on the dry ground, died.

23 And he wiped out all the substance that was on the face of the earth, from human to beast, to creeping thing, and to bird of the heavens, and they were wiped out from the earth, and only Noah and those who were with him in the ark were left.

24 AND THE WATERS GREW STRONG ON THE EARTH A HUNDRED FIFTY DAYS.

GENESIS 8:

1 AND GOD REMEMBERED NOAH AND ALL THE LIVING, AND ALL THE BEASTS THAT WERE WITH HIM IN THE ARK, AND GOD PASSED A WIND OVER THE EARTH, AND THE WATERS WERE DECREASED.

2 AND THE FOUNTAINS OF THE DEEP AND THE WINDOWS OF THE HEAVENS WERE SHUT, and the rain was restrained from the heavens.

3 And the waters receded from the earth continually, AND THE WATERS WERE ABATED AT THE END OF A HUNDRED FIFTY DAYS.

4 AND THE ARK RESTED, IN THE SEVENTH MONTH, IN THE SEVENTEENTH DAY OF THE MONTH, ON THE MOUNTAINS OF ARARAT.

5 AND THE WATERS CONTINUED RECEDING UNTIL THE TENTH MONTH; IN THE TENTH MONTH, ON THE FIRST OF THE MONTH, THE TOPS OF THE MOUNTAINS APPEARED.

6 And it was at the end of forty days, and Noah opened the window of the ark which he had made.

7   AND HE SENT OUT A RAVEN, AND IT WENT BACK AND FORTH
UNTIL THE WATERS DRIED UP FROM THE EARTH.

8   And he sent out a dove from him to see whether the waters had
eased from the face of the earth.

9   And the dove did not find a resting place for its foot, and it
returned to him to the ark, for waters were on the face of the earth,
and he put out his hand and took it and brought it to him to the
ark.

10   And he waited seven more days, and he again sent out a dove
from the ark.

11   And the dove came to him at evening time, and here was an
olive leaf torn off in its mouth, and Noah knew that the waters had
eased from the earth.

12   And he waited seven more days, and he sent out a dove, and it
did not return to him ever again.

13   AND IT WAS IN THE SIX HUNDRED AND FIRST YEAR, IN THE
FIRST MONTH, ON THE FIRST OF THE MONTH, THE WATERS DRIED
FROM THE EARTH. And Noah turned back the covering of the ark
and looked, and here the face of the earth had dried.

14   AND IN THE SECOND MONTH, ON THE TWENTY-SEVENTH DAY
OF THE MONTH, THE EARTH DRIED UP.

15   AND GOD SPOKE TO NOAH, SAYING,

16   "GO OUT FROM THE ARK, YOU AND YOUR WIFE AND YOUR SONS'
WIVES WITH YOU.

17   ALL THE LIVING THINGS THAT ARE WITH YOU, OF ALL FLESH,
OF THE BIRDS, AND OF THE BEASTS, AND OF ALL THE CREEPING
THINGS THAT CREEP ON THE EARTH, THAT GO OUT WITH YOU,
SHALL SWARM IN THE EARTH AND BE FRUITFUL AND MULTIPLY IN
THE EARTH."

18   AND NOAH AND HIS SONS AND HIS WIFE AND HIS SONS' WIVES
WENT OUT.

19   ALL THE LIVING THINGS, ALL THE CREEPING THINGS AND ALL
THE BIRDS, ALL THAT CREEP ON THE EARTH, BY THEIR FAMILIES,
THEY WENT OUT OF THE ARK.

20   And Noah built an altar to Yahweh, and he took some of each
of the clean beasts and of each of the clean birds, and he offered
sacrifices on the altar.

21   And Yahweh smelled the pleasant smell, and Yahweh said to his heart, "I shall not again curse the ground on man's account, for the inclination of the human heart is evil from their youth, and I shall not again strike all the living as I have done.

22   All the rest of the days of the earth, seed and harvest, and cold and heat, and summer and winter, and day and night shall not cease."

Each in Its Own Words

The very fact that it is possible to separate out two continuous stories like this is remarkable itself, and it is strong evidence for the hypothesis. One need only try to do the same thing with any other book to see how impressive this phenomenon is.

But it is not only that it is possible to carve out two stories. What makes the case so powerful is that each story consistently uses its own language. The P story (the one in boldface) consistently refers to the deity as God. The J story always uses the name Yahweh. P refers to the sex of the animals with the words "male and female" (Gen 6:19; 7:9,16). J uses the terms "man and his woman" (7:2) as well as male and female. P says that everything "expired" (6:17; 7:21). J says that everything "died" (7:22).

The two versions do not just differ on terminology. They differ on actual details of the story. P has one pair of each kind of animal. J has seven pairs of clean animals and one pair of unclean animals. ("Clean" means fit for sacrifice. Sheep are clean; lions are unclean.) P pictures the flood as lasting a year (370 days). J says it was forty days and forty nights. P has Noah send out a raven. J says a dove. P obviously has a concern for ages, dates, and measurements in cubits. J does not.

Probably the most remarkable difference of all between the two is their different ways of picturing God. It is not just that they call the deity by different names. J pictures a deity who can regret things that he has done (6:6,7), which raises interesting theological questions, such as whether an all-powerful, all-knowing being would ever regret past actions. It pictures a deity who can be "grieved to his heart" (6:6), who personally closes the ark (7:16) and smells Noah's sacrifice (8:21). This anthropomorphic quality of J is virtually entirely lacking in P. There God is regarded more as a transcendent controller of the universe.

The two flood stories are separable and complete. Each has its own language, its own details, and even its own conception of God. And even that is not the whole picture. The J flood story's language, details, and conception of God are consistent with the language, details, and conception of God in other J stories. The P flood story is consistent with other P stories. And so on. The investigators found each of the sources to be a consistent collection of stories, poems, and laws.

The Doorstep

The discovery that there were four separate, internally consistent documents came to be known as the Documentary Hypothesis. The process was also called "Higher Criticism."[4] What had begun as an idea by three men of the eighteenth century came to dominate investigations of the Bible by the end of the nineteenth century.

It had taken centuries of collecting clues to arrive at this stage which one could regard as fairly advanced or really quite minimal, depending on one's point of view. On the one hand, for centuries no one could easily challenge the accepted tradition that Moses was the author of the Five Books, and now people of acknowledged piety could say and write openly that he was not. They were able to identify at least four hands writing in the first five books of the Bible. Also, there was the hand of an extremely skillful collector known as a redactor, someone who was capable of combining and organizing these separate documents into a single work that was united enough to be readable as a continuous narrative.

On the other hand, what these detectives of biblical origins had arrived at was only the doorstep. They were able to see that a puzzle existed, and they were able to begin to get an idea of how complex the puzzle was going to be. True, they could identify four documents and a redactor, but who wrote those documents? When did they live? What was their purpose? Did they know each other's work? Did any of them know that they were writing a *Bible*, a work to be held as sacred and authoritative? And the mysterious redactor: was it one person, or were there several? Who were they? Why did they combine the documents in this complex way? The answers were buried in the pages of the Bible and in the soil of the Middle East. By digging into both, my predecessors and I found out how the stories in those pages were connected with that world.

Two Countries, Two Writers

The first two sources, J and E, were written by two persons who lived during the period that I described in the last chapter. They were tied to the life of that period, its major events, its politics, its religion, and its catastrophes. In this chapter I intend to demonstrate this and to identify the persons who wrote them.

First, the author of J came from Judah and the author of E came from Israel. A number of biblical scholars before me have suggested this, but what is new here is that I mean to present a stronger collection of evidence for this than has been made known before, I mean to be more specific about who the two writers were, and I mean to show more specifically how the biblical stories actually related to these two men and to the events of their world.

The mere fact that different stories in the first books of the Bible call God by different names of course proves nothing in itself. Someone could write about the queen of England and sometimes call her the queen and sometimes call her Elizabeth II. But, as I have said, there was something more suspicious about the way the different names of the deity lined up in the first few books of the Bible. The two different names, Yahweh and Elohim, seemed to line up consistently in each of the two versions of the same stories in the doublets. If we separate the Elohim (E) stories from the Yahweh (J) stories, we get a consistent series of clues that the E stories were written by someone concerned with Israel and the J stories by someone concerned with Judah.[5]

J from Judah, E from Israel

First, there is the matter of the settings of the stories. In Genesis, in stories that call God *Yahweh*, the patriarch Abraham lives in Hebron.[6] Hebron was the principal city of Judah, the capital of Judah under King David, the city from which David's Judean chief priest, Zadok, came.

In the covenant that *Yahweh* makes with Abraham, he promises that Abraham's descendants will have the land "from the river of Egypt to the . . . river Euphrates."[7] These were the nation's boundaries under King David, the founder of Judah's royal family.

But in a story that calls God *Elohim*, Abraham's grandson Jacob has a face-to-face fight with someone who turns out to be God (or perhaps an angel), and Jacob names the place where it happens Peni-El (which means "Face-of-God"). Peni-El was a city that King Jeroboam built in Israel.[8]

Both sources, J and E, tell stories about the city of Beth-El, and both kingdoms, Judah and Israel, made political *claims* on Beth-El, which was on the border between them.[9]

Both sources, J and E, tell stories about the city of Shechem, which Jeroboam built and made the capital of Israel. But the two stories are very different. According to the J story, a man named Shechem, who is the original prince of that city, loves Jacob's daughter Dinah and sleeps with her. He then asks for her hand in marriage. Jacob's sons reply that they could not contemplate this or any intermarriage with the people of Shechem because the Shechemites are not circumcised and the sons of Jacob are. The prince of Shechem and his father Hamor therefore persuade all the men of Shechem to undergo circumcision. While the men are immobile from the pain of the surgery, two of Jacob's sons, Simeon and Levi, enter the city, kill all of the men, and take back their sister Dinah. Their father Jacob criticizes them for doing this, but they answer, "Should he treat our sister like a whore?" And that is the end of the story.[10] This J story of how Israel acquired its capital city is not a very pleasant one. The E story, meanwhile, tells it this way:

And [Jacob] bought the portion of the field where he pitched his tent from the hand of the sons of Hamor, father of Shechem, for a hundred qesita.[11]

How did Israel acquire Shechem? The E author says they bought it. The J author says they massacred it.

The Origins of the Tribes

In the stories of the birth of Jacob's sons and grandsons—each of whom becomes the ancestor of a tribe—there is usually a reference to the deity as they name the child. The group of stories that invoke *Elohim* are the stories of:

> Dan
> Naphtali
> Gad
> Asher
> Issachar
> Zebulon
> Ephraim
> Manasseh
> Benjamin[12]

In short, the *Elohim* group includes the names of all of the tribes of Israel.[13] The group of stories that invoke the name of *Yahweh* are the stories of:

> Reuben
> Simeon
> Levi
> Judah

The first three of the four names on this list are the names of tribes who lost their territory and merged into the other tribes. The only name of a tribe with existing territory in the Yahweh narrative is Judah. [14]

The J story goes even further to justify the ascendancy of Judah. According to the story, Reuben is the firstborn son, Simeon is the second, Levi the third, and Judah the fourth. In the ancient Near East, birth order was extremely important, because the firstborn son was entitled to the birthright, which meant the largest portion of the father's inheritance (generally double the other brothers' inheritances). We should therefore have expected Reuben, the oldest son, to have the birthright. But there is a story that reports that Reuben sleeps with one of his father's concubines, and his father finds out. The next two sons in line for the birthright would be Simeon and Levi. But in the J Shechem story they are the ones who massacre the city and are criticized by their father. And so, in J, the birthright comes to the fourth son: Judah! In Jacob's poetic deathbed blessing of his sons, here is what he says about Reuben:

> Reuben, you are my firstborn,
> My strength and the beginning of my power,
> Preeminent in dignity and preeminent of might.
> Unstable as water, you shall not be preeminent
> Because you went up to your father's bed. [15]

And here is what he says about Simeon and Levi:

> Simeon and Levi are brothers,
> Implements of destruction are their tools of trade.
> . . . In their anger they killed a man,
> And by their will they houghed a bull.
> Cursed is their anger, for it is fierce,
> And their wrath, for it is harsh.
> I shall divide them in Jacob,
> And I shall scatter them in Israel. [16]

But he says about Judah:

> Judah, you are the one your brothers will praise . . .
> Your father's sons will bow down to you. [17]

Judah gets the birthright in J.

Who gets it in E? In the E version of Jacob's deathbed scene, Jacob bequeathes the double portion to Joseph, announcing that each of Joseph's two sons, Ephraim and Manasseh, will receive a full portion, equivalent to the portions of Reuben, Simeon, and the others. Why did the author of E favor Joseph and his sons? The answer lies in one more detail of E's story. When Jacob is giving his deathbed blessing to Joseph and his sons, Joseph sets his sons in front of Jacob in such a way that Jacob will put his right hand on the head of Manasseh, the older son. The right hand is the sign of preeminence. But Jacob crosses his arms, so his right hand is on Ephraim's head. Joseph protests the reversal, but Jacob insists that Ephraim will become greater.[18] What is it about Ephraim? Why does the author of E develop the hierarchy to culminate not in any of Jacob's sons, but in one of his grandsons who is not even a firstborn? Was there anything historically significant about the tribe of Ephraim in the writer's age? Answer: Ephraim was King *Jeroboam*'s tribe. Jeroboam's capital city, Shechem, was located in the hills of Ephraim.[19] Ephraim, in fact, was used as another name for the kingdom of Israel.[20]

Evidence from the Stories

The J stories fit the cities and territory of Judah. The E stories fit the cities and territory of Israel. I found that other details of the stories consistently fit this picture as well:

Both J and E have versions of the story of Joseph. In both, Joseph's brothers are jealous of him and plan to kill him, but one of the brothers saves him. In E it is Reuben, the oldest, who saves him.[21] But in J it is *Judah* who saves him.[22]

The E story of Jacob's deathbed testament has a pun in the Hebrew. In creating portions for Ephraim and Manasseh, Jacob tells Joseph, "I have given you one *portion* more than your brothers."[23] The Hebrew word that is translated here as "portion" is *šekem*, or as we pronounce it in English, Shechem. Telling the father of Ephraim that he is getting an extra *Shechem* is like telling the governor of

Michigan, "I have given the other states some trees, but I have given you *an arbor*."

The J stories meanwhile seem to be punning on the name of the first king of Judah after the division: Rehoboam. The Hebrew root of the name Rehoboam (r-ḥ-b) occurs six times in the J stories, usually suggesting, as does the king's name, the expanse of the country.[24] The root never occurs in E.

According to an E story, Joseph makes a deathbed request in Egypt that someday his bones should be carried back to his homeland for burial.[25] At the end of the E story of the Exodus from Egypt, the Israelites do carry his bones back with them.[26] This concern for the burial of Joseph only occurs in E. Where was the traditional location of the tomb of Joseph? In Shechem, capital of Israel.[27]

Both J and E have stories of the enslavement of the people in Egypt. The J source usually refers to the Egyptians who oversee the slaves as "taskmasters," but in a passage that appears to be E they are called "officers of *missîm*."[28] Recall that *missîm* was the term for King Solomon's forced-labor policy, a policy that was one of the main reasons for the secession of the northern tribes of Israel. The E wording appears to be an insult to Judah and its royal family.

The insult may be a double one, because the most prominent of Solomon's wives was the daughter of the pharaoh of that period. The book of 1 Kings lists her first among his wives.[29] Such a marriage would have been a notable one, further, because the kings of Egypt disdained marrying their daughters to foreigners. There is no other case recorded in the ancient Near East of a marriage of an Egyptian princess to a foreign ruler.

In E, Moses' faithful assistant is Joshua. Joshua leads the people in battle against the Amalekites; he serves as watchman inside the Tent of Meeting whenever Moses is not meeting with the deity there; he is the only Israelite who is not involved in the golden calf incident; and he seeks to prevent the misuse of prophecy.[30] In J, on the other hand, Joshua plays no role. Why the special treatment of Joshua in E but not in J? Joshua was a *northern* hero. He is identified as coming from the tribe of Ephraim, *Jeroboam*'s tribe; Joshua's tomb is in the territory of Ephraim, and, according to the last chapter of the book of Joshua, Joshua's work culminates in a covenant ceremony at *Shechem*.[31]

According to a J story, Moses sends a group of spies from the wilderness into the promised land. All but one of the spies report that the land is impregnable because its inhabitants are so huge and fierce. The one spy who challenges this report and encourages the people to have faith is *Caleb*. In the story, the spies travel through the Negev (the southern desert of the land), the hill country, as far as Hebron, then to the Wadi Eshkol. All of these places are in Judah's territory. *In J, the spies only see Judah.*[32] As for the hero of the story, Caleb, he is the eponymous ancestor of the Calebites. The Calebites held territory in the hill country of Judah. The Calebite territory in fact included Hebron, Judah's capital.[33]

The cumulative, consistent conclusion from all of this evidence, it seems to me, is: (1) the early investigators were right about the existence of the two sources, J and E; (2) the person who wrote J was particularly concerned with the kingdom of Judah, and the person who wrote E was particularly interested in the kingdom of Israel.

Still, as I said in the introduction we are interested in more than the authors' real estate preferences. The question is, why did they write these stories? What was happening in their world that prompted them to write these things?

The Twins

Take, for example, the biblical stories about the twins Jacob and Esau. In these stories, Abraham's son, Isaac, marries Rebekah, and she gives birth to twin sons. The first to come out of his mother's womb is Esau. The secondborn is Jacob. While they are still in Rebekah's womb, *Yahweh* tells Rebekah:

> *Two nations are in your womb,*
> *And two peoples will be separated from inside you;*
> *And one people will be stronger than the other people,*
> *And the greater will serve the younger.*[34]

The boys grow. On one occasion, Esau comes back from the field famished. His brother, Jacob, is making red lentil stew. Jacob tells Esau that he will give him some of the food only if Esau swears to give him his birthright in return. Esau capitulates.[35]

More time passes. Their father, Isaac, intends to give his deathbed blessing to Esau. Rebekah, however, encourages Jacob to pose as his elder brother and thus deceive his weak-eyed father into giving him the blessing instead. Jacob does it. He wears his brother's clothing, and he puts goat skins on his arms because his brother is "an hairy man." Isaac gives Jacob the blessing, *which includes dominion over his brother*. When Esau arrives, Isaac tells him that the blessing has already gone to Jacob. Esau asks for a blessing as well. His father gives him the following:

> *By your sword you will live*
> *And you will serve your brother.*
> *And it will be, when you are brought down,*
> *That you will break his yoke from your shoulders.* [36]

Why did someone write these stories, with these details? The answers are tied to the life of the writer's world.

Why red lentil stew? Because, the story says, Esau became known after that as "Red." The word for "red" in Hebrew is *Edom*. That is, Esau is traditionally regarded as the father of the Edomites.

Why twin brothers? Because the people of Israel-Judah regarded the Edomites as kin, as related to them ethnically and/or linguistically (as opposed to, say, Egyptians or Philistines, who were regarded as "outsiders").

Why the revelation to Rebekah that her younger son's descendants would dominate her older son's? Because the young kingdom of Israel-Judah, under King David, defeated the older kingdom of Edom and dominated it for two hundred years.

Why does Jacob get the birthright (a double portion) and the blessing (prosperity and dominion)? Because Israel-Judah became larger and more prosperous than Edom and dominated it.

Why does Esau/Edom get a blessing that "you will break his yoke from your shoulders"? Because Edom finally broke free and achieved its independence during the reign of the Judean King Jehoram (848–842 B.C.). [37]

These stories all refer to the deity as Yahweh or show other signs of being part of J. Why do stories about relations with Esau/Edom occur in J and not in E? J is from Judah. Judah bordered Edom, Israel did not.

On each point, the details of the stories correspond to the histori-

cal record. The J author composed the stories of his people's ancestors with an eye to explaining and justifying the world situation in
which he lived.

Sunday school versions of this story often try to vindicate Jacob.
With slight changes or reinterpretations, they make Jacob the good
son and Esau the bad one. But the J writer was more sophisticated
then his later interpreters. He told a story in which Jacob was coura-
geous and clever, but also dishonest. He did not make his heroes
perfect (any more than the Court History of David made David
perfect). His task was rather to compose a story that reflected and
explained the political and social realities of the world that he knew.
Anyone who reads the stories of Jacob and Esau can see how well he
succeeded.

CHAPTER 3

Two Kingdoms, Two Writers

THE Bible's stories have proved to be a chain of clues to the identity of their authors, and at the same time they have proved to be windows into that ancient world. The J stories reflect conditions in the time and place in which their author lived, and they show where some of this writer's interests lay.

The E stories reveal more about their author's identity than the J stories do about theirs.

The Golden Calf

The most revealing of all is the E story of the golden calf, which I summarized briefly in the Introduction. While Moses is getting the Ten Commandments on the mountain of God, Aaron makes a golden calf for the people. They say, "These are your gods, Israel, that brought you up from the land of Egypt." Aaron says, "A holiday to Yahweh tomorrow!"[1] The people sacrifice and celebrate wildly. Meanwhile, God tells Moses what is happening below, and God says that he will destroy the people and start a new people descended from Moses. Moses pleads with God to be merciful, and God relents. Moses comes down from the mountain with his assistant Joshua. When he sees the calf and the condition of the people, he smashes the tablets in anger. Then the tribe of Levi gather around Moses and carry out a bloody purge among the people. Moses makes a plea to God to forgive the people's offense and not destroy them.[2]

The story is all questions. Why did the person who wrote this story depict his people as rebellious at the very time of their liberation and their receiving the covenant? Why did he picture *Aaron* as leader of the heresy? Why does Aaron not suffer any punishment for it in the end? Why did the author picture a *golden calf*? Why do the people say "*These* are your *gods*, Israel . . .," when there is only one calf there? And why do they say ". . . *that brought you up from the land of Egypt*" when the calf obviously was not made until after they were out of Egypt? Why does Aaron say "A holiday to *Yahweh* tomorrow" when he is presenting the calf as a rival to Yahweh? Why is the calf treated as a god in this story, when the calf was *not* a god in the ancient Near East? Why did the writer picture Moses as smashing the tablets of the Ten Commandments? Why picture the Levites as acting in bloody zeal? Why include Joshua in the story? Why depict Joshua as dissociated from the golden calf event?

We already have enough information from our acquaintances with the world that produced the Bible to answer all of these questions. We have already seen considerable evidence that the author of J was from Judah and the author of E from Israel. We have also seen evidence that suggests that the Israelite author of E had a particular interest in matters that related to King Jeroboam and his policies. E deals with cities that Jeroboam rebuilt: Shechem, Penuel, Beth-El. E justifies the ascendancy of his home tribe, Ephraim. E disdains the Judean policy of *missîm*. E gives special attention to the matter of the burial of Joseph, whose traditional gravesite was in Jeroboam's capital, Shechem. Further, E is a source which particularly emphasizes Moses as its hero, much more than J does. In this story, it is Moses' intercession with God that saves the people from destruction. E also especially develops Moses' personal role in the liberation from slavery, in a way that J does not. In E there is less material on the patriarchs than on Moses; in J there is more on the patriarchs.

Let us consider the possibility that the person who wrote E was a Levitical priest, probably from Shiloh, and therefore possibly descended from Moses. Such a person would have an interest in developing these things: the oppressive Judean economic policies, the establishment of an independent kingdom under Jeroboam, and the superior status of Moses. If this is true, that the author of E was a Shiloh Levite possibly descended from Moses, then this answers every one of the questions about the golden calf story.

Recall that the priests of Shiloh suffered the loss of their place in the priestly hierarchy under King Solomon. Their chief, Abiathar, was expelled from Jerusalem. The other chief priest, Zadok, who was regarded as a descendant of Aaron, meanwhile remained in power. Northern Levites' lands were given to the Phoenicians. The Shiloh prophet Ahijah instigated the northern tribes' secession, and he designated Jeroboam as the northern king. The Shiloh priests' hopes for the new kingdom, however, were frustrated when Jeroboam established the *golden calf* religious centers at Dan and Beth-El, and he did not appoint them as priests there. For this old family of priests, what should have been a time of liberation had been turned into a time of religious betrayal. The symbol of their exclusion in Israel was the *golden calves*. The symbol of their exclusion in Judah was *Aaron*. Someone from that family, the author of E, wrote a story that said that soon after the Israelite's liberation from slavery, they committed heresy. What was the heresy? They worshiped a *golden calf*! Who made the golden calf! *Aaron*!

The details of the story fall into place. Why does Aaron not suffer any punishment in the story? Because no matter how much antipathy the author may have felt toward Aaron's descendants, that author could not change the entire historical recollection of his people. They had a tradition that Aaron was an ancient high priest. The high priest cannot be pictured as suffering any hurt from God because *in such a case he could not have continued to serve as high priest.* Any sort of blemish on the high priest would have disqualified him from service. The author could not just make up a story that the high priest had become disqualified at this early stage.

Why does Aaron say "A holiday to *Yahweh* tomorrow" when he is presenting the calf as a rival to Yahweh? Because the calf is not in fact a rival god. The calf, or young bull, is only the throne platform or symbol of the deity, not a deity itself. Why is the calf *treated* as a god in this story? Presumably because the story is polemical; the writer means to cast the golden calves of the kingdom of Israel in the worst light possible. In fact, we shall see other cases in which biblical writers use the word "gods" to include the golden calves and the golden cherubs; and in those cases, too, the text is polemical.

Why do the people say "*These* are your gods, Israel..." when there is only one calf? Why do they say "...that brought you up from the land of Egypt" when the calf was not made until they were out of Egypt? The answer seems to lie in the account of King Jeroboam in the book of 1 Kings. It states there that when Jeroboam made his two golden calves he declared to his people, "Here are your gods, Israel, that brought you up from the land of Egypt."[3] The people's words in Exodus are identical to Jeroboam's words in 1 Kings. It would be difficult for us to trace the textual history of these two passages now, but at minimum we can say that the writer of the golden calf account in Exodus seems to have taken the words that were traditionally ascribed to Jeroboam and placed them in the mouths of the people. This made the connection between his golden calf story and the golden calves of the kingdom of Israel crystal clear to his readers.

Why did the writer of E picture the Levites as acting in bloody zeal? He was a Levite. He wrote that Aaron had acted rebelliously while the other Levites alone acted loyally. Moses tells the Levites there that they have earned blessing by their actions. The story thus denigrates the ancestry of the Jerusalem priests while praising the rest of the Levites.

What is Joshua doing in this story, and why is he singled out as being dissociated from the heresy? Because, as we know, Joshua was a northern hero. His home tribe was the same as King Jeroboam's: Ephraim. His gravesite, like Joseph's, was in Ephraim. He is credited with having led a national covenant ceremony at Shechem, the place that was later to become Jeroboam's capital. The E writer therefore was adding to the golden calf story an element of praise for a northern hero who was associated in the tradition with the capital city and the preeminent tribe. The dissociation of Joshua from the golden calf heresy also explained why Joshua later becomes Moses' successor.

Why did the writer picture Moses as smashing the tablets of the Ten Commandments? Possibly because this raised doubts about

Judah's central religious shrine. The Temple in Judah housed the ark that was supposed to contain the two tablets of the Ten Commandments. According to the E story of the golden calf, *Moses smashes the tablets.* That means that according to the E source the ark down south in the Temple in Jerusalem either contains unauthentic tablets or no tablets at all.[4]

The author of E, in fashioning the golden calf story, attacked both the Israelite and the Judean religious establishments. Both had excluded his group. One might ask, why, then, was this writer so favorable to Jeroboam's kingdom in other stories? Why did he favor the cities of Shechem, Penuel, and especially Beth-El? Why did he favor the tribe of Ephraim? First, because *Shiloh* was in Ephraim, and its great priest Samuel was from Ephraim.[5] Second, presumably because the kingdom of Israel remained his only hope politically. He could look forward to a day when the illegitimate, non-Levite priests of Beth-El would be rejected, and his Levite group would be reinstated. Judah and Jerusalem offered no such hope at that time. The priests of the family of Aaron had been firmly established there since King Solomon's time. They were Levites and therefore no less legitimate than the priests of Shiloh. They were closely tied by bonds of politics and marriage to the royal family.[6] The only realistic hope for the Shiloh priests was in the northern kingdom. The E source therefore favored that kingdom's *political* structure while attacking its *religious* establishment.

Symbols of Faith

The golden calf story is not the only instance in which the author of E may have been criticizing both the northern and southern religious establishments.

In the J version of the commandments that God gives to Moses on Mount Sinai, there is a prohibition against making statues (idols). The wording of the J commandment is:

>   You shall not make for yourself molten gods.[7]

The J command here forbids only *molten* statues. The golden calves of Jeroboam in the north were molten. The golden cherubs of Solomon in the south were not molten. They were made of olive wood and then gold-plated. The J text thus fits the iconography of Judah. It may imply that the golden calves of northern Israel are inappropriate, even though they are not actually statues of a god; but it does not leave itself open to the countercharge that Judah's golden cherubs are inappropriate as well.

Meanwhile, the E source's formulation of this prohibition reads:

You shall not make with me gods of silver and gods of gold.
You shall not make them for yourselves.[8]

Perhaps this command refers only to actual statues of gods, but if it casts doubt on the throne-platform icons as well then it casts doubt on *both* the molten golden calves and the plated golden cherubs.

The relationship between the J and E sources and the religious symbols of Judah and Israel respectively is evident elsewhere as well. In a J text at the beginning of the book of Numbers the people set out from Sinai/Horeb on their journey to the promised land.[9] According to the description of their departure, the ark is carried in front of the people as they travel. Another J text also mentions the ark as important to the people's success in the wilderness. It in fact suggests that it is impossible to be militarily successful without it.[10] The ark, as we know, was regarded as the central object of the Temple of Solomon in Jerusalem. It should come as no surprise, therefore, that it is treated with such importance in J, but *it is never mentioned in E.*

E rather attributes much importance to the Tent of Meeting as the symbol of the presence of God among the people.[11] The Tent of Meeting (or Tabernacle), according to the books of Samuel, Kings, and Chronicles, was a primary site of the nation's worship until Solomon replaced the tent shrine with the Temple. The Tabernacle, moreover, was associated originally with the city of *Shiloh.* Given the other evidence for connecting the author of E with the priesthood of Shiloh, it should come as no surprise, therefore, that the Tent of Meeting has such importance in E, but *it is never mentioned in J.*

The ark does not appear in E. The Tabernacle does not appear in J. This is no coincidence. The stories in the sources treat the religious symbols of the respective communities from which they came.

Now we can also turn back to the beginning of the book of Genesis and appreciate the fact that at the conclusion of the story of Adam and Eve in the garden of Eden, which is a J narrative, Yahweh sets cherubs as the guardians of the path to the tree of life.[12] Since cherubs were in the Holy of Holies in the Jerusalem Temple, it is only natural that an advocate of Judah's religious traditions should picture cherubs as the guardians of something valuable and sacred.

The golden calf story reveals more about its author than probably any other story in J or E. In addition to all that it tells us about its author's background and about its author's skill in fashioning a story, it conveys how deep his anger was toward those who had displaced his group in Judah and in Israel. He could picture Aaron, ancestor of the Jerusalem priesthood, as committing heresy and dishonesty. He could picture the national symbols of Israelite religion as objects of idolatry. He could picture the nation who accepted these symbols as deserving a bloody purge. What he pictured Moses doing to the golden calf was what he himself might have liked to do to the calves of Dan and Beth-El: burn them with fire, grind them thin as dust.

Snow-White Miriam

There is another story in E that reflects the depth of the antagonism between the priests who identified with Moses (either as their founder or as their ancestor) and those who identified with Aaron. In this story, Aaron and his sister Miriam speak against Moses with regard to Moses' wife, and God personally reprimands them. It is worth reading this short, unusual story as it appears in the book of Numbers. It is usually left out of the Sunday school curriculum:

Snow-White Miriam, Numbers 12
E text in italics

1   *And Miriam and Aaron spoke against Moses on account of the Cushite wife he had taken, for he had taken a Cushite wife.*

2   *And they said, "Has Yahweh indeed only spoken through Moses? Has he not also spoken through us?" And Yahweh heard.*

3   *And the man Moses was very humble, more than any human on the face of the earth.*

4   And Yahweh[13] said suddenly to Moses and to Aaron and to Miriam, "Go out, the three of you, to the Tent of Meeting." And the three of them went out.

5   And Yahweh went down in a column of cloud and stood at the entrance of the tent, and he called Aaron and Miriam, and the two of them went out.

6   And he said, "Hear my words. If there will be a prophet among you, I, Yahweh, shall make myself known to him in a vision; in a dream I shall speak through him.

7   Not so my servant Moses, most faithful in all my house.

8   Mouth to mouth I shall speak through him, and vision, and not in enigmas, and he will see the form of Yahweh. And why were you not afraid to speak against my servant Moses?"

9   And Yahweh's anger burnt against them, and he went.

10   And the cloud turned back from on the tent, and here Miriam was leprous as snow. And Aaron turned to Miriam, and here she was leprous.

11   And Aaron said to Moses, "In me, my Lord, do not lay upon us the sin that we have done foolishly and that we have sinned.

12   Let her not be like someone who is half dead, whose flesh is half eaten when he comes out of his mother's womb."

13   And Moses cried out to Yahweh, saying, "God [El], heal her."

14   And Yahweh said to Moses, "And if her father had spit in her face, would she not be shamed for seven days? Let her be shut away for seven days outside the camp, and afterwards she will be restored."

15   And Miriam was shut away outside the camp seven days, and the
people did not travel until Miriam was gathered back.

Aaron and Miriam speak because of Moses' wife. What is it about
Moses' wife that bothers them? The text does not say. It only states
that she is Cushite. Since Cush is understood to mean Ethiopia in
the Bible, the issue may be that Moses' wife is black. The difficulty
is that there is also a place called Cushan in the Bible, which is a
region of Midian; and Moses' wife Zipporah has already been identified as Midianite. It is therefore uncertain whether the text here
refers to Zipporah or to a second wife. In either case, the most likely
reading of the text is that Miriam's and Aaron's opposition is based
on Moses' wife being different, whether that difference be racial or
ethnic. It is also psychologically interesting that their actual complaint never refers to the wife. That is, they do not complain out
loud about the thing that is really bothering them. Rather, they
direct their criticism at Moses himself. They question whether
Moses has any status beyond their own with regard to revelation.
("Has Yahweh indeed only spoken through Moses? Has he not also
spoken through us?")

This proves to be an error. Yahweh informs them that Moses does
indeed stand out from all other prophets in the degree of his intimacy with the divine. All other prophets only have visions, but
Moses actually sees God. The deity is described as angry at Aaron
and Miriam, and Miriam is stricken with a kind of leprosy in which
all the pigmentation of the skin disappears, leaving her "snow-
white." If the issue here is that Moses' wife is black, then the punishment to suit the crime in this case is singularly suitable.

As in the golden calf episode, Aaron does not suffer any punishment. Aaron had come to be known in the tradition as a priest, and
a person who has had leprosy is disqualified for the priestly function
thereafter. The writer therefore could not portray Aaron as sharing
his sister's punishment. Still, it remains clear in the story that Aaron
has offended, that God is angry at Aaron (verse 9), and that God
states explicitly that Moses' experience of God is superior to
Aaron's. This, too, fits the E interest in belittling the Aaronid
priesthood in Judah. Also, both here and in the golden calf story
Aaron respectfully addresses Moses as "my lord," acknowledging
Moses as his superior.

A story of a rebellion is a particularly useful means of making a point. The writer portrays a person or group as attacking the rightful authority or as being flagrantly disobedient—and then he portrays that person's or group's demise. The E stories of the golden calf and of snow-white Miriam accomplish this.

Reverence for Moses

We have covered a large amount of territory in this pursuit of two of the authors of the Bible. In story after story, we have been able to find clues connecting the story, the writer, and the writer's world. I have drawn on so many stories and pointed out all of these clues, first, simply to familiarize readers with the J and E sequence of stories. Second, it was important to demonstrate the strength of the cumulative argument. Any one of these examples might have been interesting and worth discussing, but not necessarily a compelling proof of anything in itself. The extent to which so many aspects of so many narratives converge and point in a common direction, however, is a compelling support of the multi-author hypothesis in general, and of this identification of the authors of J and E in particular. The more one reads these stories, the more one gets a sense of their authors, each in his world, and the more this explains.

When we identify the author of E as a Shiloh priest who possibly thought of Moses as his own ancestor, we are not just saying something about his pedigree. We are pursuing an understanding of why he wrote what he wrote. It helps us to understand why the E stories offer more development of Moses' personality than those of J—and not just *more* development, but more *sympathetic* development. There is nothing in J to compare with Moses' speech to God in an E account in Numbers 11. There the people complain that there is no meat for them to eat in the wilderness, and they speak nostalgically of the good food they had in Egypt, temporarily disregarding the fact that they had to work as slaves for that food. At this point, Moses apparently can no longer bear the burden that God has given him, to manage this entire community singlehanded. His plea to Yahweh is extraordinary for its anguish and for its intimacy with the deity. He says:

Why have you injured your servant, and why have I not found favor in your eyes, to put the burden of this entire people on me? Did I conceive this entire people? Did I give birth to it, that you say to me, "Carry it in your bosom," the way a nurse carries a suckling, to the land that you swore to its fathers? From where do I have meat to give to this entire people, that they cry to me, saying, "Give us meat, and let us eat"? I am not able, myself, to carry all of this people, for it is too heavy for me. And if this is how you treat me, then kill me, if I have found favor in your eyes, and let me not see my suffering. [14]

E here is more than a source. It is a powerful composition reflecting a special interest, sympathy, and affection for Moses. The E writer emphasizes the *Mosaic* covenant at Horeb and never refers to the Abrahamic covenant. The E story of the exodus from Egypt places more emphasis on the extent to which Moses himself is acting to free the people, while the J version focuses more on God as bringing the liberation about. In J, Yahweh says:

And *I am coming down to save them* from Egypt's hand and to bring them up. . . . [15]

In E, he says:

And now, go, and I shall send *you* to Pharaoh. *Take my people, the children of Israel, out of Egypt.* [16]

There is a difference of emphasis between these two. The E writer is focusing on Moses' crucial personal role. This is consistent with this writer's treatment of Moses throughout his work. For him, the arrival of Moses is the great moment of history, the time of the covenant, the time of the birth of the nation, the time of the Levites' first act of loyal service to God.

And it is the time of the world's first acquaintance with God by name.

The Name of God

I have pointed out two places where the name Yahweh occurs in E stories. Until now, I have said that the name of God was a key distinction between J and E. Now let me be more specific. In J, the deity is called Yahweh from beginning to end. The J writer never refers to him as Elohim in narration.[17] In E, the deity is called Elohim *until the arrival of Moses.* From the first time that Moses meets God, this changes. In the famous E story of the day that Moses meets God—the story of the burning bush—Moses does not know God's name, and so he asks.

> And Moses said to God [Elohim], "Here I am coming to the children of Israel, and I say to them, 'The God of your fathers has sent me to you,' and they will say to me, 'What is his name?' What shall I say to them?"[18]

The deity first gives the famous response "I am what I am." (The Hebrew root of these words is the same as the root of the name Yahweh.) And then he answers:

> Thus shall you say to the children of Israel, "*Yahweh*, the God of your fathers, the God of Abraham, the God of Isaac, and the God of Jacob, has sent me to you." *This is my name forever:* By this I shall be remembered from generation to generation.[19]

In E, Yahweh reveals his name for the first time to Moses. Prior to this scene in Exodus, he is called El or Elohim.

Why did the writer of E do this? That is controversial. Some think that this story reflects the religious system in the northern kingdom of Israel. In choosing the golden calves (young bulls) as the throne platform, King Jeroboam was perhaps identifying Yahweh with the chief Canaanite god, El. El was associated with bulls and was known as Bull El. Jeroboam was thus saying that Yahweh and El were different names for the same God. The E story would then serve this merger of the deities. It would explain why the deity had the two different names: he was called El at first, and then he revealed his personal name Yahweh to Moses. This explanation of the name change in E is attractive in that it shows another logical tie between E and the kingdom of Israel. This fits with all the other clues we have seen that E was from Israel.

However, there is a problem with this. In Judah, King Solomon used golden cherubs as the throne platform. And the god El was not only associated with bulls, but with cherubs as well. The statues that each kingdom used, therefore, do not make good evidence for explaining why E has the name revelation to Moses. Besides, all the other evidence we have seen indicates that the author of E was *against* the religious system that Jeroboam started in Israel. The E author depicted Moses *destroying* the golden calf. It is difficult, therefore, to argue that this author followed that religious system's theology on the identity of God.

Some investigators doing research on early Israelite history have concluded that, historically, only a small portion of the ancient Israelites were actually slaves in Egypt. Perhaps it was only the Levites. It is among the Levites, after all, that we find people with Egyptian names. The Levite names Moses, Hophni, and Phinehas are all Egyptian, not Hebrew. And the Levites did not occupy any territory in the land like the other tribes. These investigators suggest that the group that was in Egypt and then in Sinai worshiped the God Yahweh. Then they arrived in Israel, where they met Israelite tribes who worshiped the God El. Instead of fighting over whose God was the true God, the two groups accepted the belief that Yahweh and El were the same God. The Levites became the official priests of the united religion, perhaps by force or perhaps by influence. Or perhaps that was their compensation for not having any territory. Instead of land, they received, as priests, 10 percent of the sacrificed animals and produce.

This hypothesis, too, fits with the idea that the author of E was an Israelite Levite. His story of the revelation of the name Yahweh to Moses would reflect this history: the God that the tribes worshiped in the land was El. They had traditions about the God El and their ancestors Abraham, Isaac, and Jacob. Then the Levites arrived with their traditions about Moses, the exodus from Egypt, and the God Yahweh. The treatment of the divine names in E explains why the name Yahweh was not part of the nation's earliest tradition.

This is in the realm of hypothesis, and we must be very cautious about it. The important thing for our present purpose is that, for E, Moses has a significance far beyond what he has in J. In E, Moses is a turning point in history. E has much less than J about the world before Moses. E has no creation story, no flood story, and relatively less on the patriarchs. But E has more than J on Moses.

This is perfectly understandable from a Levitical priest. Also consistent with the priestly origin of E is the fact that E contains three chapters of law.[20] J does not. Legal material elsewhere in the Bible is by priests—*as we shall see.*

The overall picture of the E stories is that they are a consistent group, with a definite perspective and set of interests, and that they are profoundly tied to their author's world.

Likewise with the author of J, the more we read his stories the more we can see their unity and their relationship to his world. We can understand, for example, why he did not develop the distinction between the names of God before and after Moses. For him, something extremely important had happened before Moses. This writer was concerned with the ruling family of Judah, David's family. He therefore emphasized the significance of God's covenant with the patriarchs. It was tied to the city of Hebron, David's first capital. It promised inheritance of the land from river to river. In other words, it promised what was realized under King David. For this purpose, the revelation to Abraham was itself a turning point in history. It was not to be regarded as inferior to the revelation to Moses or to the people at Sinai. To depict the Sinai revelation as the first covenant sealed with the name of God would be to diminish the importance of the covenant between God and the patriarchs. J therefore uses the name Yahweh throughout.

The Similarity of J and E

The question remains as to why so many similarities exist between J and E. They often tell similar stories. They deal largely with the same characters. They share much terminology. Their styles are sufficiently similar that it has never been possible to separate them on stylistic grounds alone.

One possible explanation of this is that one of them is based on the other. Perhaps J, for example, was the Judean court account of the sacred national traditions, and so the northern Levites felt that it was necessary to produce their own national account because a legitimate kingdom should not be without such a document. Alternatively, the E document may have existed first, and the Judean court felt that it was necessary to produce its own version because the E treatment of Aaron, for example, was unsatisfactory. The point is that the E stories could hardly have been welcome in Judah on any one of a number of points; and the J stories, favoring Judah as they did, would hardly have been Israel's cup of tea either. The existence of either version in either kingdom would be likely to encourage the production of an alternative version in the other kingdom.

The two versions, nonetheless, would be just that: versions, not completely unrelated works. They would still be drawing upon a common treasury of history and tradition because Israel and Judah had once been one united people, and in many ways they still were. They shared traditions of a divine promise to their ancestors Abraham, Isaac, and Jacob. They shared traditions of having been slaves in Egypt, of an exodus from Egypt led by a man named Moses, of an extraordinary revelation at a mountain in the wilderness, and of years of wandering before settling in the promised land. Neither author was free to make up—or interested in making up—a completely new, fictional portrayal of history.

In style as well, once one version was established as a document bearing sacred national traditions, the author of the second, alternate version might well have consciously (or perhaps even unconsciously) decided to imitate its style. If the style of the first had come to be accepted in people's minds as the proper, formal, familiar language of recounting sacred tradition in that period, it would be in the second version's interest to preserve that manner of expression. In the same way, the language and style of the United States Constitution are often imitated in the constitutions of the individual states because that language is understood to be the accepted, proper form in which to compose such a document.

Another possible explanation for the stylistic similarity of J and E is that, rather than J's being based on E or E's being based on J, *both* may have been based on a common source that was prior to them. That is, there may have been an old, traditional cycle of stories about the patriarchs, exodus, etc. which both the authors of J and E used as a basis for their works. Such an original cycle would have been either written or an orally passed-down collection. In either case, once the kingdoms of Israel and Judah were established, the authors of E and J each adapted the collection to their respective concerns and purposes.

How Many Authors?

We can still be more specific about who these two persons were and when they lived. First there is the question of whether they really were only two persons. I have spoken of only one author of E and one author of J. Some scholars see J and E as each having been produced by groups, not individuals. They speak of J[1], J[2], J[3], etc., or they speak of a J school and an E school. I do not see how the evidence compels us to this analysis. On the contrary, J and E each appear to me to be unified and consistent in the texts as we have just reviewed them. Certainly an editor may have added a word or phrase or verse here or there, and the J or the E author may have inserted a received text occasionally. The author of J, for example, may not have written the deathbed Blessing of Jacob poem in Genesis 49. This author may simply have learned it, judged it to be suitable for the purpose, and inserted it into the J work. The overall J and E narratives, nonetheless, do not appear to me to require subdivision into even smaller units.

The Sex of the Authors

The author of E was almost certainly a male. We have seen how strong its connection is to the Levite priests of Shiloh. In ancient Israel the priesthood was strictly male. It is perhaps possible that a

Levite wife or daughter could have shared these interests and written about them, but the dominantly male perspective and the concentration on male characters still suggests the likelihood of male authorship. Also, given that it was a patriarchal society and a male priesthood, it is doubtful that a document that was to have formal, sacred status would have been either commissioned or accepted at the hand of a woman.

The case is much harder to judge with regard to J. Originating at—or at least reflecting the interests of—the Judean court, it came from a circle in which both men and women had a certain status. That is, even in a male-led society, women of the noble class may have more power, privileges, and education than males of a lower class.[21] The possibility of J's being by a woman is thus much more likely than with E. More important, the J stories are, on the whole, much more concerned with women and much more sensitive to women than are the E stories. There really is nothing in E to compare with the J story of Tamar in Genesis 38. It is not just that the woman Tamar figures in an important way in the story. It is that the story is sympathetic to a wrong done to this woman, it focuses on her plan to combat the injustice, and it concludes with the man in the story (Judah) acknowledging her rights and his own fault.

This does not make the author a woman. But it does mean that we cannot by any means be quick to think of this writer as a man. The weight of the evidence is still that the scribal profession in ancient Israel was male, true, but that does not exclude the possibility that a woman might have composed a work that came to be loved and valued in that land.

When Did They Live?

When did these two people live and write? Since the J narrative refers to the dispersion of Simeon and Levi but not to the dispersion of the other tribes, its author almost certainly wrote it before the Assyrians destroyed and exiled Israel in 722 B.C. It might conceivably have been written as early as the reign of David or Solomon, but the emphasis on the importance of the ark and the command against molten gods sound like polemic against the kingdom of Israel. That means composition after the division of the kingdoms. Also, the J stories of Jacob and Esau reflect Edom's independence from Judah ("You shall break his yoke from your shoulders"). That occurred during the reign of the Judean king Jehoram, 848–842 B.C.[22] This would put the author of J between 848 and 722. The author of E composed in Israel, which stood from 922 to 722 B.C. It is difficult to narrow it much further within this period.[23]

The most important point is that both J and E were written before the Assyrians destroyed Israel. At that time, the Assyrians carried out a deportation of the Israelite population. Also, there would of course have been many Israelites who fled south to Judah as refugees. The City of David archeological excavations in Jerusalem confirm that the population of Jerusalem grew substantially in this period. The likely historical scenario is that the E text came to Judah in this flow of people and events. Levites fleeing the Assyrians would hardly leave their valuable documents behind.

The assimilation of recently arrived Israelites into the Judean population after 722 B.C. need not have presented insurmountable difficulties in itself. The Israelites and the Judeans were kin. They spoke the same language: Hebrew. They worshiped the same God: Yahweh. They shared ancestral traditions of the patriarchs and historical traditions of exodus and wilderness. But what were they to do with two documents, each purporting to recount sacred national traditions, but emphasizing different persons and events—and occasionally contradicting each other? The solution, apparently, was to combine them.

The Combination of J and E

One might ask why the person or persons responsible for this did not simply exclude one or the other. Why not just make E, or more probably J, the accepted text and reject or ignore the other version? A common answer to this question is that the biblical community had too great a respect for the written word to ignore a received document that bore the stamp of antiquity. The problem with this view is that neither J nor E is complete in the text as we have it anyway. The editor(s) clearly were not averse to applying scissors and paste to their received texts. It is therefore difficult to argue that they retained texts that they did not want simply out of reverence for documents that had been passed down.

A more probable reason why both J and E were retained is that both of them may have become sufficiently well known that one simply could not get away with excluding one or the other. One could not tell the story of the events at Sinai without referring to the golden calf incident, for example, because someone in the audience (especially a former northerner) would remember the story and protest. One could not tell the story of Abraham without telling the story of the events at Hebron, because someone else in the audience (especially someone from Hebron) would object. To whatever extent J and E narratives had become known by this time, to that extent it was necessary to preserve both.

One may ask then: why combine them at all? Why not just preserve both J and E separately? Why were they cut and combined in the manner that we observed in, for example, the flood story? Presumably, because preserving J and E separately would challenge the authenticity of both. If both were to be kept side by side on the same shelf, that would be a reminder of the dual history that produced two alternate versions. And that would diminish the authoritative quality of each of them.

In short, the editing of the two works into one was as much tied to the political and social realities of its day as the writing of the two had been in their days. The uniting of the two works reflected the uniting (better: the *re*uniting) of the two communities after two hundred years of division.

There is still much to be discovered about who wrote J and E. We do not know the precise dates when they lived, and we do not know their names. I think that what we do know is more important. We know something about their world and about how that world produced these stories that still delight and teach us. Still, we may be dissatisfied until we can be more specific about the writers. So let me turn to source D. We can know even more about the person who assembled it than about those who wrote J and E—perhaps even his name.

CHAPTER 4

The World That Produced the Bible: 722–587 B.C.

Change

WHEN the Assyrian empire destroyed the kingdom of Israel in 722, the world that had produced J and E ended forever. Judah, now left without its sister-companion-rival, changed. The political change also meant economic and social change and, as always, religious change. And that meant changes in the way the Bible would come out as well.

The land and the people were different after 722. The land was smaller. The kings of Judah ruled a territory that was about half the size of the united Israelite kingdom that David and Solomon had ruled. There was a different sort of international politics. Judah now operated from a position of weakness. It was an age of great empires in Mesopotamia: first Assyria and then Babylonia. And these empires were capable of, and interested in, conquest in the west. Subjugating Judah meant income (spoils initially, tribute thereafter), control of a trade route between Africa and Asia, and strategic placement on Egypt's doorstep. (See the map, p. 11.)

The new international politics had an impact on religion as well.

When a small kingdom became a vassal to a large empire, the vassal state might place statues of the empire's gods in their temple. It was a symbol of the vassal's acceptance of the empire's hegemony. In modern times, the equivalent would be that a small subject nation would have to fly the flag of a nation that subjugated it. But an idol is not quite the same as a flag. Periods when Assyria dominated Judah often meant religious conflict in Jerusalem. The king of Judah would honor a pagan god in the Temple, and then Judean prophets would attack him for promoting idolatry. A modern historian would say that the Judean king was accepting Assyria's suzerainty. But the biblical historian, who told history from a religious point of view, would say that the king "did what was bad in the eyes of Yahweh."

Another difference in life in Judah was that the fall of Israel was a fact, a specter to be reckoned with. Different Judeans (and refugee Israelites) may have interpreted it in different ways, but no one could ignore its implications, politically or religiously. To some, the fact that Israel fell and Judah stood showed that Judah was better, ethically or in terms of fidelity to Yahweh. To others, it showed that it was *possible* to fall, and this was a warning to Judah. Presumably, it would be harder to laugh off a prophet who predicted the fall of Judah after the catastrophe of 722.

The king's power and stature were diminished. David's descendants on the throne in Jerusalem were, most of the time, vassals to the emperors of Assyria or Babylonia. They were at all times dependent on the flow of events among the great powers—Assyria, Babylonia, Egypt—rather than being major political forces in their own region, much less in the ancient Near East as a whole. Even during the days of the divided kingdoms, Judah and Israel had each seen periods of strength in the region, but very little of that remained now that Assyria's shadow extended to the Mediterranean Sea.

Other roles changed. There was no more role at all after 722 for tribal leaders. For virtually all intents and purposes, there were no more tribes. As for the priests, it is difficult to say if there was rivalry among priestly groups in Judah (like the rivalry in Israel) prior to 722. After 722, though, any influx of northern Levites would have brought new issues, balances, and competitions among the priestly houses.

There was one more new factor after 722: the presence of JE, the combined narrative of the nation's sacred recollections. This work itself was to play a part in the creation of other works. There was also one other book in Judah now that was going to play a part in this story.

King Hezekiah

Political events and religious events continued to have an impact on one another. King Hezekiah ruled Judah from around 715 to 687. According to the biblical books of Isaiah, 2 Kings, and 2 Chronicles, he carried out a religious and political reform. We have archeological evidence that confirms and adds to this picture. Hezekiah's religious reform apparently included the elimination of various forms of religious practice other than the sanctioned worship at the Temple in Jerusalem. The political reform included rebellion against Assyria and an attempt to extend Judah's control over areas that had been part of the now defunct kingdom of Israel and over Philistine cities. Both the religious and the political actions had enormous consequences for the country's historical fate and for the Bible.

The religious reform meant more than breaking idols and cleansing the Temple. It also meant destroying the places of worship of *Yahweh* outside of the Temple in Jerusalem. In addition to the Temple, there had been various local places where people could go to sacrifice to God. These places of worship in the local communities were called "high places." Hezekiah eliminated them. He promoted the centralization of the religion at the Temple in Jerusalem.

In order to understand why this made such a big difference, one must know something about sacrifice in the biblical world. The function of sacrifice is one of the most misunderstood matters in the Bible. Modern readers often take it to mean the unnecessary taking of animal life, or they believe that the person who offered the sacrifice was giving up something of his or her own in order to compensate for some sin or perhaps to win God's favor. In the biblical world, however, the most common type of sacrifice was for *meals*. The apparent rationale was that if humans wanted to eat meat they had to recognize that they were taking life. They could not regard this as an ordinary act of daily secular life. It was a sacred act, to be performed in a prescribed manner, by an appointed person (a priest), at an altar. A portion of the sacrifice (a tithe) was given to the priest. This applied to all meat meals (but not fish or fowl).

The centralization of religion meant that if you wanted to eat lamb you could not sacrifice your sheep at home or at a local sanctuary. You had to bring the sheep to the priest at the Temple altar in Jerusalem. This also would mean a sizable gathering of Levite priests at Jerusalem, which was now the only sanctioned location where they could conduct the sacrifices and receive their tithes. It also meant considerable distinction and power for the High Priest in Jerusalem and for the priestly family from which he came. This idea of centralizing religion around one temple and one altar was an important step in the development of Judah's religion, and over two thousand years later it became an important clue in unraveling who wrote the Bible.

There was one more item in Hezekiah's religious reform worth special mention. According to the book of 2 Kings, there was a bronze snake in Judah that was reputed to have been made by Moses himself. This corresponds to a story that appears in the E source.[1] In that story, the people speak against God and Moses in the wilderness. God sends poisonous snakes that bite and kill many of the people. The people repent. God tells Moses to make a bronze snake and set it on a pole. Then, whenever an Israelite is bitten by a snake, he or she is to look at the bronze snake and will be healed. The association of Moses and the snake in E is doubly interesting because recently a small bronze snake was uncovered archeologically in Midian. Midian is Moses' wife's home, and he is associated with the Midianite priesthood through his father-in-law, Jethro, the Midianite priest. Now, according to 2 Kings, King Hezekiah

smashed the bronze snake that Moses had made, because the children of Israel were burning incense to it until those days.[2]

How could Hezekiah dare to destroy a five-hundred-year-old relic that was regarded as having been made by Moses himself? If the people were acting improperly by burning incense to it, why could he not forbid them to do so, or put it away in the Temple or palace? The answer to this will be tied to the search for two of the authors of the Bible.

Hezekiah's political action, rejecting Assyria's suzerainty, brought a massive military response. Assyria's emperor, Sennacherib, brought a huge force to bring Judah to its knees. He was largely successful, but not entirely. The Assyrians captured the Judean fortress of Lachish in a powerful military assault that was not unlike the famous Roman capture of Masada eight hundred years later. Lachish was situated on a high mound commanding the area (see the map, page 10), and the Assyrians constructed a ramp out of huge stones leading up the side of the mound to the very doorstep of Lachish. The excavations of Lachish which are now in progress tell part of the story.

The other side of the story comes from the excavations of Nineveh, the capital city of the Assyrian empire. The Assyrian emperor decorated the walls of the palace there with depictions of the battle of Lachish. The wall depictions, which are impressive both in size and in artistic skill, are among the few known depictions of what Jews looked like in biblical times. They are now located in the British Museum, and there are casts of them in the Israel Museum. Together these two archeological sources, Nineveh and Lachish, tell of the Assyrians' extraordinary might and determination.

Nevertheless, the Assyrians failed to bring down the kingdom of Judah as they had brought down Israel. The showdown between the Assyrians and the Judeans (or Jews) at Jerusalem is of special interest because it is one of the very rare cases in which we have both biblical and archeological witness to the same event.

The biblical account of what happened appears in three places in the Bible.[3] The Assyrian account appears in a document that was found in the excavations of Nineveh, the Prism Inscription of Sennacherib. It is called the Prism Inscription because it is an eight-sided clay stele. On its eight sides, Sennacherib inscribed his account of his military campaigns. The inscription is in Akkadian, the dominant language of Mesopotamia in that era. It is written in cuneiform script. It is now located in the British Museum. We are thus in the very rare position of having each side's version of what happened: the Judean view from inside the besieged walls of Jerusalem, and the Assyrians' view from the other side of the walls. The biblical report concludes:

And it was, that night, that an angel of Yahweh went out and struck one hundred eighty-five thousand in the Assyrian camp, and

they rose in the morning and here they were all dead corpses. And
Sennacherib traveled and went and returned, and he lived in Nineveh.[4]

Thus the Bible reports that Jerusalem, under King Hezekiah, was
saved from Assyrian capture and possible destruction. Now here is a
translation of the relevant portion of the Sennacherib Prism Inscription:[5]

And Hezekiah the Judean, who did not submit to my yoke: I
besieged and captured forty-six of his strong walled cities, and the
small cities of their environs which were without number, by the
spanning of a ramp, the approach of siege machines, the battling of
infantry, breaches, breaks and stormladders. 200,150 people, small
and great, male and female, horses, asses, mules, camels, oxen,
and sheep and goats without number I brought out from them and I
counted as spoil.
   *Himself, I locked him up like a caged bird in the midst of Jerusalem,
his royal city.* I connected siegeworks against him so that I turned
those going out of his city gate into a taboo for him. I cut off the
cities that I despoiled from the midst of his land, and I gave them
to Mitinti King of Ashdod, Padi King of Ekron, and Silli-Bel King
of Gaza, so that I diminished his land. To the former tribute I
added and fixed against him the giving of their annual tribute,
greeting-gifts of my lordship.
   The fear of the splendor of my majesty overcame Hezekiah, and
the Arabs and crack troops that he had brought in for the
strengthening of Jerusalem his royal city ceased working. He sent a
heavy tribute and his daughters and his harem and singers, together with thirty talents of gold, eight hundred talents of silver,
choice antimony, blocks of stone, ivory couches, ivory armchairs,
elephant hides, ivory, ebony, boxwood, and all sorts of things to
the midst of Nineveh, my lordly city, and he sent his ambassadors
for the giving of tribute and the performance of vassal service.

On the face of it, these two reports from the ancient Near East
sound as contradictory as reports from the modern Near East. The
Bible says that the Assyrians went home after an angel struck much
of the army dead. The Prism Inscription says that the Assyrians were
victorious and took home a handsome tribute.

What can we do to get at the event behind these two versions? We are not in a position to determine the historicity of a report of the activity of an angel. Nor is the Assyrian spoil available for us to count. We can, though, examine what the two reports share. Sennacherib claims in the first two sentences that he captured many of the fortified cities of the Judean countryside. The biblical account acknowledges this in 2 Kings 18:13. It says:

> And in the fourteenth year of King Hezekiah, Sennacherib King of Assyria went up against all the fortified cities of Judah and captured them.

There is no contradiction here between our sources regarding the initial military successes. The question is what happened in the siege of Jerusalem. The key line in Sennacherib's inscription is his claim that he kept King Hezekiah "locked up liked a caged bird in the midst of Jerusalem his royal city." This wording is suspicious. The function of a siege elsewhere (such as at Lachish) is not to keep one's enemy "locked up." The idea of a siege, rather, is to *get in*. The fact is that Sennacherib does not claim to have captured Jerusalem. He rather appears to be saving face by the "caged bird" image and by concentrating on the quantity of tribute paid.

Perhaps the siege was a standoff in which the Assyrians were unable to take the city and the Judeans were unable to leave it. The Judeans paid a sum that the Assyrians extracted as the price of their withdrawal. The book of 2 Kings in fact reports that Sennacherib had initially demanded a sum of thirty talents of gold and three hundred talents of silver, and the biblical text is not completely clear as to whether Hezekiah was in fact able to raise the full amount.[6] This is close enough to Sennacherib's claim of receiving thirty talents of gold and eight hundred of silver that we can believe that some such transaction took place.

Jerusalem's ability to withstand the siege owed partly to its excellent strategic position on a hill looking down over a valley from which the Assyrians would have to attack *up*. Another crucial factor for siege warfare was the water supply. Hezekiah constructed a tunnel under the city to provide water from the spring below.[7] Hezekiah's tunnel, an important architectural achievement in its time, is now open to the public as part of the City of David excavations in Jerusalem.

The point of this is that the reign of King Hezekiah in Judah was a turning point in history. In the face of Assyria's power, Israel had fallen and Judah had survived—albeit as a tributary to Assyria. Though the Judean countryside had suffered, Jerusalem had withstood Assyria's siege. Jerusalem's population grew in this period. It became the only sanctioned religious center in the country. From all of Judah, people had to bring their sacrifices there, and so there would have been a great flow of livestock and produce to the city.

The End of the Reform

Hezekiah's son and grandson who ruled after him in Jerusalem did not follow in his footsteps. Perhaps they were not able to. Assyrian forces returned to Judah during the reign of Hezekiah's son Manasseh. According to biblical reports, the Assyrians even imprisoned King Manasseh for some period of time in Babylon. (The Assyrian emperor's brother ruled Babylon at that time.) Whether because of Assyrian insistence, domestic pressures, or religious conviction, Manasseh and his son Amon reintroduced pagan worship in Judah, including pagan statues in the Temple. They also rebuilt the high places, the sacrificial locations outside of Jerusalem, thus ending Hezekiah's religious centralization.

King Amon's reign was cut short by assassination. He became king at the age of twenty-two and was murdered at twenty-four. His son Josiah became king of Judah. Josiah was eight years old.

King Josiah

We do not know who governed the country or who influenced the king until he came of age. Perhaps a member of the royal family or a priest acted as regent. According to the reports of the books of Kings and Chronicles, in an earlier case of an underage king (King Joash, who became king at the age of three), the High Priest served as regent. There may well have been priestly influences in Josiah's case as well, because when he became old enough to rule he did a turn-about from his father's and grandfather's religious policies. He behaved more like his great-grandfather Hezekiah.

Like Hezekiah he instituted a religious reform. Like Hezekiah he smashed idols, cleansed the Temple, and extended his sphere of influence into the territory that had been the kingdom of Israel before 722. Like Hezekiah he centralized the religion at Jerusalem. Once again the local high places were destroyed. The people were required to bring all sacrifices to the one central altar at the Temple. The priests from all the high places were brought to Jerusalem to work at second-level jobs beside the Temple priests.

In addition to the human influences on Josiah—including the court and priestly circle, the domestic and international political forces around him—there was one other thing that influenced his reform: a book. According to the biblical historians, in the eighteenth year of Josiah's reign, 622 B.C., Josiah received word from his scribe Shaphan that the priest Hilkiah had found a "scroll of the *torah*" in the Temple of Yahweh.[8] When Shaphan read the text of this book that Hilkiah had found to the king, King Josiah tore his clothes, a sign of extreme anguish in the ancient Near East. He consulted a prophetess concerning its meaning, and then he held a giant national ceremony of renewal of the covenant between God and the people. According to one of the biblical sources, Josiah's destruction of the high places followed the reading of this book. Josiah also destroyed the altar at Beth-El where one of King Jeroboam's golden calves had once stood. This religious act was also a political act. It blatantly expressed the Judean monarch's interest in the land that had once been the kingdom of Israel.

What was this book? Why did it inspire acts of religious reform? Who was the priest Hilkiah? Where had the book been before he found it? The identity of that book and its author is the subject of the next chapter. First, though, it is necessary to know more about the world of King Josiah and his successors on the throne of David.

An important change was taking place in international politics. The Assyrian empire was weaker, and Babylon was threatening to replace it as the major power of the Near East. Perhaps it was Assyria's weakness that made it possible for Josiah to behave so independently.

Egypt, meanwhile, became an ally of its old rival Assyria against the rising power of Babylonia and others. When the Egyptian army passed through Judah on its way to support the Assyrians, Josiah went out to confront the Egyptians at Megiddo. An Egyptian arrow killed him. He was only forty at the time.

The Last Years of Judah

Josiah's early death meant an early end to his country's political independence and religious reform. The high places were rebuilt. Three of his sons and one grandson ruled in the next twenty-two years. All started young and did not reign for long.

The first, Jehoahaz, ruled for three months. Then the Egyptian king overpowered him, dethroned him, carried him to Egypt, and placed his brother, Jehoiakim, on the throne in his place.

Jehoiakim, an Egyptian vassal, ruled for eleven years. Then the Babylonians, who had meanwhile brought the Assyrian empire to an end, overpowered him. He died during the Babylonian campaign against Judah.

His son, Jehoiachin, succeeded him and ruled for three months, long enough to be captured and dethroned by the Babylonians. The Babylonian emperor, Nebuchadnezzar, exiled Jehoiachin to Babylon along with thousands of other Judeans: the upper class, military leaders, artists; i.e., those who could be threatening in Judah or useful in Babylon. Nebuchadnezzar placed another of Josiah's sons, Zedekiah, on the throne.

Zedekiah, a Babylonian vassal, ruled for eleven years. Around his ninth year, he rebelled against Nebuchadnezzar. The Babylonian army returned and destroyed Jerusalem. They exiled thousands more of the population to Babylon. The last thing that Zedekiah saw was the death of his children. Nebuchadnezzar executed Zedekiah's sons in front of him and then blinded him.

In this horrible manner, King David's family's rule in Jerusalem ended. Nebuchadnezzar placed no more members of this family on the throne. Instead he appointed a Jewish governor, Gedaliah son of Ahikam son of Shaphan. Note that he is the grandson of Shaphan, the man who had reported to King Josiah the finding of the "scroll of the *torah*" years earlier. Josiah was a king who had opposed the Assyrians and the Egyptians, which is to say that he would be perceived as pro-Babylonian. The Shaphan family, too, had a record over at least three generations of being part of a pro-Babylonian party in Judah. This party included the famous prophet Jeremiah as well. The biblical book of Jeremiah speaks well of King Josiah but not of his successors on the throne. Shaphan, Jeremiah, or Gedaliah might have described themselves simply as pro-Judah, but the fact remained that they favored an anti-Assyrian king and spoke against opposing the Babylonians. And so Nebuchadnezzar would have perceived them as pro-Babylonian. Nebuchadnezzar therefore made Gedaliah, a member of this party, his local governor.

This was an overwhelming affront to the house of David. Two months later, a relative of that family assassinated Gedaliah.

This left the remaining population of Judah in an impossible position. Nebuchadnezzar, the great emperor, had left his handpicked governor in charge. His governor had been assassinated. The people of Judah could only feel terrified at the emperor's possible response. There appeared to be only one place where they could go that was outside his grasp: Egypt. The books of 2 Kings and Jeremiah report that virtually the entire population that was left in Judah fled as refugees to Egypt. It was an extraordinary and ironic fate for a people who, according to their own traditions, had started as slaves there.

The year in which Nebuchadnezzar captured and burned Jerusalem was 587 B.C. That year therefore stands as another turning point in the destiny of the people of Israel-Judah. The city was destroyed, the population was exiled as captives in Babylonia or as refugees in Egypt, their Temple was destroyed, the ark was lost, which is a mystery to this day, their four-hundred-year-old royal family was dethroned, and their religion was about to face perhaps the greatest challenges it had ever known.

The biblical world's landmarks seem to be its disasters. The historical junctures that begin and end this chapter are the fall of Israel in 722 and the fall of Judah in 587. Perhaps this tells us more about the perceptions of modern historians than about the biblical world. Or perhaps it tells us that great historical crises played critical roles in the formation of the Bible. In any case, we should still note that the years between 722 and 587 were not unceasingly bleak. These were times of powerful persons and great events, of the rise and fall of great empires. This period included times of hope and vision, especially, it appears, during Hezekiah's and Josiah's reigns. These times produced an Isaiah, a Jeremiah, and an Ezekiel. Precisely in this age of empires in conflict, of rebellions, of violence, and of cruelty, a man conceived of an era when

> *They will beat their swords into plowshares*
> *and their spears into pruning-hooks.*
> *A nation will not raise a sword against a nation,*
> *and they will not learn war anymore.* [9]

In this age, among these persons and events, a biblical writer would be expected to conceive of his kings, his people, and his God differently from the way writers saw these things in the days of David, Solomon, and Jeroboam. One writer who lived in this age assembled a history of his people form Moses to the writer's own day. As with the authors of J and E, the world in which this writer lived had an impact on the story that he told and on the way in which he told it.

CHAPTER 5

In the Court of King Josiah

The Book from the Temple

THE book that the priest Hilkiah said he found in the Temple in 622 B.C. was Deuteronomy.

This is not a new discovery. Early church fathers, including Jerome, said that the book that was read to King Josiah was Deuteronomy. Thomas Hobbes, the first modern investigator to argue that the majority of the Pentateuch was not by Moses, also said that it was Deuteronomy's law code that Josiah heard. Hobbes still claimed that Deuteronomy really was by Moses himself, that it had been long lost, and that Hilkiah rediscovered it. But later investigators denied that.

In Germany in 1805, W. M. L. De Wette investigated the origin of Deuteronomy. He argued that Deuteronomy was the book that Hilkiah handed over to King Josiah. But De Wette denied that the book was by Moses. He said that Deuteronomy was not an old, Mosaic book that had been lost for a long time and then found by the priest Hilkiah. Rather, De Wette said, Deuteronomy was written not long before it was "found" in the Temple, and the "finding" was just a charade. The book was written to provide grounds for Josiah's religious reform.

For example, the first commandment in the law code of Deuteronomy is to sacrifice to God only at a single place. Josiah did just that. He tore down all places of worship outside of the Temple. But this brought all the influence and income of the religion to the Jerusalem Temple priesthood, and *it was a Jerusalem Temple priest who had found the book.*

Was centralization of worship an old practice that had been lost some generations before Josiah? Or was it something new, conceived by the priestly leaders of Josiah's own time to justify a religious reform that was in their own interest?

De Wette pointed out that in the books of Samuel and Kings the early figures in Israel's history know nothing of any centralization law. Samuel, the prophet-priest-judge who anoints Saul and David, sacrifices in more than one place. The first three kings, Saul, David, and Solomon, also sacrifice at altars in various places. The text of the history in the books of Samuel and Kings, nonetheless, does not criticize Samuel, Saul, David, or Solomon for this at all. De Wette concluded that, from the earliest period of the history of the people in the land, there was no evidence of the existence of a law requiring that worship be in only one central place.

From the law of centralization and other matters, De Wette concluded that the book of Deuteronomy was not a long-lost document, but rather was written not long before its "discovery" by Hilkiah. Though it may have been written for legitimate purposes, it was nevertheless falsely attributed to Moses. De Wette referred to it as "pious fraud."

"Pious fraud" is strong language to use about a part of the Bible. The "pious" softens the impact of the "fraud," but only slightly. Did Hilkiah or someone from his circle compose a book and then pretend to find it in order to trick the king into supporting it? Or did the king and Hilkiah both plan the book's composition and discovery for their mutual purposes? Or was the book really composed before the time of Josiah and Hilkiah, and only made known and put into force by them?

In order to get answers and identify authors, we have to know more specifically what was written on the scroll that was read to King Josiah. We need to see more evidence that it was Deuteronomy, and we have to know what the book of Deuteronomy contains.

And Not Only Deuteronomy

The book of Deuteronomy is presented as Moses' farewell speech before his death. It is set in the plains of Moab, just across the Jordan River from the promised land. Moses and the people have arrived there after forty years of travel in the wilderness. Moses reviews the events of the forty years that he and the people have known each other. He gives them a code of laws by which to live in the new land. He appoints Joshua as his successor. Then he climbs a mountain from which he can see the land, and there he dies.

The first key breakthrough in finding out the identity of the person who produced this account was the recognition of a special relationship between Deuteronomy and the next six books of the Bible: Joshua, Judges, 1 and 2 Samuel, and 1 and 2 Kings. These six books are known as the Early Prophets.

In 1943, a German biblical scholar, Martin Noth, showed that there was a strong unity between Deuteronomy and these six books of the Early Prophets. The language of Deuteronomy and parts of these other books was too similar for coincidence. Noth showed that this was not a loose collection of writings, but rather a thoughtfully arranged work. It told a continuous story, a flowing account of the history of the people of Israel in their land. It was not by one author. It contained various sections, written by various people (such as the Court History of David, and the stories of Samuel). The finished product, nonetheless, was the work of one person.

That person was both a writer and an editor. He (the person was male, as we shall see) selected the stories and other texts that he wanted to use from sources available to him. He arranged the texts, shortening or adding to them. He inserted occasional comments of his own. And he wrote introductory sections which he set near the beginning of the work. Overall, he constructed a history that extended from Moses to the destruction of the kingdom of Judah by the Babylonians.

For this man, Deuteronomy was *the* book. He constructed the work so that the laws of Deuteronomy would stand as the foundation of the history. When he rated the kings of Israel and Judah as "good in the eyes of Yahweh" or "bad in the eyes of Yahweh" it was according to how obedient they were to Deuteronomy's laws. He characterized the entire fate of the nation as hanging upon how well they kept the commandments of Deuteronomy. The tie between Deuteronomy and the six books that follow it appeared to be so crucially integral that Noth referred to the full seven-book work as the *Deuteronomistic history*.

Noth's analysis and the term "Deuteronomistic history" came to be widely accepted among investigators. The case was strong. The first book of the Early Prophets, the book of Joshua, begins where Deuteronomy leaves off. It develops themes that are begun in Deuteronomy, and it refers to matters first mentioned in Deuteronomy. Key passages in Joshua, Judges, Samuel, and Kings use terminology that comes from Deuteronomy and refer to specific passages in Deuteronomy.

And so, *the answer to the question "Who wrote Deuteronomy?" should also tell us who produced six other books of the Bible.*

Covenant

The Deuteronomistic history covers the period from Moses to the end of the kingdom. It pictures Moses' last days, it has stories of the conquest of the land, stories of the judges, the kings, the division of the country into Israel and Judah, the fall of Israel, and finally the fall of Judah. It is a fabulous collection of stories: battles, romances, miracles, politics. It is history, but told from a religious perspective. What, specifically, is the religious perspective? The Deuteronomistic historian presents his history consistently in terms of *covenant*. He depicts the fate of the kings and the people as dependent on how faithfully they keep their covenants with God.

It is difficult to overestimate the importance of covenant in the Bible. In the Christian tradition, the very names Old *Testament* and New *Testament* reflect this importance, for the Latin word *Testamentum* means "covenant." In addition to the theological, literary, and historical significance of the biblical covenants, they provide evidence that helps in the search for who wrote the Bible.

In the Bible, covenants are written contracts between God and humans. They are written according to the form and standard terminology of legal documents in the ancient Near East. J portrays a covenant between God and Abraham. Both J and E portray a covenant between God and the people of Israel at Mount Sinai (or Horeb) in Moses' time. In the book of Deuteronomy, the Mosaic covenant is understood to mean not only the laws given at Sinai/ Horeb. It also includes laws that Yahweh gives to Moses in the plains of Moab, at the end of the forty years of travel through the wilderness. In other words, it includes the laws of Deuteronomy. Later in the Deuteronomistic history, one more covenant comes in: a covenant between God and King David. This covenant provided a clue concerning the identity of the Deuteronomistic historian.

According to 2 Samuel 7, God promises David that, as a reward for his loyalty, David and his descendants will rule the kingdom forever. David's predecessor, King Saul, dies, and Saul's son Ishbaal is assassinated and never replaced by another member of Saul's family. But David receives a divine promise that his son, grandson, great-grandson, etc. will occupy the throne continually. The promise states unequivocally:

Your house and your kingdom will be secure before you forever.
Your throne will be established forever.[1]

There is no mistaking the message: David's dynasty is to rule his kingdom forever. There will always be a descendant of David (a "Davidide") on the throne. Even if a Davidide king behaves improperly, he may suffer for it, but he and his family will not lose the throne. That is an unconditional covenant promise from God.

The Deuteronomistic historian explains the division of David's kingdom at the time of Rehoboam and Jeroboam in light of this promise. Because of Solomon's offenses, his family suffers the loss of the northern tribes, but the royal family cannot lose the throne altogether. They must retain at least the tribe of Judah. Why? Because God made a covenant with David. According to the Deuteronomistic historian, when the prophet Ahijah of Shiloh tells Jeroboam that Yahweh means to take the kingdom of Israel away from Solomon's son Rehoboam and give it to Jeroboam instead, Ahijah says:

> I shall take the kingdom from his son's hand and give it to you— the ten tribes. But I shall give one tribe to his son *so that there may be a holding for my servant David always* before me in Jerusalem, the city that I have chosen for myself to set my name there.[2]

And so, according to the Deuteronomistic covenant tradition, even when a king from the house of David goes wrong, the throne, the kingdom, and its capital, Jerusalem, remain secure—forever.

The Deuteronomistic historian reminds us of this fact several times in his history. In his report of David's grandson Rehoboam and great-grandson Abijam, the historian criticizes these two kings. He says that they lacked David's faithfulness. He explains, nonetheless, that they were able to hold on to their kingdom thanks to the terms of the Davidic covenant:

> Abijam...went in all his father's crimes that he had done before him, and his heart was not whole with Yahweh his God as the heart of David his father was. *But, for David's sake, Yahweh his God gave him a holding in Jerusalem* to establish his son after him and to establish Jerusalem.[3]

In his report of David's great-great-great-great-grandson King Jehoram, the historian says:

> ...he did bad in the eyes of Yahweh, but Yahweh was not willing to destroy Judah for the sake of David his servant, *as he had promised to give a holding to him and to his son always.*[4]

This matter of the eternal covenant with David is interesting in itself, but my interest in it for our present purpose is that it raised a mystery in the Deuteronomistic history. According to Martin Noth, the Deuteronomistic historian had constructed a history of the people that went from Moses to the Babylonian conquest of Judah. In the conquest, the Babylonian emperor had killed the Davidide King Zedekiah's children, blinded him, and led him in chains to Babylon. David's kingdom had fallen. Now the question is: why would the

Deuteronomistic historian, a person who had seen the fall of the king, write a work claiming that Yahweh would *never* take away the king's holding in Judah, even if the king "went in crimes," "did evil in the eyes of Yahweh," and "his heart was not whole with Yahweh"? Why would a person who had seen the fall of the kingdom write a work claiming that the kingdom was *eternal*? These were not figurative or apocalyptic claims of a distant, messianic sort, such as those that developed later in Judaism and Christianity. In these Davidic covenant passages, the context is the security of specific kings on the throne of an existing kingdom. Why would someone write that after 587?

The First Edition

These questions were raised by the American biblical scholar Frank Moore Cross of Harvard University, in 1973.[5] Cross reasoned that it was hardly likely that an individual who had seen the destruction of the country would set out to develop a theme of the country's eternal security. Cross also pointed to other evidence against looking for the Deuteronomistic writer in the years after the destruction.

He referred to a problem that earlier investigators had reckoned as a clue as well. The Deuteronomistic writer occasionally speaks of things as existing "to this day," when the things in question existed only while the kingdom was standing. Why would someone writing a history in, say, 560 B.C. refer to something as existing "to this day," when that something had ended back in 587? For example, 1 Kings 8:8 refers to the poles that were used for hoisting and carrying the ark. It states there that the poles were placed inside the Temple of Solomon on the day it was dedicated and that "they have been there unto this day." Why would someone write these words after the Temple had burned down? Even if the words were not his own, but rather appeared already in one of his sources, why would he leave them in? Why not edit them out?[6]

Cross suggested that the reason for these apparent contradictions was that there had been two editions of the Deuteronomistic history. The original edition was by someone who was living during the reign of King Josiah. It was a positive, optimistic account of the people's history, emphasizing the security of the Davidic covenant and believing that the kingdom would thrive under Josiah and survive into the future. But after Josiah's death, his sons' disastrous reigns, and the fall of the kingdom, this original version of the national history was out of date. Tragic events had made its optimism look ironic, or even foolish. So someone wrote a new edition of the history after the destruction in 587.

The second edition was about 95 percent the same as the first edition. The main difference was that the editor added the last chapters of the story—the last two chapters of the book of 2 Kings —which give a very brief account of the reigns of Judah's last four kings. The updated history now concluded with the fall of Judah. The person who produced the second edition of the Deuteronomistic history also added a few short passages at earlier points in the text, which made the text more relevant in light of the new historical situation.

The first edition referred to things as existing "to this day" because in Josiah's time they really still existed. The editor of the second edition did not bother to edit them out because that was simply not his concern. He was not rewriting the whole history or looking for contradictions to clean up. He was just adding the end of the story and adding a few lines at the beginning.

If Cross was right, then investigators had been looking for the Deuteronomist in the wrong time and the wrong place.

In the Court of King Josiah

What is the evidence for looking for the author-editor of the original version of the story in Josiah's time? Why not the reign of Hezekiah or any one of the other kings?

First of all, there already was considerable evidence for connecting the book of Deuteronomy itself with Josiah, as Hobbes and De Wette had shown long ago. The "book of the *torah*" that the priest Hilkiah found in the Temple had long been identified as Deuteronomy, or at least as Deuteronomy's law code (chapters 12–26).

Cross also pointed to the length of the text dealing with Josiah as a factor. There are two full chapters dealing with this king in the Deuteronomistic history, even though there were other kings who lived longer and did more. His reform was short-lived. The books of Jeremiah, Ezekiel, 2 Kings, and 2 Chronicles all indicate that many of his innovations were disregarded after he died. For example, the high places were rebuilt. Why then the emphasis on this particular king and his attempt at reform? According to Cross, because he was the king when the history was written. It was written to culminate in him.

There is another piece of evidence that the Deuteronomistic writer had a particular interest in King Josiah. The text itself points to him by name early in the history. 1 Kings 13 tells a story about King Jeroboam. He has recently set up the golden calves at Dan and Beth-El. He goes to Beth-El to celebrate a festival, and he goes up to the altar to burn incense. And then something strange happens:

> And here was a man of God coming from Judah by the word of Yahweh to Beth-El as Jeroboam was standing on the altar to burn incense. And he called out upon the altar by the word of Yahweh, and he said, "Altar, altar. Thus says Yahweh: 'Here a son will be born to the house of David, *Josiah by name*, and he will sacrifice on you the priests of the high places who burn incense on you. He will burn human bones on you.'"[7]

The reference to "Josiah by name" in a story that takes place three hundred years before he is born is remarkable even in a book filled with prophecies and miracles. No other case of such explicit prediction of a person by name so far in advance occurs in biblical narrative. Also, the Deuteronomistic writer made a special point of this reference later in the history. In describing the events of Josiah's religious reform, the Deuteronomist reported that Josiah goes to Beth-El and destroys the high place and altar that have been there since Jeroboam's days. He wrote:

> And also the altar that was in Beth-El, the high place that Jeroboam son of Nebat, who had caused Israel to sin, had made: he [Josiah] also smashed that altar and the high place, and he burned the high place, made [it] thin as dust . . .
>
> And Josiah turned and saw the graves that were there in the

mountain, and he sent and took the bones from the graves and burned [them] on the altar and defiled it, according to the word of Yahweh that the man of God had called out, who had called out these things. And he [Josiah] said, "What is that monument that I see?"

And the people of the city said to him, "The grave of the man of God who came from Judah and called out these things that you have done upon the altar of Beth-El."

And he said, "Leave it alone. Let no one disturb his bones."[8]

It is not just that the Deuteronomistic historian has put a prediction of Josiah near the beginning of the story and a fulfillment near the end. This writer rates every one of the kings in between, both of Israel and of Judah, throughout the history, below Josiah. He rates every king as good or bad. Most are bad. The good are still imperfect. Even David is criticized for adultery with Bathsheba and causing her husband's death so that he could have her for himself. Even Hezekiah is criticized through the prophet Isaiah.[9] The Deuteronomistic historian rates Josiah, and Josiah alone, as unqualifiedly good. He says it explicitly:

And there was none like him before him, a king who returned to Yahweh with all his heart and with all his soul and with all his might according to all the torah of Moses, and none arose like him after him.[10]

Cross thus argued that the original edition of the Deuteronomistic history was the work of someone who lived at the time of Josiah, and the second edition was the work of someone living after the kingdom fell. He called the first edition Dtr[1] and the second edition Dtr.[2]

Moses and Josiah

Cross' analysis was not widely accepted at first. Cross' colleague at Harvard, G. Ernest Wright, disagreed. Wright questioned the existence of Dtr[1] and Dtr[2]. He did not accept Cross' key argument: that the Deuteronomistic idea of an *eternal*, *unconditional* Davidic covenant had to be written before the fall of the kingdom. Wright doubted that any covenant could be completely unconditional. For example, if a king went so far as to worship other gods, forsaking Yahweh, would God's promise to support the king still be in force?

Wright asked one of his students to work on this question. The student produced a paper arguing that in fact no covenant was completely unconditional. Wright then had the student present the paper in the department seminar. The seminar is a course that all of the Bible faculty and students of the Harvard Department of Near Eastern Languages and Civilizations attend. Each week a different student presents a paper which must then face the criticism of the faculty and student peers. This young student found himself standing between two giants. I was the student.

It had an ironic finish. I defended Professor Wright's position that day, but in my investigations years later I found evidence that convinced me that Cross had been right. The person responsible for seven books of the Bible was someone from Josiah's reign. I found that this person deliberately designed his history of the people to culminate in Josiah. Josiah was not just good, and he was not just important. In this writer's picture, Josiah, in many ways, was someone to be compared to Moses himself. Specifically:

1.   The words "none arose like him" are applied to only two people in the Bible: Moses and Josiah. The conclusion of Deuteronomy is: "And there did not arise a prophet again in Israel like Moses..."[11] The closing comment on Josiah is: "...and none arose like him after him."[12] There arose no prophet like Moses; there arose no king like Josiah.

2.   In Deuteronomy Moses tells the people, "Love Yahweh your

God with all your heart and with all your soul and with all your might."[13] Only one person in the Hebrew Bible is described as fulfilling this: Josiah. The Deuteronomist says that Josiah was "a king who returned to Yahweh with all his heart and with all his soul and with all his might."[14] This threefold expression occurs nowhere in the Old Testament but in these two places.

3.   Moses says in Deuteronomy that, in difficult matters of law, when one is uncertain about what course to take, one must "inquire" of the priests or judge at the place where Yahweh will choose, and then one must follow whatever instruction they give.[15] The Deuteronomist depicts only one king in one situation as ever fulfilling this: Josiah. When the book of the *torah* that was found is read to him, he inquires of a prophetess via the priest Hilkiah at Jerusalem, the place that Yahweh has chosen, as to what course to take. He tells Hilkiah, "Go, *inquire* of Yahweh for me . . ."[16]

4.   Moses says in Deuteronomy that once one has inquired of the priests, one must do exactly as they say. He says, "Do not turn from the thing that they tell you, right or left."[17] Moses also says in the Law of the King that the king must read a copy of the law all the days of his life "so that he will not turn from the commandment, right or left."[18] The warning about turning right or left occurs in two other places in Deuteronomy and twice more in the book of Joshua. It then never occurs anywhere else in the Holy Scriptures except in the case of one person: Josiah. The first thing that the historian says about Josiah is: "He did what was right in the eyes of Yahweh; he went in all the way of David his father, and he did not turn, right or left."[19]

5.   The book of the *torah* is mentioned only in Deuteronomy, in Joshua, and then never again in the Hebrew Bible except in one story: Josiah. Moses writes it, gives it to the priests, and says, "Take this book of the *torah* and place it at the side of the ark . . ."[20] The book then stays near the ark and ceases to be an issue in the story until, six hundred years later, the priest Hilkiah says, "I have found the book of the *torah* in the house of Yahweh."

6.   In Deuteronomy, as Moses hands the book of the *torah* over to the priests, he instructs them to read the book publicly every seven years. Literally, he says, "Read it in their ears."[21] This expression for public reading then does not occur again in the Deuteronomistic history until the story of Josiah. The historian says that King Josiah assembled all the people at Jerusalem, "and he *read in their ears* all

the words of the book of the covenant that was found in the house of Yahweh."[22]

7.   In Deuteronomy, Moses describes what he did to the golden calf that Aaron made. He burned it, he smashed it "thin as dust," and he cast the dust into a wadi.[23] In 2 Kings, Josiah goes to the altar and high place at Beth-El, the site of the golden calf that Jeroboam set up. Josiah burns the high place and smashes it "thin as dust." Aaron's golden calf and Jeroboam's golden calf (or its high place) thus suffer similar fates. The Deuteronomistic writer used the language describing Moses' actions in Deuteronomy to describe Josiah's actions in 2 Kings. Josiah's grandfather Manasseh had set a statue of the goddess Asherah in the Temple. Josiah burns the statue, at a wadi, "and he made it thin as dust."[24] Manasseh and other Judean kings had made altars. Josiah smashes the altars and casts their dust into a wadi.[25] The expression "thin as dust" occurs nowhere in the Bible but in the passages mentioned here. The historian is specifically depicting Josiah's action in the language of Moses' words and deeds in Deuteronomy. Moses says, ". . . you shall smash their altars . . . and burn their Asherim with fire . . ."[26] Josiah smashes the altars and burns the Asherah.

8.   Finally, in Deuteronomy Moses repeatedly refers to the law against making statues. It is one of the Ten Commandments, which he quotes.[27] He states it several more times in other parts of the book.[28] A statue of a pagan deity must be burned.[29] The very term "statue" only occurs a few times after that. It appears only once in the four books of Samuel and Kings, until King Manasseh sets the statue of Asherah in the Temple.[30] *Josiah* removes the statue, and he burns it.

I considered the possibility that the wordings of Deuteronomy and 2 Kings are so similar in all of these cases simply because these were the natural words to use to describe these acts. But this was not a sufficient explanation. Just a few chapters before Josiah in 2 Kings is the story of Hezekiah's reform.[31] Hezekiah performs many of the same acts that Josiah does, or similar acts. Yet Hezekiah and his activities are described in different language—language that does not repeat the expressions of Moses' words and actions. On the contrary, the Deuteronomistic historian paints Josiah in special colors—Mosaic colors. He is a culmination of that which began with Moses. His actions in his day emulate Moses' actions in his own day. He is the hope that the covenant that began with Moses will be fulfilled as never before.

A Full Stop at Josiah

To some, all of this might prove only that Josiah was *important* to the Deuteronomistic writer, not that the work originally ended at Josiah. To my mind, the weight of all the evidence listed so far suggests that King Josiah was more than just one important character in a story. The emphasis on the eternal covenant, the cases of "to this day," the length of the Josiah section, the prediction of Josiah by name three centuries before he is born, the totally positive rating of Josiah alone out of all the kings, the parallels between Moses and Josiah—the weight of all of these factors argues that the writer originally designed the work to culminate in Josiah.

Also, I found clues in the text that there was once a full stop at Josiah and then a resumption of the story from a different point of view after his death.

The first clue was in the writer's critical ratings of the kings. The most important factor from his point of view seems to be centralization of the religion. The first law of Deuteronomy's law code is that there is to be only one place for sacrifice, one place "where Yahweh sets his name."[32] The writer therefore regards Jeroboam's establishment of the golden calves at Beth-El and Dan as a tremendous sin. He rates *every* king of Israel as having "done bad in the eyes of Yahweh," because none of them removed the calves. As for the kings of Judah, he rates several of them as having "done bad in the eyes of Yahweh" for various offenses—which always include building or retaining the "high places" for worship outside of Jerusalem. Even when he rates a king of Judah as having "done what is right in the eyes of Yahweh," he still says, "except that he did not do away with the high places."[33] Of all the kings of Israel and Judah, only two do not receive this criticism: Hezekiah and Josiah, the two kings who are said to have destroyed the high places.

The one consistent criterion, applied to every king, is centralization of religion. But after *Josiah*, this criterion disappears.

The last two chapters of 2 Kings do not even mention high places. According to the books of the prophets Jeremiah and Ezekiel, the high places were reestablished in this period.[34] Yet the Deuteronomistic writer does not mention it, neither to praise any of the last four kings for rejecting high places, nor to attack them for rebuilding them.

If all of the Deuteronomistic history were the work of one person, why would he set up this criterion and apply it to every single king except the last four—the very four in whose reigns the kingdom finally fell?

That is not the only thing that changes after the story of Josiah. King David figures in a fundamental way in the Deuteronomistic history. Half of the book of 1 Samuel, all of the book of 2 Samuel, and the first chapters of 1 Kings deal with his life. The majority of the kings who come after him are compared to him. The historian states explicitly, several times, that because of David's merit even a bad king of Judah cannot lose the throne for the family. Especially among the last few kings down to the time of Josiah, the historian reminds us of David. He compares Josiah himself to David, saying, "He went in all the path of David his father."[35] He compares Josiah's great-great-grandfather Ahaz, his great-grandfather Hezekiah, and his grandfather Manasseh to David.[36] Altogether the name David occurs about five hundred times in the Deuteronomistic history. Then, in the story of the last four kings, it stops. The text does not compare these kings to David. It does not refer to the Davidic covenant, let alone explain why it does not save the throne now the way it did in the reigns of Solomon, Rehoboam, Abijam, and Jehoram. It just does not mention David at all.

Thus two common, crucial matters in the Deuteronomistic history—centralization and David—disappear after the Josiah section.

Now, we must be careful how we interpret this. "Argument from silence" must be used cautiously. That is, it is stronger to deduce evidence from what a text does say than from what it does not. In the present case, though, the argument from silence is a loud one. When every king is rated with reference to centralization of religion down to Josiah but not therafter, when David figures regularly and essentially down to the time of Josiah but not thereafter, we have evidence of a real break and a change of perspective that are connected to that king. And this agrees with all the other evidence for identifying a culmination and break at Josiah. The evidence indicates that the author-editor of the original edition of this work was someone who lived during Josiah's reign. And it was someone who was *favorable* to Josiah.

This was the trail of clues that my predecessors and I followed through the Bible in order to know when and where to look for the person who gave us Deuteronomy and the next six books of the Bible. Now we knew when: around the year 622 B.C. And we knew where: Judah, almost certainly in the city of Jerusalem. The question that still remained was: who?

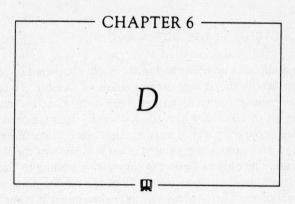

CHAPTER 6

D

We have learned that someone fashioned Deuteronomy and the next six books of the Bible as one continuous work. And we have learned that the person who fashioned this work was someone who lived during the reign of King Josiah. The original edition of the work told the story from Moses to Josiah.

In order to figure out who this author-editor of Deuteronomy and the next six books of the Bible was, it is necessary to look at what this person's work contained.

It included, first of all, the code of laws at the core of the book of Deuteronomy.

The Contents of the Law Code

The law code takes up about half of the book, chapters 12–26.

Its first law is the law of centralization of worship. It tells the worshiper that if he wants to eat meat he is not free simply to slaughter his sheep or cow himself. Rather, he must take the animal to the one approved place of worship, the "place where Yahweh sets his name," and there a consecrated priest will perform the slaughter at the altar. The only exception to this rule, according to Deuteronomy, is when someone lives too far from the official place to bring the animal there. Then he may slaughter the animal at home as long as he spills the blood onto the ground.[1]

The Deuteronomic law code also contains the "Law of the King." It requires that the king must be chosen by Yahweh (which presumably means designation by a prophet), that the king must not be a foreigner, that he must not acquire large numbers of horses, that he must not have many women (wives and concubines) nor great quantities of silver and gold, and he must write a copy of this law in front of the Levites and read it regularly.[2]

Deuteronomy's code of laws also contains prohibitions against practicing pagan religion. It contains instructions concerning prophets, especially false prophets. It deals with charity, justice, laws of family and community, holidays, dietary laws, laws concerning war, and a variety of laws on a wide range of matters from the treatment of slaves to agricultural matters to the practice of magic. Also, it regularly refers to the well-being of the *Levites*; it instructs the people to provide for the Levite.

Who Wrote the Law Code?

When it was Baruch Halpern's turn to present a paper to the Harvard Near East Department seminar in 1974, he presented research in which he attempted to find out from where this law code came.

He asked first: did it come from someone in the royal court? Did Josiah or some other king have it written to serve his own political purposes? This seemed unlikely. After all it contains the Law of the King. This law says that the king "shall not multiply silver and gold for himself very much." Why would a king who is establishing a "pious fraud" law code for his own political advantage include a law saying that he cannot have a lot of money? The law also prohibits him from having many women or from acquiring many horses, and it requires him to write out a copy of the law in front of the Levite priests. Why would a king want to encumber himself with all these restrictions?

The law code of Deuteronomy does not have the look of a book that was produced at the court. In fact, it contains material that relates to conditions that existed before there were any kings in Israel or Judah.

An example of this is the group of laws of war that appears in Deuteronomy 20 and 21. These laws are concerned with the summoning of the people to battle. Before going into battle, judges are to make an announcement to the people: any man who has built a house but has not yet dedicated it, or who has betrothed a woman but has not yet married her, should go home to his house or to his wife. He should not have to risk dying in war and leaving his new wife or his new home to be taken by someone else. It also exempts from conscription any man who is afraid. The man who is frightened should go home rather than weaken the spirit of others as well. The laws of war also state that after a military victory an Israelite is forbidden to rape a captured woman. The women of the group that has been defeated must be given time to mourn their lost family members, and then they may be taken as wives, or else they must be set free.

Now, this group of laws of war assumes universal military conscription—i.e., a draft. It is referring to ordinary citizens who are
being gathered into an army. There was in fact such a system of
mustering the Israelite tribes' forces in the country's early years. In
times of emergency, the Israelites were drafted for military service.
With the rise of the monarchy, however, this sort of conscription
was replaced by professional armies. The kings wanted to have
standing professional forces who were responsible to the king, rather
than to be obliged to turn to the tribes for support. The laws of war
in the book of Deuteronomy, therefore, do not reflect the kings'
interests. These laws rather suggest an early, nonmonarchic point of
view. There are instructions regarding lawsuits in this law code that
likewise appear to come from somewhere other than the palace.
They give jurisdiction in legal matters to the Levites, not to the king
or his appointees.

The Levites, Israel's priestly tribe, seem to be a more likely group
in which to look for the author of Deuteronomy than the royal
courtiers. The book appears to be written in their interests at many
points. It opens with the religious-centralization laws, which pro-
hibit lay persons from doing their own sacrificing. It repeatedly requires the people to care for the Levite. It includes laws of religious
tithes and offerings. It requires that the king write his copy of the
law in front of the Levites. It declares the Levites to be the rightful
priestly tribe. It regularly deals with this group's concerns. Most investigators, therefore, have related Deuteronomy's law code, in one
way or another, to Levites.

Which Priests?

But which Levites? There had been several different priestly circles
in Israel and Judah. In Jerusalem there was a priesthood that was
identified as descendants of Aaron. At Beth-El there had been
priests whom King Jeroboam had appointed. There were the Levites
of the northern kingdom who had functioned at Shiloh. There were
the rural Levites, local clergy who functioned at the various high
places for most of Israel's and Judah's history. Halpern asked, to

which priestly house and to which period could the search for the author of Deuteronomy's law code be narrowed down?

It was not likely that the author would be found among the Jerusalem Temple priests. True, this group might have liked the idea of centralizing the religion at their Temple; but this group also was Aaronid. They traced their lineage to Aaron, and they distinguished between Aaronids and all other Levites. The law code in Deuteronomy, however, makes no such distinction between Levite families, and it never even mentions the name Aaron. It also never refers to the ark, the cherubs, or any other religious implements that were housed in the Jerusalem Temple. It also never refers to the office of High Priest, and the High Priest of Jerusalem had been Aaronid ever since the day when King Solomon expelled the priest Abiathar and made the Aaronid priest Zadok the sole High Priest. The law code of Deuteronomy thus does not represent the point of view of the Aaronid priests of any period.

The laws do not reflect the views of the priests who functioned at Beth-El during the two hundred years between Jeroboam and the fall of Israel in 722 either. Those priests were not Levites. Deuteronomy's laws favor the Levites and regard *only* Levites as legitimate priests.

The author of the Deuteronomic law code did not come from the rural Levites either. The first and perhaps foremost law of the code is the centralization of the religion, the requirement that all sacrifices be brought to one central altar. This was the law that put the rural Levites out of business. It meant the destruction of the high places at which they functioned. The Deuteronomic law code shows *concern* for such Levites; it instructs the people to care for them. But it does not *enfranchise* them. That is, it does not allow them to be official priests, presiding over the sacrifices at the central place of worship. The person who wrote Deuteronomy's laws certainly did not represent this group's interests.

The Priests of Shiloh

The place to look for the author of Deuteronomy, therefore, was in a group (1) that wanted centralization of religion, but not tied to the ark or to the Jerusalem priesthood; (2) that cared about all Levites' livelihood, but would enfranchise only a group of *central* Levites; (3) that accepted having a king, but wanted limitations on his rule; (4) that had a premonarchy approach to matters of war.

This sounds like the priests of Shiloh—the same group that produced E.

The priests of Shiloh believed in centralization of worship, because Shiloh had once been the national religious center, in the days of Samuel.

They did not relate centralization to the ark or to the Jerusalem priesthood, because their leader Abiathar had been expelled from Jerusalem by Solomon, and ever since then the Jerusalem priesthood had been Aaronid.

They insisted that only Levites were legitimate priests, for they themselves were Levites, and they had been preempted by non-Levites at Beth-El.

They had good reason to urge the people to care for needy Levites, because they *were* needy Levites, without land or employment.

They accepted having a king, since their leader Samuel had designated and anointed the first two kings of Israel. They wanted limitations on royal rule, since Samuel's acceptance of the monarchy had been reluctant, and King Solomon and King Jeroboam had treated them badly.

They took a premonarchy approach to war, preferring the tribal musters to a professional army, because it was with the rise of professional armies that the kings had become independently powerful and no longer had to depend on the people for support.

At least the *law code* of Deuteronomy, then, was probably written by someone connected to the priests of Shiloh. It need not have been written as a pious fraud shortly before its discovery by Hilkiah.

It reflected the interests of the Shiloh priests at just about any time after the division of Israel and Judah.

Other investigators before Halpern had said that Deuteronomy might have been written in Israel before the Assyrian destruction of the kingdom, and then brought south to Judah in 722. But, Halpern asked, what did "brought south to Judah" mean? If the law code of Deuteronomy was really written by an out-of-power group of priests in a kingdom that was then destroyed, how did this document find its way into the Temple in Judah? How did it become the law of the land?

It was necessary to trace the fate of this scroll and to see what was done with it. It turned out that the Shiloh connection was strengthened by investigation of how the law code came to be in the middle of Deuteronomy. This also led to discovering the identity of the Deuteronomist himself.

The Shiloh Connection

The Deuteronomistic historian took the law code and added an introduction. The introduction, Deuteronomy 1–11, says that this is the last speech of Moses. It then pictures Moses as reviewing the main events of his forty years with the people.

Then the Deuteronomistic writer pictured Moses as giving them the law code, Deuteronomy 12–26, and added a list of blessings and curses, for fidelity or infidelity to the code respectively, in Deuteronomy 27–28.

Then he added a conclusion, picturing Moses' last words and acts. Moses encourages the people. He writes "this *torah*" on a scroll. He gives it to the *Levites*. He tells them to put it *next to the ark*. And then he dies.

The Deuteronomistic historian writer then set Deuteronomy at the beginning of the history that flows through the books of Joshua, Judges, Samuel, and Kings. And then he wrote the climactic finish: the priest Hilkiah finds the scroll, and King Josiah fulfills it.

How did this strengthen the Shiloh connection? Because the

Deuteronomistic historian turned out to be connected with the priests of Shiloh himself.

First, the Deuteronomistic historian seems to have had the same unadmiring attitude toward the Aaronid priesthood that the Shiloh priests had. In his introduction and conclusion to the book of Deuteronomy, he mentioned Aaron only twice: once to say that he died,[3] and once to say that God was mad enough to destroy him in the matter of the golden calf.[4] The Deuteronomist also added a gratuitous allusion to the case of snow-white Miriam, another story in which Aaron had acted badly and God had been angry at him.[5]

Second, the Deuteronomist—and his hero King Josiah—shared the Shilonite priests' antipathy toward Solomon and Jeroboam, the two kings who had removed the Shilonites from authority. In the case of Solomon, the historian said that Solomon went wrong in his old age, that he turned to pagan religion, that he followed the Sidonian goddess Ashtoreth, the Moabite god Chemosh, and the Ammonite god Milcom, and that he built high places to these deities on a hill opposite Jerusalem.[6] Then the historian reported at the end of the history that part of Josiah's reform was to eliminate these very high places. His language made it clear that he meant to picture Solomon's acts in the worst light possible. He wrote that Josiah

> defiled the high places that were opposite Jerusalem . . . that Solomon King of Israel had built to Ashtoreth, *the Sidonians' disgusting thing*, and to Chemosh, *the disgusting thing of Moab*, and to Milcom, *the Ammonites' abomination*.[7]

So much for Solomon. The Deuteronomist also wrote critically about Jeroboam's religious building activities, namely the golden calf high places of Dan and Beth-El, and he reported that Josiah destroyed at least the Beth-El high place as well.[8]

The priests of Shiloh could not have asked for more from Josiah. He was righting the wrongs that had been done to them three centuries earlier. And the Deuteronomistic historian was picturing this king as the culmination of three centuries of history.

Jeremiah

There was one other person who was connected with King Josiah and with the Deuteronomistic history. This person's association with them further confirmed the Shiloh connection, and it brought us a step closer to knowing the Deuteronomist's identity. The person was the prophet Jeremiah.

According to the book of Jeremiah, this prophet admired King Josiah and began his ministry as a prophet during Josiah's reign.[9] According to the book of Chronicles, Jeremiah composed a lamentation for Josiah when he was killed.[10]

Jeremiah was connected with Josiah's counselors who were involved with "the book of the *torah*." Recall that Hilkiah the priest had discovered the book, and Shaphan the scribe had carried it to King Josiah and read it to him. When Jeremiah sent a letter to the exiles in Babylon, it was delivered for him by Gemariah, son of *Hilkiah*, and by Elasah, son of *Shaphan*.[11] When Jeremiah wrote a scroll of prophecies against Josiah's son Jehoiakim, it was read at the chamber of Gemariah, son of *Shaphan*.[12] Gemariah, son of Shaphan, stood by Jeremiah at critical moments in his life, as did Ahikam, son of Shaphan, who saved Jeremiah from being stoned.[13] And Gedaliah, son of Ahikam, son of Shaphan, when he was appointed governor of Judah by Nebuchadnezzar, took Jeremiah under his protection.[14]

Jeremiah was somehow tied to Josiah and to the book of the *torah*. What does this have to do with the Shiloh connection?

First of all, Jeremiah is the one prophet in the Bible to refer to Shiloh (four times).[15]

Second, he calls Shiloh "the place where I [God] caused my name to dwell," which is the Deuteronomic term for the central place of worship.[16]

Third, the last thing that we heard about the Shiloh priesthood was that their leader, Abiathar, who had been one of David's two chief priests, was expelled from Jerusalem by Solomon. Solomon banished Abiathar to his family estate in the town of Anathoth,

which to this day is a small village outside of Jerusalem. In Anathoth, Abiathar presumably could be observed and kept out of trouble, because it was a town of Aaronid priests.[17] What is the
connection between the last Shiloh leader's ending up in Anathoth,
on the one hand, and Jeremiah and the book that Hilkiah found, on
the other? The first verse of the book of Jeremiah is:

> The words of Jeremiah, *son of Hilkiah*, of the priests who were in
> *Anathoth*.

Jeremiah, the prophet who favored Josiah, and who was close to
the people who discovered the *torah*, and who referred to Shiloh as
the great central place of old, was a priest from Anathoth. And his
father was a priest named Hilkiah. (Not to overstate the case, we do
not know if Jeremiah's father was the same priest Hilkiah who found
the book.) And the residents of Anathoth, an Aaronid city, were
hostile toward Jeremiah.[18]

Jeremiah is a priest, but he never sacrifices — which is also consistent with the position of the priests of Shiloh. Also, he is the only
prophet to allude to the story of Moses' bronze snake.[19] The story of
that snake comes from E, the Shiloh source. King Hezekiah had
smashed that snake. His destruction of an old relic that was associated with Moses himself was probably a blow to the priests of Shiloh. They were the ones who told its story, they held Moses in
particularly great esteem, and they may have been Moses' descendants. King Josiah, on the other hand, who was the darling of the
Shiloh priests, had a different record on the bronze snake. The term
in Hebrew for the bronze snake was "Nehushtan." Josiah married his
son to a woman who may have been connected with the Shiloh
circle, because she was named Nehushta.[20]

I would add to Halpern's observations that not only is Jeremiah
the only prophet to refer to Shiloh and to allude to Moses' bronze
snake; he is also the only prophet to refer to Samuel, the priest-
prophet-judge who was the greatest figure in Shiloh's history. Jeremiah speaks of Samuel alongside Moses as the two great men of the
people's history.[21]

There is one more thing connecting the prophet Jeremiah to
Deuteronomy and the events surrounding it, and it is probably the
strongest evidence of all. As many readers, both traditional and critical, have observed, the book of Jeremiah seems to be written, at

several points, in the same language and outlook as Deuteronomy. Parts of Jeremiah are so similar to Deuteronomy that it is hard to believe that they are not by the same person. Just to give a few examples:

Deuteronomy	Jeremiah
And it will be, if you really listen to Yahweh's voice... (Deut 28:1)	And it will be, if you really listen to me, says Yahweh... (Jer 17:24)
Circumcise the foreskin of your heart... (Deut 10:16)	Be circumsised for Yahweh and take away the foreskins of your heart... (Jer 4:4)
...to all the host of the heavens... (Deut 4:19; 17:3)	...to all the host of the heavens... (Jer 8:2; 19:13)
...and he brought you out of the iron furnace, from Egypt ... (Deut 4:20)	...in the day I brought them out from the land of Egypt, from the iron furnace... (Jer 11:4)
With all your heart and with all your soul... (Deut 4:29; 10:12; 11:13; 13:4)	...With all my heart and with all my soul... (Jer 32:41)

On the weight of this collection of evidence, Halpern concluded that Deuteronomy's law code came from the Levitical priests of Shiloh. The evidence also indicated that this group was connected with the full Deuteronomistic history, comprising seven books of the Bible, as well as the book of Jeremiah—or at least part of it.

E and D

Halpern's investigations on D and mine on E came out complementing one another. We each had identified a biblical source with the same group: the priests of Shiloh. And the fact is that these two sources, E and D, have many things in common.

They both refer to the mountain where Moses and the people go in the wilderness as Horeb[22] (as opposed to J and P, which call it Sinai).

They both use the crucial expression "place where Yahweh sets his name" (or "causes his name to be mentioned," or "causes his name to dwell").[23] (The expression does not occur in J or P.)

They both regard Moses as good, and more than good. He is at a turning point in history and singularly crucial to it. His personality is carefully and extensively developed. (There is nothing comparable in J or P.)

They both place great emphasis on the role of prophets—which makes sense, given that their heroes included such figures as Moses, Samuel, Ahijah, and later Jeremiah. (The very word "prophet" occurs only once in P and never in J.)

They both favor and support the Levites. (In J. the Levites are dispersed as recompense for Levi's having massacred the people of Shechem; in P, the Levites are separate from, and lower than, the Aaronid family of priests.)

They both regard Aaron as bad, referring to his role in the golden calf episode and to the snow-white Miriam episode. (Neither of these is mentioned in J or P.)

The Priests of Shiloh

The laws and stories of D, therefore, were as tied to the life of the biblical world as J and E were. They expressed the convictions and the hopes of an old and distinguished priestly family through generations of frustration. And, in the later parts (Dtr[1]), they reflected a happy day when, through King Josiah, some members of that family finally returned to positions of authority and respect.

One might ask: could the Shilonite priests really have maintained their identity through three hundred years of being out of power and without a major religious center? Answer: yes. This has happened with families, especially politically active families, in many countries at various times in history. Indeed, there are families who trace their lineage to the biblical priests or Levites to this day, even though these groups have been out of power for nineteen hundred years. If anything, the priestly families of biblical Israel and Judah would have been even more conscious of lineage because the priestly role itself was hereditary. Moreover, the Shiloh priests were very possibly Mushite—i.e., descended from Moses—and a family with such a famous, noble ancestor would be even more likely to be conscious of its heritage.

Further, the particular fate of the Shilonite priests over those centuries can account for peculiarities of the sources. For example, the ark is not mentioned in E or in the Deuteronomic law code, both of which were written when the Shilonite priests did not have access to the ark. But the ark *is* mentioned in the parts of Deuteronomy that were written during the reign of Josiah (Dtr[1]), when the Shilonites *did* have access to the ark.

The priests of Shiloh were apparently a group with a continuing literary tradition. They wrote and preserved texts over centuries: laws, stories, historical reports, and poetry. They were associated with scribes. They apparently had access to archives of preserved texts. Perhaps they maintained such archives themselves, in the same way that another out-of-power group of priests did at Qumran centuries later. The Qumran archives, known as the Dead Sea

Scrolls, were the Qumran group's collection of laws, stories, and poetry; and it, too, included a code of laws that would apply at such time that the Qumran group would return to a position of authority in Jerusalem: the Temple Scroll, which the archeologist Yigael Yadin recovered and published in 1977.

The Creation of the Deuteronomistic History

The Deuteronomistic historian, in the days of King Josiah, assembled his history out of the texts available to him. The beginning of his history was the book of Deuteronomy, and the conclusion was the story of Josiah.[24] The way he handled the texts that came in between these also demonstrates the impact of the events of the ancient world on the way that the Bible's story came to be written.

He took texts that told the story of his people's arrival in the land—the stories of Joshua, Jericho, and the conquest—and he added a few lines at the beginning and at the end to set the story in a certain light. This became the book of Joshua.

He did the same with the next set of texts, which told the story of the people's early years in the land: the stories of Deborah, Gideon, and Samson. This became the book of Judges.

Next he placed the stories of Samuel at Shiloh: the stories of Saul and of David, the first kings. This became the book of 1 Samuel.

After that he set the Court History of David. That became the book of 2 Samuel.

Then he took several texts that told the stories of the kings who came after David, and he assembled one continuous history out of them that went down to the time of his own king: Josiah. And that became the books of 1 and 2 Kings.

I was able to establish this picture of his work by isolating the lines that he added to these archive texts. It is only possible to find them in the puzzle now by careful examination of wording, grammar, syntax, theme, and literary structure. I refer here only to those lines about which there is a relatively high degree of certainty. As a general rule we do not rush to call a line an insertion unless two or more of these clues are present. It is impressive to read these lines and see how he gave a shape and direction to six hundred years of history with just a few short insertions—short, but carefully worded and artfully inserted.

The insertions in the book of Joshua are in God's first words to Joshua when he replaces Moses, in a passage concerning a national covenant ceremony that Joshua leads at Mt. Ebal, and in speeches that Joshua makes to the people at Shiloh before he dies.[25] All of the inserted lines refer to the *torah* of Moses. They point out that Joshua read every word of it to the people and carved it in stone. They warn that the people's destiny in the land depends on how carefully they observe it.

The insertion at the beginning of the book of Judges says that the people often failed to follow Yahweh, that they would turn to other gods, that Yahweh would then allow other peoples to overpower them, that they would then be sorry for their infidelity, and that Yahweh would then forgive them and provide a judge to save them. This pattern of infidelity-defeat-repentance-forgiveness became a *Leitmotif* into which all the stories of the book of Judges then fit. The Deuteronomistic historian then added other short notices at subsequent locations in the book of Judges that demonstrated that this pattern was operative in history. That is, he noted that misfortunes that the people suffered were the result of their infidelity.[26]

Thus the Deuteronomistic historian made it clear with only a small quantity of writing in Deuteronomy, Joshua, and Judges that (1) God had given the people instruction, (2) they had been warned that their fate depended on their fidelity to this instruction and (3) their subsequent history was the record of how well they fared when they heeded or failed to heed this warning.

The Deuteronomist's insertions into the book of 1 Samuel were few but important. As in the book of Joshua, he placed them in communications that were made at important moments in history: in Samuel's speech to the people after the establishment of the ark, in Yahweh's instructions to Samuel to give the people a king, and in Samuel's speech to the people on the day of the inauguration of the monarchy. Each of these insertions involved the issue of the people's faithfulness to Yahweh alone.[27]

In 2 Samuel he made only one insertion, the promise of the Davidic covenant, that David and his descendants after him would hold the throne, *eternally* and *unconditionally*.[28]

In the books of Kings, his task was more complicated. He was not just inserting occasional lines into an otherwise continuous text. Rather, he had to fashion this section of his history out of several different texts from his archive. Apparently there was no single history of the two kingdoms of Israel and Judah. There were only histories of one kingdom or the other. The Deuteronomist took one history of the kings of Israel and one history of the kings of Judah, and he sliced them up and wove them in between each other.

For example, he tells the story of Asa, king of Judah. At the end of it he turns to Israel and says, "Ahab, son of Omri, became king over Israel in the thirty-eighth year of Asa, king of Judah."[29] Then he tells the story of Ahab, king of Israel, and at the end of it he turns back to Judah and says, "Jehoshaphat, son of Asa, became king over Judah in the fourth year of Ahab, king of Israel."[30] And so on.

He united the stories by beginning each with the formula "He did bad in the eyes of Yahweh" or "He did what was right in the eyes of Yahweh." And he only gave information that he regarded as relevant to his story about each king. For those readers who might want more facts, he referred them back to his sources, saying, for example, "And the rest of the acts of Ahab and all that he did . . . are they not written in the book of the Chronicles of the Kings of Israel?"[31]

He was therefore not just recording annals. He was fashioning a history of his people, a history with a purpose and a message. He made the message clear with a few more insertions in these books. He inserted several more references to the Davidic covenant, some of which I quoted at the beginning of this chapter. They reemphasized the eternal and unconditional promise of this covenant, that David's family would always have a "holding" to rule, even if they did wrong. This was an important point for the Deuteronomist to develop. It enabled him to criticize the kings of Judah for wrongdoing and still be able to account for the historical fact that their family remained on the throne for hundreds of years.

The Covenant

Modern investigators were confused over these insertions about the Davidic covenant. Sometimes the insertions reiterated this promise that the Davidic kings would rule forever, even if they sinned; but sometimes they seemed to be saying just the opposite, that the kings could rule only if they did *not* sin.

For example, the covenant promise in 2 Samuel 7 says explicitly that even if the king does wrong he keeps the throne:

> I shall chastise him with the rod of people and the lashes of humans if he does wrong, but my fidelity will not turn from him. . . . Your house and kingdom will be secure before you forever. Your throne will be established forever.

But the covenant promise in 1 Kings 8:25 says that the king's tenure on the throne does depend on his behavior:

> There will not be cut off from you a man before me sitting on the throne of Israel *only if* your sons keep their way, to go before me as you went before me.

How could the Deuteronomist insert lines that blatantly contradicted each other? Was the covenant conditional or unconditional?

If we examine all of the passages that mention the Davidic covenant, we will find that all of the *conditional* passages spoke of the kings' holding the throne *of Israel*. All of the *unconditional* passages spoke of the kings' holding *the throne*. This petty difference of wording was not so petty to the writer. He had to deal with the historical fact that David's family started out ruling the whole united kingdom of Israel, but that they had lost all of it except their own tribe of Judah. He therefore pictured the covenant promise to David to be partly conditional and partly unconditional. The throne of Judah in Jerusalem was unconditional. It was to belong to David's descen-

dants forever. But the throne of all Israel was to belong to them only
if they were worthy. Which they were not. And so they lost it.

The Deuteronomistic writer added a slight, enigmatic twist on
this point. When he pictured the prophet Ahijah of Shiloh taking
the throne of Israel away from the Davidides and giving it to Jeroboam, he wrote that Ahijah says to Jeroboam:

> I shall give Israel to you. And I shall humble David's seed on
> account of this, *but not for all time.*[32]

Ahijah seems to be saying that the Davidic kings' loss of Israel
will not last forever. And in fact King *Josiah* attempted to take back
the northern territory of Israel. Again the events of the biblical
world had an impact on the way a biblical author told the story. In
this case, the political fortunes of the country affected the writer's
formulation of the covenant between God and his anointed king, his
messiah—which became one of the central elements of Judaism and
Christianity. The man who assembled the Deuteronomistic history,
like those who write J, E, and the Deuteronomic law code, was
inextricably tied to the issues of the world around him, its moments
of joy and its catastrophes. And those issues and events had an
impact on the way he pictured God and history.

Some would say that this makes this writer guilty of "pious fraud,"
making up a covenant between God and King David and concocting
its terms to fit later events in history. It does not seem that way to
me. The Deuteronomistic writer did not make up the Davidic covenant tradition himself. He only wrote about it. The *tradition* was
much older than he was. Davidic covenant traditions appear in some
biblical Psalms that were composed before the Deuteronomist ever
picked up his quill.[33] Also, it is hard to imagine that the Deuteronomist could have gotten away with making up a Davidic covenant in
622 B.C. and claiming that it had been around for four hundred
years without anyone's having heard of it. Who would have believed
him? Rather, the process of writing history was more complex than
that. The Deuteronomistic writer was governed by both events and
tradition. His task was both to record history and to interpret history
in the light of tradition.

Giving Shape to History

The Deuteronomistic historian developed other matters in the books
of Kings besides David's covenant. At several junctures he identified
Jerusalem and its Temple as the "place where Yahweh causes his
name to dwell"—which is to say, he used the language of Deuteronomy's law code. In the law code the expression "the place where
Yahweh causes his name to dwell" refers to the one central place
where all sacrifice is supposed to take place. The Deuteronomistic
historian made it clear that the Temple in Jerusalem had become
that place. He also added more references to the *torah*.

And so he shaped his history of his people around the themes of
(1) fidelity to Yahweh, (2) the Davidic covenant, (3) the centralization of religion at the Temple in Jerusalem, and (4) the *torah*. And
then he interpreted the major events of history in light of these
factors. Why did the kingdom split? Because Solomon had forsaken
Yahweh and his *torah*. Why did David's descendants retain Jerusalem
and Judah? Because God had made an unconditional covenant
promise to David. Why did the northern kingdom of Israel fall?
Because the people and their kings did not follow the *torah*. Why
was there hope for the future? Because the *torah* had been rediscovered under Josiah, and now it would be fulfilled as never before. All
of the Deuteronomist's major themes—fidelity, *torah*, centralization,
Davidic covenant—culminated in Josiah.

And then Josiah died from an Egyptian arrow.

CHAPTER 7

A Priest in Exile

JOSIAH, the culminating hero of the Deuteronomistic history, had died.

The Deuteronomistic history looked ironic, even foolish, twenty-two years later. The Babylonians had destroyed and exiled Judah. The "eternal" kingdom had ended. The family that would "never be cut off from the throne" was cut off from the throne. The place "where Yahweh causes his name to dwell" was burned down. And the things that were said to exist "to this day" did not exist anymore. What was to be done with the positive, hopeful history book that culminated in Josiah? *Someone* decided to make a second edition of it.

Probably the nearest modern analogy would be if someone who admired the American President John Kennedy assembled a history of the United States from George Washington to Kennedy, constructing the story to climax in Kennedy's presidency as a culmination of things past and as the beginning of something new and hopeful. And then the president's early death left that history ironic and obsolete, even painful to read. It would not be enough just to add a chapter or two at the end, briefly describing the next few presidencies. Rather, someone would have to go back through the work and make changes at critical points so that it would no longer point so specifically to Kennedy. The changes would have to prepare the readers for the new ending and provide a context in which to understand the new events.

Such was the task of this person who fashioned the second edition of the biblical history. He could not just add a summary of the last four kings' reigns. He had to explain why the dream had failed.

Reshaping History

Clues in the text reveal how he did it. They were the same sort of clues that other investigators and I had used to find the hand of the creator of the first edition of the history (Dtr[1]): grammatical breaks (for example, when a text that has been speaking in the singular suddenly shifts to plural), special terminology (terms and phrases that occurred only in passages that were also suspected to be additions on other grounds), theme (destruction and exile), syntax, and literary structure.

The clues were harder to trace in the case of the postdestruction writer than they had been with the Josiah writer because the postdestruction writer imitated the language and style of the earlier edition perfectly. (I shall discuss how he was able to do it later.) Also, he only added occasional paragraphs here and there to the Josiah edition. He was not writing a whole new version. Therefore, there were no obvious doublets or contradictions like those of J and E.

In order to identify a line as a Dtr[2] insertion, it was necessary to find converging lines of evidence, such as grammar, theme, and terminology, all pointing in the same direction. Just because a passage predicted an exile, that did not mean that one could conclude that it had been inserted by the exiled writer to explain his current situation. On the contrary, exile was a known and feared reality in the ancient Near East, and it could have been threatened at almost any time. But if a passage that predicted exile also broke the context in which it appeared, and there was a shift in grammar, and it used phrases that appeared only in other suspected passages, then the converging evidence was strong.[1]

Identifying Dtr[2] insertions in this way, and using considerable caution, I uncovered the following picture of how the exiled writer reshaped the history.

Exile

First the writer developed the idea of exile itself. He was not prepared just to add a statement at the end saying that the Babylonians conquered and exiled Judah—which would have been an unexpected, unrelated finish. Rather, he inserted references to the possibility of exile in various places in the history, so that conquest and exile now became a fundamental part of the story, a threatening sword hanging over Israel's and Judah's heads for centuries:...

you will perish quickly from the land...
(Deut 4:26; Josh 23:16)

Yahweh will scatter you among the nations...
(Deut 4:27)

Yahweh will drive you and your king...to a nation that you have not known...
(Deut 28:36)

You will be lifted off the land...
(Deut 28:63)

Yahweh will scatter you among all the peoples from one end of the earth to the other...
(Deut 28:64)

You will not lengthen days on the land...
(Deut 30:18)

I shall cut off Israel from the face of the land that I gave
them . . .
(1 Kings 9:7)

This writer was not merely listing facts of history. He was producing
an *interpretive* history. In it, exile was not just a one-time event. It
was a theme.

Other Gods

Then the writer developed the reason for the exile. Why had this
calamity happened? Answer: because the people had worshiped
other gods. On this point he only had to emphasize what was already
written in Dtr[1]. The worship of Yahweh alone was the first of the
Ten Commandments in Dtr[1] (as it was in the E Ten Commandments
and the J Ten Commandments[2]), and it was called for in every book
from Deuteronomy to 2 Kings. The exiled writer added ten more
references to the command against apostasy, and he tied every one of
them to a reference to exile.[3]

He placed them at significant points in the story: in God's last
speeches to Moses, among Joshua's last words to the people after
settling in the land, in God's words to Solomon after building the
Temple, and in the chapter describing the fall of the northern kingdom.

Strongest of all, he made this the point of God's last words to
Moses before summoning him to his death. This is the last prophecy
that Moses hears:

When you are lying with your fathers, this people will rise and
will whore after alien gods of the land into which they are coming,
and they will leave me and break my covenant which I have made
with them.

And my anger will burn against them in that day, and I shall
leave them, and I shall hide my face from them, and they will be
devoured, and many evils and troubles will find them.

And they will say in that day, "Is it not because our God is not among us that these evils have found us?"

But I shall hide my face on that day because of all the wrong that they have done, for they turned to other gods. [4]

The scene was set. God had commanded the people not to worship other gods, and he had made destruction, exile, and abandonment—"hiding the face"—the penalty for breaking this command.

Manasseh

Next, the exiled writer looked back through the history for some possible explanation, already existing in the story, for the kingdom's fall—something that had happened before Josiah, something that had been so terrible that Josiah's attempt at reform was not enough to counterbalance it.

He found it in the story of King Manasseh, Josiah's grandfather. According to the Dtr[1] story, Manasseh had undone all the good things that his father, King Hezekiah, had accomplished. Manasseh rebuilds the high places, he sets up a statue of the goddess Asherah, and he builds altars to pagan gods in the Temple precincts. In Dtr[1] this had set up the story of Josiah nicely, because in the next two chapters Josiah sets all of this right again. He tears down the high places, burns the statue of Asherah, and smashes the pagan altars. But the person who produced the new edition, Dtr[2], now elaborated upon Manasseh's crimes *and on their consequences.* He added these words:

Manasseh instigated them to do wrong, more than the nations that Yahweh had destroyed before the children of Israel.

And Yahweh said by the hand of his servants the prophets, "Because Manasseh King of Judah has done these abominations . . . he has caused Judah to sin by his idols. Therefore I am bringing such evil on Jerusalem and Judah that the ears of whoever hears about it will tingle . . . I shall wipe Jerusalem the way one wipes a plate and turns it over on its face. And I shall reject the remnant of my possession and put them in their enemies' hand, and they will be a spoil and booty for all their enemies, because they have done wrong in my eyes and have been angering me from the day their fathers went out of Egypt to this day."[5]

Manasseh had been so bad, and he had caused the people to be so bad, that he had brought about a prophecy that the kingdom would fall.

The person who inserted these remarks about Manasseh's crimes then turned back to end of the scroll. It had concluded that "no king ever arose like Josiah," but he now added these words:

But Yahweh did not turn back from his great fury which burned against Judah over all the things in which *Manasseh* had angered him.[6]

Without taking anything from Josiah, the Dtr² historian had explained why Judah was still due to fall: the crimes of the past outweighed the good of the short-lived reform. He then added two short chapters describing Judah's last four kings, noting in the manner of Dtr¹ that each "did what was bad in the eyes of Yahweh." The reform was over, and the country was back on the road to disaster.

The Two Covenants

But there was still the matter of David's covenant. According to the Dtr¹ history, it was eternal and unconditional. No matter what Manasseh or any other Davidide king did, the throne and the royal city were supposed to be secure forever. The person who was now redoing that history was apparently not willing to cross out that promise as if it had never been there—which is another indication that he was not simply committing pious fraud. How then was he to explain the fall of the kings, the Temple, and Jerusalem?

He did it by drawing his readers' attention to another covenant: the Mosaic covenant. This covenant that Yahweh had made with the people in the wilderness, according to tradition, was definitely

conditional. It required the people to obey God's commandments or
else suffer severe consequences. The Dtr[2] writer added several lines
to Deuteronomy, emphasizing that destruction and exile were among
these consequences.

This pulled the carpet out from under the Davidic covenant. The
fate of the nation ultimately depended on the people, not on the
king. The Davidic family's rule was assured, yes, but if the people's
own actions brought about the destruction of the country, then *over
whom* was this family to rule?!

The Davidic covenant thus logically came second after the Mosaic covenant. The first question was whether the nation was going
to survive. Only after that came the question of who was going to
govern it.

There was a similar problem awaiting the exiled historian in the
story of King Solomon. According to the Dtr[1] account, God appears
to Solomon after he finishes building the Temple, and God repeats
the Davidic covenant promises, adding that the Temple will last
forever. He says:

> I have sanctified this house that you have built to set my name
> there *forever*, and my eyes and my heart will be there *all the days*.[7]

The exilic historian again was not prepared to cross out this eternal promise even though it obviously had failed—the Temple was
lying in ruins. Instead, he buried it in the folds of the conditional
Mosaic covenant. He added four sentences in which he pictured
God as now speaking not only to Solomon but to the entire people.
God warns the people that if they do not keep the commandments
he has given them he will exile them and reject the Temple. He
says:

> I shall cut off Israel from the face of the land that I gave them, and
> I shall cast out the house that I sanctified to my name from before
> my face.[8]

Notice the difference between the two quoted sentences on this
page. They both refer to the Temple as the place sanctified to Yahweh's name. But the second one, the exilic one, leaves out the word
"forever."

Again the events of the biblical world had enormous impact on the way the Bible was developing—and the form that the Bible took ultimately was also to have enormous impact on the character of Judaism and Christianity. In this case, the fall of David's family after centuries of rule resulted in an increased emphasis in the Bible on the covenant that Moses mediated between God and the people. The historical reality—now reflected in the wording of the Deuteronomistic history—was that any hopes the people might have for security could no longer be based on the Davidic covenant. Their survival and well-being depended not on a promise to a king of an eternal royal holding and Temple in Jerusalem, but on their fidelity to their own covenant with God. The Davidic covenant, therefore, became a promise only that the throne was eternally *available* to David's family. Even if it was unoccupied at the present, there was always the possibility that a descendant of David, a messiah, might come someday and rule justly. The implications for Judaism and Christianity were, of course, tremendous.

From Egypt to Egypt

It remained for the exiled Deuteronomist to write the finish: the people's fate. He reported that the Babylonians deported the last kings and several thousand of the people to Babylonia. He reported last that the Babylonian emperor's appointed governor, Gedaliah, was assassinated and that the entire people then fled to Egypt.

He did not add any interpretation of these last events, no summation, long or short, saying something like "And so Judah was exiled from its land because they worshiped other gods." This unelaborated finish was possible precisely because the exiled Deuteronomist had already prepared the way for it. In his carefully placed insertions he had told his readers that worshiping other gods was the worst possible offense, that it would lead to defeat and exile, and that the kings, particularly Manasseh, had caused the people to go wrong. The short, straightforward report of the kingdom's calamity, in the light of this preparation, was powerful. The end of the kingdom had been predictable—and predicted.

One of the exiled writer's insertions in particular prepared the way for the terse conclusion. He added a curse to the text of Deuteronomy. Deuteronomy already contained a horrifying list of curses in the Dtr[1] version. This list of consequences of not keeping the covenant is still terrible to read: diseases, madness, blindness, military defeats, destruction of crops and livestock, and starvation to the point that people will eat their own children. The exiled Deuteronomist added references to exile in general, and he added one more specific curse to the end of the list. What is the worst possible thing that could be said to an Israelite as a threat? The last curse of Deuteronomy is:

> And Yahweh will send you back to Egypt . . . in the road that I had told you that you would never see again; and you will sell yourselves there to your enemies as slaves, and no one will buy.[9]

Back to Egypt! The ultimate curse for the people who started out as slaves there. The exiled writer then simply reported the people's fate at the end of 2 Kings. The Babylonian emperor appointed Gedaliah as governor of Judah. Gedaliah was assassinated. The people fled in terror of the Babylonians' reprisal. The last sentence of the story is:

> And the entire people, from the smallest to the biggest, and the officers of the soldiers, arose and came to Egypt, because they were afraid of the Babylonians.[10]

The exilic writer had made the new edition of the history into the story of the people of Israel from Egypt to Egypt. He had given a whole new shape and direction to the story without, apparently, deleting a word of the original edition.

The Mercy of Yahweh

Was this the end of the story then? Did this as yet unnamed person see the people's exile to Babylonia and Egypt as the termination of the covenant and the demise of the people? Definitely not. He left open a channel of hope. His insertions into the text included a reminder that Yahweh is a merciful God, compassionate and forgiving. This was hardly a new idea in the biblical world. Both J and E had pictured the God of Israel as merciful and long-suffering. So had Dtr[1] in Josiah's days. The person who produced Dtr[2] now emphasized to his readers that if they would turn back to Yahweh, repent, and give up other gods, then their God would forgive them.[11] Thus he designed his history not only to tell the past, but to give hope for the future.

The Same Man

Who was he? How did he come to have a copy of the original version of the history? How was he able to imitate the language and style of that earlier edition so perfectly? Why did he choose to produce a new version of an old history in the first place, instead of writing an all-new work?

The most likely answer to all of these questions is that both editions of the Deuteronomistic history were by the same person.

He had a copy of Dtr[1] because he wrote it. He chose to build on the earlier edition instead of writing an all-new work because he had created that earlier edition, and he was still able to be satisfied with all but a few sentences of his original work. (And, besides, what writer was ever eager to throw out a seven-book work he had produced and write a new one from the beginning?) The language and styles are similar because the same man wrote them.

Biblical scholars argue generally that, rather than one man, it was a "school" that produced the Deuteronomistic material. They suggest that there may have been a circle of people who shared a particular outlook and set of interests, and that various Deuteronomistic sections of the Bible were produced by various members of this group. The various members of the "Deuteronomistic school," they suggest, wrote in similar styles and language because of their common membership in a group.

Now it is true that different members of a common school of thought may write in quite similar styles. (The Pythagoreans in

Greece are cited as an example.) Still, in the case of the Deuteronomistic history, the degree of similarity of Dtr¹ and Dtr² is phenomenal. Further, there is no compelling reason why we should hypothesize the existence of an otherwise unknown "school" when it was perfectly possible and logical for a single person to have done it. The first edition of the history, Dtr¹, had to be written before Josiah died in 609 B.C. The second edition, Dtr², had to be written after the Babylonian destruction and exile in 587 B.C. That is only a difference of twenty-two years. One person could easily have been alive and writing from the time of Josiah to the exile.

The Identity of the Deuteronomist

It is time to name that person. In the first place, we know of a man who was alive and writing in precisely those years: the prophet Jeremiah. He was in the right places at the right times. He was a priest, of the priests of Shiloh-Anathoth. He was in Jerusalem during the reign of Josiah, when Dtr¹ was produced. He was in Egypt after the destruction and exile, when Dtr² was produced. His book is filled with the language of the Deuteronomistic history, the same favorite terms and phrases, the same metaphors, the same point of view on practically every important point. He was quite possibly the son of the man who unveiled the law code of Deuteronomy. He favored Josiah but not his successors on the throne.

The book of Jeremiah, further, is filled *throughout* with the language of *both* Dtr¹ and Dtr². How could phrases that are typical to Dtr¹ appear in the book of Jeremiah, regularly intertwined with phrases that are otherwise unique to Dtr², unless all three came from the same source? To call it the result of a "Deuteronomistic school" of persons who all drew on a common bank of terminology is to ignore all of the evidence associating Jeremiah with this history. And, again, where is the evidence for the existence of such a literary school? What we have in the text of the book of Jeremiah, rather, is only a picture of the prophet Jeremiah associated with a particular scribe, named Baruch son of Neriyah. We have an explicit portrayal of his dictating prophecies to Baruch, who writes them on a scroll.[12]

The ancient Jewish traditions concerning who wrote the Bible are reported in a volume of the Talmud.[13] According to that work, recorded some fifteen hundred years ago, the author of the Five Books of Moses was Moses, and the author of the book of Joshua was Joshua. That view comes as no surprise in a pious work of that period. What is intriguing, however, is that in that discussion the author of the books of Kings is identified as Jeremiah. Either the rabbis who produced the Talmud had a tradition that associated Jeremiah with the history, or they assumed the association because of the obvious similarity of language and outlook of the two works. Either way, the fact is that the association of Jeremiah with at least a large part of the Deuteronomistic history is an ancient one.

There are numerous scholarly hypotheses regarding the authorship of the book of Jeremiah. The book is partly the oracles of the prophet, which are mostly in poetry, and partly the stories about the prophet's life, which are in prose. Some suggest that Jeremiah himself composed the poetry and that the scribe, Baruch son of Neriyah, was the composer of much of the prose.[14] Baruch is mentioned numerous times in the book of Jeremiah. He is described as writing documents for Jeremiah. And it is reported that he went into exile in Egypt with Jeremiah.[15] If it is true that Baruch wrote much of the prose of the book of Jeremiah, then he would presumably be the author-editor of the Deuteronomistic history as well. In the first edition of *Who Wrote the Bible?* I raised the possibility that Jeremiah might be the Deuteronomistic historian. I now admit that I was wrong and that such a speculation is extremely unlikely. It is far more probable that the author of the prose history in the book of Jeremiah was also the author of the Deuteronomistic history, whose prose resembles it so strikingly. What I do retain from my earlier views is the idea that it may be best to think of the Deuteronomistic writings as a collaboration, with Jeremiah, the poet and prophet, as the inspiration, and Baruch, the scribe, as the writer who interpreted history through Jeremiah's conceptions.

Whether Baruch son of Neriyah was the recorder, the author, or the collaborator, it is important to take note of a fabulous archeological find concerning him which was made very recently. In 1980, the archeologist Nachman Avigad published a clay seal impression which he had acquired (see photograph below). In biblical times, documents were sometimes written on papyrus scrolls, which were then rolled up and tied with string. The string was then pressed into a ball of wet clay, and then someone would press his or her seal from a ring or cylinder into the clay. We can date the seals and the clay impressions by the script. The seal impression that Avigad published is in a Hebrew script of the late seventh and early sixth century B.C. It reads:

lbrkyhw bn nryhw hspr

In translation, this means "belonging to Baruch son of Neriyah the scribe." It was the first archeological discovery ever of an object that was identifiable as having belonged to someone who is mentioned in the Bible. It is, in effect, his signature. It is now located in the Israel Museum. It means that we have the signature of the recorder—and possibly the author/editor—of eight books of the Bible.

Located now in the Israel Museum, this clay stamp reads "Belonging to Baruch son of Neriyah the scribe"—possibly the author/editor of eight books of the Bible.

If we are right in identifying Baruch and Jeremiah with the fashioning of these books, then we not only have the connection between the biblical world and the formation of these books, as we had with J and E, but can also have some sense of the man who played a part in giving birth to them, his personality and his life story. One gets an impression of Jeremiah from the book that is called by his name—both from the text and from between the lines. It is quite often an impression of a tortured man, spiritual, bound to his mission, rejected by humans, persecuted. He gives the impression that he would rather be doing anything else than his appointed task, that he wishes that he could not see the future, and that he could escape his present, even by death. He must tell the truth no matter what the consequences. People fear him. He is profoundly solitary.

One thing that Jeremiah does *not* appear to be is a fraud. And indeed he and Baruch were no frauds, pious or otherwise. The Deuteronomistic historian built his history around the Deuteronomic law code, which was an authentically old document, and which he may well have believed to be by Moses himself. He used other documents as well, and he fashioned a continuous history out of them. His own additions to that history gave it structure, continuity, and meaning. His last chapters told of events that he had witnessed personally. There need not be anything fraudulent in any of this. Quite the contrary. It rather appears to be a sincere attempt, by a sensitive and skillful man, to tell his people's history—and to understand it. The historian painted his people's heritage. The prophet conceived of their destiny.

CHAPTER 8

The World That Produced the Bible: 587–400 B.C.

━━ 📖 ━━

The Least-Known Age

THE period that followed the disasters of 587 B.C. is the hardest for us to know. Even though it is more recent than the other periods I have described, it is the hardest to write about. There are two reasons for this. The first is simply the lack of sources. Neither the Bible nor archeology has told us very much.

There is very little in the narrative books of the Bible that tells us about what happened to the generation of exiles and refugees from Judah. The story ends in the books of Kings and Chronicles with the fall of the kingdom, and the next books of historical narrative in the Bible (Ezra and Nehemiah) pick up the story fifty years later. A small portion of the book of Daniel deals with those years, but it refers only to a few events in the lives of Daniel and his friends. It does not deal with the fate of the nation. Probably our best means is deducing information from parts of the books of the prophets Jeremiah and Ezekiel.

Archeology, too, has revealed little about the fate of the exiled community in Babylonia or about those in Egypt. We are not even sure about what was happening back in the land of Judah itself. We have some evidence that Judah's old neighbor Edom had not been very neighborly, but had shared in the Babylonian conquest of Judah and was encroaching on Judah's territory. And we know that the Samaritans continued to occupy the northern territory that had once been the kingdom of Israel. But we know hardly anything about how many of the Jews were able to remain in Judah or about what their lives were like there.

The second reason why it is so difficult to talk about this period is that, for most of us, it is barely possible to know how it *felt*. Outside of those of us who have actually had the experience of being an exile or refugee, it would take an enormous leap of sympathy (in the true Greek sense of the word *sym-pathos*, "to feel with") to know what the exiles felt. We would have to imagine seeing the defenses of the city where we have lived all our lives torn down. All the public buildings and all the most beautiful homes are burned. The religious leaders of our community are executed. The national leader's children are butchered in front of him, then his eyes are put out, and then he is led away in manacles. We are carried away in a group of thousands, probably never to see our country again. And then we live as outsiders in our conquerors' country. It is a horror.

What were the exiled people of Judah to do? How were they to maintain their identity as a national group and not simply be assimilated into the mass of the Babylonian empire? Or to put it more practically, what did they have to hold on to?

Religion

Probably the most important single thing was religion. Other countries that the Babylonians conquered also had their own particular national religions, but one of the remarkable characteristics of pagan religions in the ancient world is that they were all extremely compatible. The god who was identified with the wind may have been called Marduk in Babylon and Baal-Haddad in Canaan and Zeus in Greece, but he was still essentially the same god. He was the wind. The Mesopotamian goddess Ishtar was essentially the same as the goddess Ashtoreth in Canaan and Aphrodite in Greece. She was fertility. And so on. The interchangeability of the pagan deities made it possible for a conquered people to assimilate to their conquerors' religion.

But the religion of the people of Judah was different. There was no god in the pagan pantheon who corresponded to Yahweh. Scholars still debate the specific character of Judah's religion in this period. Was it completely monotheistic in the modern sense? Was Yahweh believed to be all-powerful? Were other lesser deities tolerated? But, whatever Judah's religion was, it was not compatible with pagan religion. Yahweh was not a force in nature. He was outside the natural realm, controlling its forces. And so, by holding on to their national religion in exile, the people of Judah, intentionally or not, reinforced their ethnic identity.

Life in Exile

Were they content in exile? Whatever tranquillity or acceptance they found in Babylonia, the community still expressed longing for home. They instituted five annual fast days to commemorate their misfortune.[1] And they expressed their feelings in literature, which is preserved in several places in the Bible. The literature of the exile includes Psalm 137 and the book of Lamentations, as well as several sections from the prophets: the last part of the book of Jeremiah, reflecting the refugees' life in Egypt; and the entire book of Ezekiel and the latter part of the book of Isaiah, reflecting the exiles' life in Babylonia. It is not happy literature. Some of it expresses bitterness. Much of it expresses guilt. (Why did this happen to us? It must be that we did something wrong.) Just about all of it expresses sadness.

Psalm 137, written by a Judean poet and preserved by the community among their psalms, is one indicator of the experience of exile:

> By the rivers of Babylon
> There we sat
> Also, we wept
> When we remembered Zion

By the willows in her midst
We hung up our harps

For there our captors required of us words of song
And our conquerors, joy
"Sing us a song of Zion"

How shall we sing a song of Yahweh on foreign soil?

If I forget you Jerusalem
Let my right arm forget

Let my tongue stick to the roof of my mouth
If I don't remember you
If I don't hold up Jerusalem
Over my highest joy

Remember, Yahweh, the Edomites
With the day of Jerusalem
Who said, "Tear up, tear up
To the foundation of it"

Despoiled daughter of Babylon
Happy is he who pays you back
Your payment
As you paid us

Happy is he who takes hold and smashes
Your suckling babies
Against a rock

The poem does not exude affection for the Babylonians. And it takes bitter note of the Edomites, Judah's kin and neighbor who abetted the conquering enemy.

As for those of Judah who fled to Egypt, things did not go well for them either, because nineteen years later the Babylonians invaded Egypt. We only know of a colony of Judean mercenaries at Elephantine, which was located at the first cataract of the Nile. This fits with the report in Kings and Jeremiah that it was the Judean army that led the community to Egypt.

God, Temple, King, and Priest

How were the exiles and refugees to relate their fate to God? Questions of theology were not matters of purely theoretical speculation in this moment. Theology and history were now on a collision course. The way in which one understood God made a difference to the way in which one understood the situation in which the exiles found themselves. Is Yahweh a *national* God? If so, he is left behind in Judah, and the people are cut off from him in exile. This very question is asked by the author of Psalm 137, translated on the previous pages: "How shall we sing a song of Yahweh on foreign soil?"

Or is Yahweh a *universal* God? And if so, why did he let this disaster happen? That is, if Yahweh is the one true God of the whole world, why did he allow the Babylonians to destroy his Temple, carry off his anointed kings and priests, and exile the people? Since the exiled community was hardly likely to believe that the Babylonians were stronger than Yahweh, the answer that was regularly suggested to them was that it was their own fault. *They* had failed to keep their covenant with Yahweh. *They* had worshiped other gods. The Babylonians were merely Yahweh's tool, which he was using to fulfill the covenant curses because Judah had broken its contract. One of the logical consequences of monotheism is guilt.

There were also practical problems. Now that the Temple was destroyed, how were the people to worship God? The Egyptian group at Elephantine actually built a Temple there—which was clearly against the law of centralization in Deuteronomy. The extraordinary thing about the Elephantine Temple is that they worshiped Yahweh and two other gods, one male and one female, there. The Jews in other parts of the world apparently were not happy with this development, because when the Elephantine Temple was destroyed in the fifth century they would not help rebuild it. As for the Babylonian community, the prophet Ezekiel, who was one of the Babylonian exiles, envisioned a plan for a rebuilt Temple in Jerusalem. He described the new Temple in detail, including its measurements in cubits, but the Temple that he pictured was never built.[2]

The other practical and pressing problem was: now that the monarchy was gone, who was to lead the people? King Jehoahaz was imprisoned in Egypt. He died there. King Jehoiachin and King Zedekiah were imprisoned in Babylon. We do not know what happened to Zedekiah, but, according to the very last sentences of the book of 2 Kings, Jehoiachin was released from prison thirty-seven years after his capture. Still, that did not mean that he was reinstated as king.

The priests, too, had lost their center, the Temple, and that meant that there were no more sacrifices to perform. It meant that their authority, their income, and most of their functions were threatened. It also meant that the rival priesthoods, the Mushites (those who traced their ancestry to Moses) and the Aaronids, did not have much left to fight over.

In short, the Babylonian destruction of Judah had brought horrors and tremendous challenges and crises to this nation. They were forced to reformulate their picture of themselves and of their relationship with their God. They had to find a way to worship Yahweh without a Temple. They had to find leadership without a king. They had to learn to live as a minority ethnic group in great empires. They had to determine what their relationship was to their homeland. And they had to live with their defeat.

And then, after only fifty years, the impossible happened. The exile ended, and they were allowed to go home.

The Persian Empire: The Age of Mysteries

In 538 B.C. the Persians conquered the Babylonians. Babylonia, Egypt, and everything in between, including Judah, now were part of a tremendous, powerful Persian empire. The ruler of this empire was Cyrus the Great. In the same year that he took Babylon, Cyrus allowed the Jews to return to Judah. By royal decree, Cyrus permitted the exiles to rebuild their homeland and their Temple. The precious implements of the Temple, which the Babylonians had carried away, were returned—with one exception: the ark.

For some reason, the biblical sources do not tell what happened to the ark containing the tablets of the Ten Commandments. Archeology, too, has shed no light on this at all. The disappearance of the ark is the first great mystery of this period, and it remains one of the great mysteries of the Bible. There is no report that the ark was carried away or destroyed or hidden. There is not even any comment such as "And then the ark disappeared, and we do not know what happened to it," or "And no one knows where it is to this day." The most important object in the world, in the biblical view, simply ceases to be in the story.

Did it ever really exist? For the purposes of our search, it is necessary to recognize at least that the earlier historical books *portray* it as existing, enshrined in the Temple. The books of Kings and Chronicles say explicitly that the ark was placed in the inside room (the Holy of Holies) of the Temple on the day that King Solomon dedicated the Temple. It then ceases to figure in any direct way in the story, and there is no report of what happened to it when the Temple was destroyed. And now, in the report of the exiles' return to Judah, it is not mentioned, while the less important Temple utensils are. The community that returned to Jerusalem rebuilt the Temple, but this second Temple did not contain the ark. Nor did it have cherubs, the giant golden statues of winged sphinxes whose purpose, after all, was at least partly to spread their wings over the ark. The second Temple's Holy of Holies apparently was an empty room. All of this will be relevant to the search for who wrote the Bible.

The second great mystery of this period is the disappearance of the Davidic dynasty. According to the biblical books of Ezra and Nehemiah, those who returned from Babylonia were led by two men named Sheshbazzar and Zerubbabel.[3] Both of these men were from the royal house of David. They were descendants of King Jehoiachin. Zerubbabel is also mentioned in the biblical books of the prophets Haggai and Zechariah, who prophesied in this period.[4] But Sheshbazzar and Zerubbabel cease to be mentioned after the fifth chapter of Ezra. There is no report of the disappearance of these men, no explanation of what happened to the royal family. Rather, as with the ark, the monarchy simply ceases to be mentioned. Neither the biblical nor the archeological sources indicate what happened to the family of the messiah, the descendants of David.

Also, prophecy diminishes, and perhaps disappears, in this period. The age of the great prophets is past. The prophets Haggai and

Zechariah preached at the time of Zerubbabel, but as the kings dis-appeared, so did the prophets.

The fifty years of exile in Babylonia and Egypt are not described. The nation's most sacred object and its royal family disappear. Prophecy diminishes. And there are more unknowns. The entire period seems to be an age of mysteries. How many of the people who were in Babylonia actually took advantage of the opportunity to return to Judah? Did the majority stay or leave? The Bible's figures are confusing. According to the book of Jeremiah, 4,600 had been deported from Judah to Babylonia in 587; according to the book of 2 Kings, it was 11,600.[5] But according to the book of Ezra, 42,360 returned just fifty years later.[6] That is a very prolific community. It is possible that this number of returnees includes some who came from Egypt. Or it may include people from the northern tribes of Israel who were deported to Mesopotamia by the Assyrians in 722 B.C. and who were now reunited with the exiles from Judah. We just do not know. We also do not know who was already in the land of Judah when the new returnees arrived. Had *everyone* left the land for Babylonia or Egypt? Probably not. But who—and how many—stayed?

Back in the Promised Land

We do know something about how life developed in the land as the exiles returned and began to rebuild. They completed building the second Temple, and it was dedicated on Passover, 516 B.C. This was seen, at least by some, as the fulfillment of a prophecy of Jere-miah's.[7] We do not know the size of the second Temple, whether it was the same as the first Temple or not. We do know that it did not have the ark, the cherubs, or the Urim and Thummim. (The Urim and Thummim were sacred objects that were used by the High Priest, apparently to obtain oracles.) We know that it had a High Priest. We know that the High Priest was an Aaronid, not a Mu-shite.

Most important, our sources indicate that the entire Temple

priesthood was Aaronid at this time. All other Levites were not recognized as legitimate priests. Levites were regarded as secondary clergy, assistants to the Aaronids, who alone exercised the priestly prerogatives. The struggle between the Mushite and Aaronid priests was over. Somehow, the Aaronids had won completely. Their old claim that they alone were the legitimate priests was now the accepted view. The triumph of the Aaronid priesthood in this period was to have tremendous implications for the formation of the Bible.

How did the Aaronid priests come to be so completely in control? Perhaps it was because they were the priesthood in power at the time of the fall of the kingdom. Since the Babylonians took the upper classes into exile, it would thus be the Aaronid priests who would have been carried off to Babylon. For example, the prophet Ezekiel was an Aaronid priest, and he was among the Babylonian exiles. The Mushite priests, meanwhile, would have been more likely to be among the refugees in Egypt. For example, the prophet Jeremiah, who was apparently a Mushite priest, was among the Egypt refugees. Since it was now the Babylonian group that was leading the return and governing the new community (initially under Sheshbazzar and Zerubbabel), the Aaronid priests would be, at the very least, in a position to dominate, and perhaps in a position to define who was a priest and who was not.

Another reason why the Mushite priests lost to the Aaronids in this period may be that Mushites, notably Jeremiah, had been perceived to be pro-Babylonian. Now that the Persians had conquered the Babylonians, the Persian authorities might well have preferred to empower the Aaronid priests. The Aaronids had been anti-Babylonian, as indicated by the fact that the Babylonians had executed the chief priests in 587.

There is one more reason to be taken in to account to explain the success of the Aaronid priests in rebuilt Judah. That is the influence and power of one man: Ezra.

Ezra

In the entire Bible, two men are known as lawgivers: Moses and
Ezra. Ezra came from Babylon to Judah eighty years after the first
group of exiles returned, in 458 B.C. He was a priest and a scribe.
The biblical record states explicitly that he was an *Aaronid* priest. It
also indicates that he was no ordinary scribe. His writing skills were
associated with one document in particular: "the *torah* of Moses."

Ezra arrived in Jerusalem with two important documents in his
hand. One was this "*torah* of Moses," and the other was a letter from
the Persian emperor, Artaxerxes, giving him authority in Judah.
The emperor's authorization empowered Ezra to teach and to enforce
"the law of your God which is in your hand." The enforcement
powers included fines, imprisonment, and the death penalty.

What was this "*torah* of Moses," this "law of your God which is in
your hand"? References to it in the biblical books of Ezra and Nehemiah include material from JE, D, and P.[8] It is therefore likely that
the book that Ezra brought from Babylon to Judah was the full
Torah—the Five Books of Moses—as we know it.

Ezra's political authority was somehow shared with a governor,
Nehemiah, who also was appointed by the emperor. With the backing of the emperor, who was perhaps the most powerful man in the
world, Ezra and Nehemiah wielded considerable authority. They rebuilt the city walls of Jerusalem that the Babylonians had torn down.
They enforced the observance of the Sabbath. They forced inter-
marriages between Jews and others to be dissolved. In the absence of
any Judean kings, these two men were the leaders of the people.
Judah was not an independent country. It was now a province of the
Persian empire. And Ezra and Nehemiah were the emperor's designated authorities.

Temple and Torah

In the second Temple period, centralization was achieved. There apparently was no competition from any other religious center in Judah. What Hezekiah and Josiah had tried to do was now actually achieved. One God, one Temple. The Elephantine Temple was far away, and in any case it was destroyed around the time that Ezra was in Jerusalem.

Ezra called a public assembly at the water gate of Jerusalem. He held it on the fall holiday, when the people would come from all over Judah to Jerusalem. On that occasion he brought out the scroll of the Torah and read it to the assembled mass. This was followed by a covenant ceremony in which the people renewed their commitment to their God and to their pact with him as written in this Torah.

The period of restoration, the age of the second Temple, appears from biblical and postbiblical sources to have been a time of dedication to the book as never before. Why? Presumably because political authority was now more in the hands of the priests, who had more of an interest in it than the kings had had. Perhaps, also, the book came to be especially treasured by the people at this time because it was a link to the past. It was the connection that meant for the ex-exiles that this was a rebuilding, not just a new start. As a work of history, it gave a feeling of heritage from an extraordinary past. As a work of law, it showed a way to participate in the covenant—which is to say, in the heritage—in the present.

How did Ezra come to have a copy of this book? How did it come to have all the sources combined? How was he able to promulgate it successfully as "the torah of Moses," which was then accepted for two and a half millennia? When we know who produced P and who combined all the sources into one work, we shall know the answers to these questions, and much more.

CHAPTER 9

A Brilliant Mistake

UNTIL now I have spoken almost exclusively in terms of the facts themselves—meaning the evidence from the text and from archeology—and not of the history of how we found out what we know. I took this approach because I wanted this to be a presentation of evidence and conclusions rather than a history of scholarship. But now I must tell about one wrong turn that was taken in the search for who wrote the Bible, because it dominated the investigation for a hundred years. The great majority of biblical scholars, myself included, accepted it. Most still accept it, at least partly.

This is the most controversial part of the story, for, from this point on, the controversy is not just with religious fundamentalists but with other critical investigators as well. Also, it is necessary to tell the story of this wrong turn because it played a part in arriving at what I believe is the solution. Oddly enough, it is sometimes necessary to go through a mistake to get to a discovery. Or to put it more in terms of the respect I hold for the great biblical scholars of the past: even when we think that we see farther than our predecessors, we should remember that it is only because we are sitting on their shoulders.

The central and most controversial question in this search all along has been over when P, the Priestly source, was written. It has been generally accepted that J and E came from the early period—the days of the two kingdoms, Judah and Israel. And it has been even more universally accepted that D came primarily from the middle period—from Josiah's time. But finding the writer (or writers?) of the P laws and stories has proved to be the hardest task.

P is the largest source, about the size of the other three put together. It includes the creation story in the first chapter of the Bible. It includes the cosmic version of the flood story, the version in which the windows of the heavens and the fountains of the deep are opened to flood the world. It has stories of Abraham, Jacob, the exodus, and the journey through the wilderness, *most* of which are doublets of stories in J and E. (The differences are extraordinary, but more on that later.) And it contains a tremendous body of law, covering about thirty chapters of Exodus and Numbers and all of the book of Leviticus. And so this is no minor question. Simply put, the search for the writer of most of the Five Books of Moses begins with a mistake.

The Mistake

It began in a lecture in Strassburg in 1833. Professor Eduard Reuss told his students that the biblical prophets do not refer to the Priestly (P) law. The prophets do not quote P, nor do they even give the impression that they are familiar with it. He concluded that *the law was later than the prophets.* P was written when prophets were no longer prophesying; in other words, in the days of the second Temple.

The law was later than the prophets. That was the first step of the mistake.

Reuss was actually afraid to state his critical views in print at that time. He waited forty-six years before publishing a long work on the subject, in 1879, but by then one of his own students had already developed and published the idea independently.

The student, Karl Graf, was convinced by his teacher's arguments, and in his own investigations he developed them further. By that time, scholars had already concluded that D was from Josiah's time, and Graf accepted that as a starting point. Then he scrutinized sections of J, E, and P in order to see which of them came before D and which came after. He concluded that J and E were written before D, which, as we know, became the general view to the present day. But, following his teacher Reuss, Graf claimed that the great P corpus of law was written after D, late in the biblical world, in the days of the second Temple. Graf was suggesting a whole new picture of the history of biblical Israel, in which the elaborate legal and ritual system and the centrality of the priests and the Temple to the life of the people were developments of the end of the biblical period, not of its beginning.

There was one particularly serious problem with this idea that the person (or persons) who wrote P came from the post-exile community. True, it was a time when priests were in charge and a time of centralization of the religion around the Temple. But the question was: if P was written by someone from the time of centrality of the Temple, why is a Temple never mentioned once in P? Yahweh never commands Moses to tell the people to build a Temple when they get to the land. There is not one law whose fulfillment requires the presence of a Temple. Priests, yes. An ark, an altar, cherubs, Urim and Thummim, and other sacred instruments, yes. But not a single reference to a Temple. Graf's solution to the problem of the missing Temple was critical to his analysis. He argued that the Temple *was* mentioned in P, many times, but in disguise. It was not called the Temple; it was called the *Tabernacle*.

The Tabernacle is the tent that Moses builds in the desert to house the ark. In the E source it is mentioned only three times. In J and D it is not mentioned at all. P, on the other hand, mentions it over two hundred times. P gives elaborate information on its materials and construction and the laws relating to it. It figures regularly in P's stories. In P, all assemblies of the people take place at the Tabernacle. The Tabernacle is simply essential to P.

According to Graf (and then others) the Tabernacle never existed. Graf concluded that the Tabernacle was a fiction, made up by someone living in the days of the second Temple. This second Temple writer wanted to establish a law code that was in the interests of the Temple priests of that time. In order to give such laws a claim of antiquity, and thus give it authority, this writer wanted to claim that this was the *torah* that God gave to Moses at Mount Sinai. In short, it was another case of "pious fraud."

But this presented a problem. How could this writer compose a story in which God gives Moses laws about a Temple when no Temple was actually built until over two hundred years after Moses was dead? In order to make anyone believe that the Priestly laws came from Moses' quill, the second Temple writer had to invent some device that would connect the era of Moses with the era of the Temples. The Tabernacle was that device.

And so, in this writer's conception, Moses built the Tabernacle and gave the laws concerning it. Then, after Moses' time, the Tabernacle continued to serve as the people's central shrine until the Temple was built *as its successor*. Then the ark was transferred from the Tabernacle to the Temple, and the laws that required the presence of the Tabernacle now required the presence of a Temple instead. The Priestly Tabernacle was thus a literary and legal fiction created by the post-exile author (or authors) of P to support the rebuilt Temple and the reestablished priesthood in Jerusalem of their day.

One of the arguments given in favor of this idea was that the Tabernacle, as described in the book of Exodus (chapter 26), was too big for the Israelites really to have carried through the desert during their forty years of wandering there with Moses. A second argument came from comparing the measurements of the Tabernacle with those of the Temple. Scholars determined that, according to Exodus 26, the Tabernacle was thirty cubits long and ten cubits wide. According to 1 Kings 6, the Temple was sixty cubits long and twenty cubits wide. The two structures thus have the same proportions, the Tabernacle being half as long and half as wide as the Temple. Investigators thus saw the Tabernacle as a fictional miniature of the Temple.

The Tabernacle was a fiction, a symbol of the second Temple. That was the second step of the mistake.

And then came Wellhausen. As Freud is to psychology or Weber to sociology, Julius Wellhausen stands out as a dominant figure of modern biblical scholarship. Much of what Wellhausen said came from those who preceded him. He took and used conclusions from

Graf, De Wette, and others. His own contribution does not so much constitute a beginning as a culmination. He brought all the pieces together, along with his own investigations and arguments, into a clear, organized synthesis. His books were extremely influential. Across Europe and England, people who had not accepted the critical investigation into who wrote the Bible began to be persuaded. Wellhausen's reputation was tremendous. He actually resigned his academic position in Greifswald partly because of the impact he was having on his students. In his letter of resignation he said:

I became a theologian because I was interested in the scientific treatment of the Bible; it has only gradually dawned upon me that a professor of theology likewise has the practical task of preparing students for service in the Evangelical Church, and that I was not fulfilling this practical task, but rather, in spite of all reserve on my part, was incapacitating my hearers for their office.[1]

What was he saying that was so powerful? He identified the sources J, E, D, and P, and he laid out a neat scheme of the history of the biblical world in which each found its place. And that scheme culminated in the laws and stories of P.

Once Wellhausen accepted Reuss' claim that the law was later than the prophets, and he accepted Graf's claim that the Tabernacle was nothing more than a symbol of the Temple, the scene was set. Wellhausen took the case one step further. For him, the Tabernacle was the key to the whole puzzle. The history of the centralization of the religion around the Tabernacle (meaning around the Temple) was the clue to the history of the writers:

In the stories and laws of J and E, there was no idea of centralization. Why? Because they were written in the early days of Israel, when anyone could sacrifice anywhere.

In D, centralization was strictly demanded: "You must only sacrifice at the place where Yahweh causes his name to dwell." Why? Because it was from the time of King Josiah, a time when centralization was first introduced and needed firm insistence.

In P, Wellhausen said, centralization was not demanded. It was *assumed.* Over and over in the laws and stories of P, it was simply understood that there was only one place on earth where one could sacrifice, and that one place was the Tabernacle (meaning the Temple). Why? Because it came from the time of the second Temple, a time when it was an accepted fact that people were supposed to sacrifice only at the Temple.

The laws and stories of P take centralization for granted. That was the third step of the mistake.

There were other arguments for this, of course. In the P list of different kinds of sacrifices there is one called a "sin offering" and one called a "guilt offering." There are no such sacrifices mentioned in J, E, or D. Wellhausen reasoned that it was only logical that sin and guilt sacrifices would be instituted after the experience of exile. It was then that the people felt guilty, believing that the destruction and exile were punishment for their own sins. And so this was another proof that someone wrote P in the second Temple days.

Also, in the P list of holidays there is a holiday that has come to be known as the Fall New Year, followed by a Day of Atonement ten days later. These holidays also are not mentioned in J, E, or D; and these extra two holidays also involve atonement for sin. Wellhausen argued that this, too, reflected the days when Judah felt guilty in the wake of the destruction and exile.

There was one more piece of evidence for looking for the writer of P in the days of the second Temple. That evidence was the book of the prophet Ezekiel. Like the prophet Jeremiah, Ezekiel was a priest. Unlike Jeremiah, Ezekiel was an *Aaronid* priest. Like Jeremiah, Ezekiel went into exile. Unlike Jeremiah, Ezekiel was exiled in Babylonia. There he produced his book. That book, the book of Ezekiel, is written in a style and language remarkably similar to P's. It is almost as much like P as Jeremiah is like D; there are whole passages in Ezekiel that are nearly word-for-word like passages in P.

For Wellhausen, one passage in Ezekiel was particularly important. Ezekiel declares that, in the future, only certain Levites may be priests. All others are disqualified from the priesthood because of their past transgressions. The only Levites who may function as priests are those who are descendants of Zadok.[2] Zadok was David's *Aaronid* priest. And so, according to Ezekiel, only Aaronid priests are legitimate. All others are excluded.

And this, Wellhausen said, is just the point of view in P. It is quite clear in P that only Aaronids are priests. Several P stories (which I shall tell below) and many P laws make this point crystal-clear. P simply does not recognize Moses' descendants or anyone else as legitimate priests. Wellhausen concluded that P was written in the days of the second Temple, when the Aaronid priests came to power. They took Ezekiel's prophecy as their inspiration, and, once and for all, the competition between the priestly families was over. The Aaronids had won, and one of them wrote a "*torah* of Moses" that reflected their victory.

Wellhausen's picture was very attractive. It placed a priestly source in a priestly period. It identified guilt sacrifices and holidays of atonement in a period of guilt and atonement. It placed Ezekielian ideas in the period that came right after Ezekiel. It explained the concentration on the Tabernacle in P in terms of the period of concentration on the Temple. It was logical, coherent, persuasive— and wrong.

What is Wrong with This Picture?

Reuss simply was mistaken. Prophets do quote P. Notably, Jeremiah quite plainly alludes to it. The famous opening of P's story in the first chapter of the Bible is:

In the beginning of God's creating the heavens and the earth, the earth was unformed and void. . . . And God said, "Let there be light."[3]

In one of Jeremiah's prophecies, he refers to a coming time of destruction. He speaks poetically of a time when nature will be turned upside down. He begins with the words:

> *I looked at the earth,*
> *And here it was unformed and void,*
> *And to the heavens,*
> *And their light was gone.*[4]

The two are too similar for coincidence. And it hardly seems likely that the P story of the creation of the universe was based on a line from a destruction prophecy in Jeremiah. It is rather Jeremiah who is dramatically dismantling the picture that is found in P.

Jeremiah in fact seems to enjoy such reversals on P's language. P several times uses the expression "Be fruitful and multiply,"[5] and P emphasizes the ark, which the Tabernacle houses.[6] But Jeremiah prophesies:

> It will be, when you will multiply and be fruitful in the land in those days, says Yahweh, that they will no longer say, "the ark of the covenant of Yahweh," and it will not come to mind, and it will not be made anymore.[7]

Recall that Jeremiah is from the priests of Shiloh, who brought us E, the source that never mentions the ark, and D, the source that mentions it rarely (only in chapters 10 and 31). Then it is not surprising to find Jeremiah eschewing the ark in a twist of P's own language.

P in Leviticus begins with seven full chapters of rules of sacrifices. It lists kinds of sacrifices, it tells which animals to sacrifice, and it tells when and how to sacrifice them. It concludes:

> This is the *torah* of offering, grain offering, sin offering, trespass offering, installation offerings, sacrifice, and peace offerings which Yahweh commanded Moses in Mount Sinai in the day that he commanded the Israelites to offer their sacrifices to Yahweh in the wilderness of Sinai.[8]

But Jeremiah says:

> For I did not speak with your fathers and I did not command them in the day that I brought them out of the land of Egypt about matters of offering and sacrifice.[9]

Why is Jeremiah hostile to P? Let me get to that later. For now, the important thing is that he *knows* P.

Jeremiah is not the only prophet who knows P. Ezekiel knows it, quotes it, and bases prophecies on it. Take Ezekiel 5 and 6. In these chapters, Ezekiel indicts his people for not keeping their covenant with God. This sort of prophecy is known among biblical scholars as a "covenant lawsuit." The prophet acts as a prosecuting attorney in a divine court, accusing the people of breach of their contract with God. In the case of Ezekiel 5 and 6, the contract in question is a chapter in P (Leviticus 26). There, the P record of the covenant between God and Israel gives a list of blessings and curses. It says that the blessings will come:

> If you walk according to my statutes and you keep my commandments and do them.[10]

And the curses will come:

> If you despise my statutes and disdain my judgments so as not to do all my commandments.[11]

Those are the words of the covenant. The words of the indictment in Ezekiel's covenant lawsuit are:

> You did not walk according to my statutes, and you did not do my judgments.[12]

The P covenant curse says:

> You will eat the flesh of your sons.[13]

Ezekiel's covenant lawsuit includes the judgment:

> Fathers will eat sons in your midst.[14]

The P covenant curses say:

> And I shall send the wild beast among you, and it will bereave you. . . . And I shall bring the sword over you. . . . And I shall send pestilence in your midst.[15]

Ezekiel's covenant lawsuit includes the judgment:

> And I shall send hunger and evil beast over you, and they will bereave you, and pestilence and blood will pass through you; and I shall bring the sword over you.[16]

And so on. Ezekiel's indictments and judgments of the people appear to be based nearly verbatim on the words of the P text—which is exactly what one would expect a covenant lawsuit to do. But investigators following Reuss, Graf, and Wellhausen concluded that P was written *after* Ezekiel. How could they explain the fact that this meant that a *contract* had to be based on the *lawsuit* of that contract? Most said that this particular portion of P (Leviticus 26) must have been written earlier than the rest of P.

But Ezekiel quotes other portions of P as well, notably the P version of the story of the exodus from Egypt. In the P story, God tells Moses:

I shall bring you to the land which I have lifted up my hand to give to Abraham, Isaac, and Jacob, and I shall give it to you.[17]

In Ezekiel, God says to Ezekiel:

I brought them to the land which I lifted up my hand to give to them.[18]

There are numerous other parallels of wording between P's exodus story and Ezekiel's review of the story.[19] It appears that Ezekiel's source for the exodus event is P. But, again, investigators since Reuss, Graf, and Wellhausen concluded that P was written *after* Ezekiel. How can they explain the fact that this meant that the *telling* of the story in P had to be based on the *retelling* of the story in Ezekiel? I do not think that they *can* explain it. It seems to me that what we would naturally expect is that a prophet would quote the *torah*, not the opposite. (And Ezekiel does quote *torah* explicitly.[20]) We would naturally expect the retelling of a story to be based on the telling, and not the opposite. We would expect a contract litigation to be based on its contract, and not the opposite. The biblical investigators of the nineteenth century were attributing enormous influence to the prophet Ezekiel. Yet all sorts of crucial matters in Ezekiel are ignored or even contradicted in P. Notably, Ezekiel gives a plan for the rebuilding of the Temple in elaborate detail, but the P Tabernacle-Temple does not correspond to Ezekiel's model at all.[21]

I believe that new methods of linguistic analysis now put any last arguments on this point to rest. In 1982, Professor Avi Hurvitz of the Hebrew University in Jerusalem demonstrated that P is written in an earlier stage of biblical Hebrew than Ezekiel.[22]

Of course, one might argue that perhaps Jeremiah did not write Jeremiah and Ezekiel did not write Ezekiel. But that is not the defense that the Wellhausen proponents have made. Rather, there is a tremendous investigation of the books of the prophets to determine exactly what *portions* were written at which point in history. The texts that I have cited here from Jeremiah and Ezekiel seem to me to resist cutting and reassignment; and, in any case, the linguistic evidence does not only place P before the prophets in relative chronology, it places it before the *time* in which Wellhausen pictured it. Besides Hurvitz's book, five other scholars in recent years, two in Canada and three in the United States, have uncovered linguistic evidence that most of P is written in the biblical Hebrew of the days before the exile to Babylon.[23] Reuss' claim, that the P law came after the prophets, was simply wrong. The evidence from the prophets rather indicated that the author of the P laws and stories was to be sought before the time of Jeremiah and Ezekiel—i.e., before the Babylonian exile.

Wellhausen's claim, that P assumes centralized religion, was also wrong. P constantly commands that sacrifices and other religious ceremonies must take place at the Tabernacle—or the Tent of Meeting, as it is also known. Just as D regularly commands the people to come to "the place where Yahweh causes his name to dwell," P regularly commands them to come to the Tabernacle. The point is the same. They are only using different euphemisms for the same idea: there can be only one approved religious center.

P commands this repeatedly in the early chapters of Leviticus and Numbers. P says it especially clearly in Leviticus 17:

Any man from the house of Israel who slaughters an ox or sheep or goat, in the camp or outside the camp, and does not bring it to the Tent of Meeting to offer it as a sacrifice to Yahweh before the Tabernacle of Yahweh, blood[guilt] will be reckoned to that man. He has spilled blood. And that man will be cut off from his people.[24]

If you do not come to the central place, you will be cut off. It is as if you have committed murder (spilled blood). That hardly assumes centralization. It demands it.

How did Wellhausen explain this? He said that this section of Leviticus was not really part of P. It had much style and language in common with P, but it was an older, originally separate work, called the Holiness Code, which was edited into the P law code later. But that answer does not really solve the problem. Wellhausen still said that this "Holiness Code" was written by someone after Ezekiel, so it is still part of the world of the exile and second Temple period. And, in any case, there are still all the other commands about the Tabernacle all through P. P by no means takes centralized religion for granted. And that means that P does not have the comfortable fit in the days of the second Temple—the days of successful centralization of religion—that Wellhausen pictured.

Wellhausen's other interpretations of the evidence are not compelling arguments either. He related P's sin and guilt sacrifices to the days after the exile, when the people of Judah felt guilty about their fate. That is a dangerous kind of reasoning. It is extremely precarious to date a piece of literature based on a guess as to when the author's community felt a certain way. It is especially precarious when the feeling in question is guilt. People, whether as individuals or communities, can feel guilt at just about any moment in history. It is easy to imagine Judean priests adding guilt sacrifices to the ceremonies in Jerusalem, say, in 722 B.C., after the northern kingdom of Israel had been destroyed by the Assyrians. At that time there would have been Israelite refugees in Jerusalem who could have felt at least as guilty as the Judeans did after 587.

The same goes for the addition of holidays of atonement in P. In fact, the period after the fall of Jerusalem is, if anything, the hardest time to imagine the creation of such a holiday, because there is a matter of *promulgation*. If the Day of Atonement was made up because of the people's feelings of guilt after their fall, how could the writer of P's laws possibly have hoped to convince anybody that it was an ancient law? Who would have believed that it was written by Moses but somehow unknown to anyone until after 587 B.C., just when they happened to be feeling guilty? It is easier to picture successful promulgation of new laws in the days of the *first* Temple, when religious reforms such as those of Kings Hezekiah and Josiah were presenting new laws and newly discovered documents.

The prophets *do* quote P, and the Priestly laws and stories do *not* take centralized religion for granted. This seriously weakens the scenario pictured by Reuss, Graf, and Wellhausen. We cannot confidently look for the writer of P—of the majority of the Five Books of Moses—in the days of the second Temple.

But this does not tell us where we *should* look for this person either. The third part of the structure of the brilliant mistake, however, holds the clue to where to look for this writer. Wellhausen was right about one thing: the key to the whole puzzle was the Tabernacle.

CHAPTER 10

The Sacred Tent

GRAF and Wellhausen thought that the work known as P, the largest of the sources of the Pentateuch was also the last of the sources to be written. They argued that the author of P must have lived in the days of the second Temple. The Temple was the center of the community's life in that period. Yet P's laws and narrative never mention a Temple. And so it became a cornerstone of the Graf/Wellhausen hypothesis that whenever P mentioned the Tabernacle it meant the Temple. The Tabernacle had never really existed. It was a fiction that the Priestly writer had invented in order to avoid the anachronism of using the word "Temple" in a supposedly Mosaic text.

They were right to be so concerned with the Tabernacle. In the Five Books of Moses there is more on the Tabernacle than on any other subject. There are all the commandments about sacrifices and other ceremonies that must be performed there. There are whole chapters just describing the materials out of which it is made. There are stories that take place in it or in front of it. After Mount Sinai, it is the place where God communicates with Moses. It is sacred; it is the shrine that houses the ark, the tablets of the Ten Commandments, and the cherubs. It is constructed of precious wood, gold, brass, wool and linen woven with gold, scarlet, and purple, and a covering of red leather. Only priests may enter it; anyone else who enters it must be killed.

Was all of this a fiction, made up by a late Priestly writer as a symbol of the second Temple?

But the Priestly source emphasizes the ark, the tablets, the cherubs, and the Urim and Thummim in connection with the Tabernacle; and none of these things were in the second Temple. Why would a second Temple priest, composing a pious-fraud document, emphasize the very components of the Tabernacle that the second Temple did not have?

Counting Cubits

There are some peculiarities about the description of the Tabernacle in P (Exod 26). Those who followed Graf and Wellhausen said that its proportions matched those of the second Temple, but that is not really true. The measurements they gave were:

Temple:	width 20 cubits	length 60 cubits
Tabernacle:	width 10 cubits	length 30 cubits

And so they said that the Tabernacle was obviously a one-to-two scale model of the Temple. There are three things wrong with this. The first is that buildings have three dimensions, not two, and the third dimension is:

Temple:	height 30 cubits
Tabernacle:	height 10 cubits

One-to-three. If the Tabernacle was a pious-fraud copy of the second Temple, why copy only two of the three dimensions?

That is the smallest problem with the Tabernacle-Temple equation. The second problem is that the Temple dimensions that they used (twenty by sixty) are not the dimensions of the second Temple. The dimensions of the second Temple are not given anywhere in the Bible. What, then, are these twenty-by-sixty dimensions? They are the measurements of the *first* Temple, given in 1 Kings 6.[1] The proof that the Tabernacle was a scale model of the second Temple was based on the dimensions of the first Temple.

The third problem is that the Tabernacle dimensions that they used (ten by thirty) are not the dimensions of the Tabernacle. The dimensions of the Tabernacle are not given in the Bible. The biblical Tabernacle is actually one of the great puzzles of all time. The book of Exodus (chapter 26) lists all the materials out of which it is made—wooden frames, metal rings, wooden poles, sheets of fabric—but it does not tell how to set it all up. It gives the equipment but not the blueprint. That is the puzzle. Seminary students, amateurs, and various cubit counters have tried their hands at it over the centuries. In my student days it occurred to me that if I would ever be able to read that list of materials and cubits and *care*, then I would be a scholar. And then it turned out years later that these cubits contained a key clue in the investigation into the authors of the Bible.

The Tabernacle is a tent that is made by setting up a series of wooden frames in a rectangle and then spreading a fabric over them (see opposite).

According to Exodus 26, the frames are each one and a half cubits wide. Twenty frames are used to make up each of the two sides of the Tabernacle. The back, it says, is made of six frames, plus two frames for the corners. (Presumably the two extra frames in the corners are for stability.) Now it is easy to see why investigators thought that the Tabernacle was thirty cubits long: twenty frames, each one and a half cubits wide. But how did they figure that it was ten cubits wide? If they figured six frames in the back, that is only nine cubits. If they figured eight frames in the back, that makes twelve cubits. How did they get ten? Presumably it was just a guess—which they formulated with a preconceived notion of what the proportions should be.

The dimensions did not match, the Temple dimensions they used were not the dimensions of the second Temple, and the Tabernacle dimensions they used were not the dimensions of the Tabernacle.

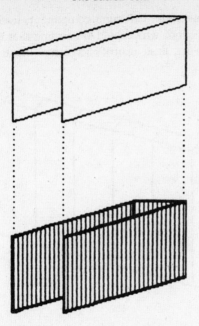

The architectural evidence for the Tabernacle's being a symbol of the second Temple was faulty.

And besides, why would the biblical writer give all of these precise measurements in such detail if it was all of something that never was?

Reconstructing the Tabernacle

It is not enough just to reject the Tabernacle component of the Graf-Wellhausen scheme. It is still necessary to come to terms with the fact that the Tabernacle is so important in the Bible. If it was not a symbol of the second Temple, what was it?

Bear with me for just a little more counting of cubits. First, the one-and-a-half cubit width of the Tabernacle's frames is strange. Presumably, the ancient Israelite carried a cubit string. So why design a structure with one-and-a-half-cubit components instead of one-cubit or two-cubit? Second, why should we assume that the frames stood shoulder to shoulder, flush against each other, like this:

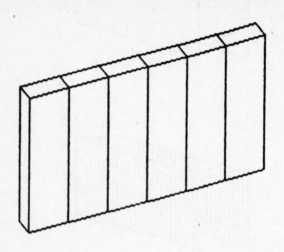

Instead of overlapping, like this:

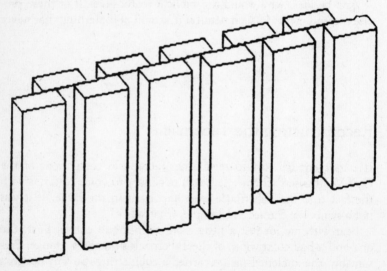

Architects I have consulted tell me that the latter arrangement has advantages of stability and ventilation. That could also explain the need for the unusual one-and-a-half cubit width. The extra half cubit is for the overlap. If this is correct, then the twenty-frame side of the Tabernacle would be twenty cubits long. And the six-plus-two back of the Tabernacle would be six to eight cubits, depending on how the two corner frames are arranged. The text says that the frames are ten cubits tall, so, drawn to scale, the Tabernacle structure would look like this:

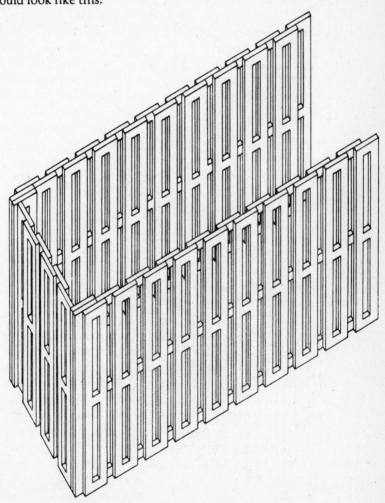

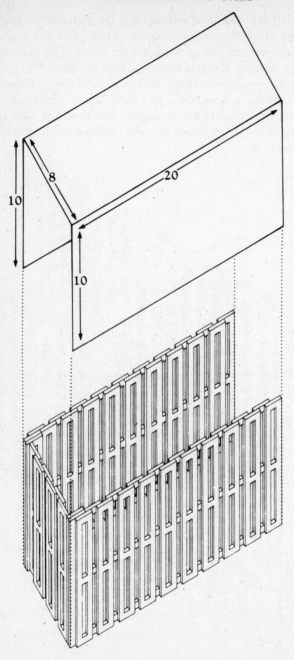

There is a way to confirm that these measurements and this arrangement are correct. That is to measure the fabric that is spread
over the structure. It is a giant double layer of fine linen, embroi-
dered with pictures of cherubs in blue, purple, and scarlet. Each of
its two layers is the same size. The two layers are joined together by
fifty gold rings that connect loops along their edge. When this great
fabric is spread over the frames, the gold rings surround the entrance. The size of this double fabric is twenty by twenty-eight
cubits—which matches the overlapping arrangement of the frames.
The twenty-cubit width of the fabric falls along the twenty-cubit
length of the Tabernacle frames. The fabric's twenty-eight-cubit
length covers each of the ten-cubit-high walls plus an eight-cubit
ceiling. See opposite.

There is a point to all of this besides an interest in tent architecture. When I first worked out the Tabernacle measurements a few
years ago, I was stymied. The Tabernacle was twenty by eight by ten
cubits—what did that prove? It was not proportional to either Temple or to anything else in the Bible. A few days later, though, I
realized that there is in fact a space described in the Bible that is just
these measurements: the space under the wings of the cherubs inside
the Holy of Holies of the Temple.

The *first* Temple was divided into two rooms. The outer room was
called the Holy, and the inner room was called the Holy of Holies.
The Holy of Holies was twenty cubits square:

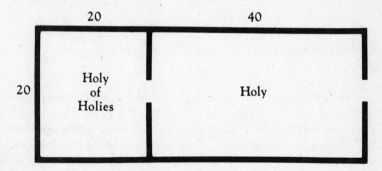

Inside the Holy of Holies were the two golden cherubs. They were
each ten cubits tall. Cherubs generally have the head of a human,
the body of a four-legged animal, and the wings of a bird. In extant

examples, the wings are generally folded back against the cherub's body. The Temple cherubs' wings, however, are spread. Their wing-spread is ten cubits each, so their wings touch the walls of the room on each side and touch each other in the middle—like this:

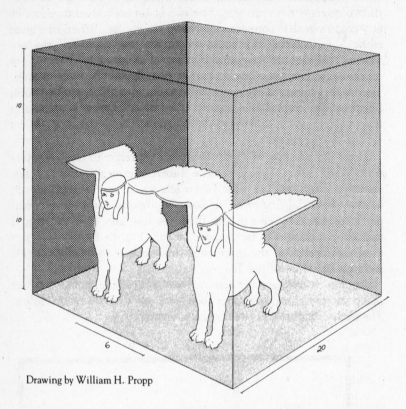

Drawing by William H. Propp

The space under the wings of the cherubs would be twenty cubits long (the length of the Holy of Holies), ten cubits high, and *less* than ten cubits wide, because the bodies of the cherubs would take up some of the center space. The measurements of the Tabernacle match those of the most sacred place, the space under the wings of the cherubs inside the Holy of Holies of the Temple. This was the first clue that *the Tabernacle was actually in the first Temple.*

I first published these findings concerning the Tabernacle measurements in an article in the journal *Biblical Archeologist* in 1980. Many scholars were receptive to these findings, but at least one scholar suggested that these dimensions were "arbitrary." Some time later, Baruch Halpern, who was familiar with my findings, was studying the reports of the Israeli archeologist Yohanan Aharoni of the University of Tel Aviv. Aharoni had excavated the cite of Arad, a city in the Judean desert. At Arad he discovered a temple that had functioned through the biblical period. Halpern called me to tell me that the measurements of the Arad temple were six cubits wide by twenty cubits long—matching the Tabernacle measurements. There were other similarities connecting the recently discovered temple with the Tabernacle as well, and Aharoni had commented, "The similarity between the Tabernacle and the Arad sanctuary is most striking." Striking indeed—this provided further confirmation that the Tabernacle measurements that I had calculated were hardly arbitrary. The Arad temple, the Tabernacle, and the inner sanctum of the first Temple were built to matching specifications.

More evidence that the Tabernacle was actually in the first temple came from the Bible itself. If we look at the report of the events of the day that King Solomon dedicated the Temple, which appears in both the books of 1 Kings and 2 Chronicles, it says:

And they brought up the ark of Yahweh *and the Tent of Meeting* and all of the holy implements that were in the Tent.[2]

It says explicitly that the Tabernacle was brought up to the Temple along with the ark and the implements. The Tabernacle may then have been set up under the cherubs' wings, or it may have been stored away in the Temple precincts while the correspondingly measured space under the wings stood for it. Either way, the Tabernacle was linked to the first Temple.

Josephus, the Jewish historian of the first century A.D., also says explicitly that the Tabernacle was brought into the Temple. And he states that the effect of the cherubs' having their wings spread was precisely to appear as a tent.[3]

Also, the Babylonian Talmud, compiled in the fifth century A.D., says that the Tent of Meeting was stored away beneath the Temple.[4]

What have the investigators made of these explicit statements connecting the Tabernacle with the Temple? The evidence of Josephus and the Talmud, when considered at all, are regarded skeptically because they are relatively late sources. As for the biblical

statement, most have said that it is a "gloss," that it was added by
some later editor who wanted to make it *appear* that the Tabernacle
was tied to the Temple. There are, however, other references to the
presence of the Tabernacle in the Temple to be found in the Bible,
and some of them are in poetry that takes this presence for granted,
rather than as something to be impressed upon the readers. Psalm
26:8, for example, says:

> *Yahweh I love the dwelling of your House,*
> *The place of your glory's Tabernacle.*

"Yahweh's House" regularly means the Temple. Here the House is
identified as the place of the Tabernacle. Most English translations,
not knowing what to make of this, translate the second line as "The
place where your glory dwells." But the Tabernacle reference makes
perfect sense if it refers to the Tabernacle in the Temple.

Psalm 27:4–5 also connects the Tabernacle and the sacred Tent:

> *I ask one thing of Yahweh; that I shall seek:*
> *That I may dwell in Yahweh's House all the days of my life,*
> *To envision Yahweh's beauty and to visit in his Temple,*
> *For he will conceal me in his pavilion in a day of trouble;*
> *He will hide me in the covert of his Tent.*

One might answer that this is poetry, after all, and that the Tabernacle here in these psalms may be meant merely figuratively, as a
symbolic parallel to the Temple. But consider another parallel, in
Psalm 61:5:

> *I shall dwell in your Tent forever;*
> *I shall trust in the covert of your wings.*

Here God's Tent is in parallel not with the Temple but with that
which is hidden by the wings—which fits the arrangement of the
Tabernacle under the wings of the cherubs.

Even the Psalm that mourns the destruction of the Temple, Psalm
74:7, refers to the Tabernacle:

> *They cast your sanctuary into the fire;*
> *They profaned your name's Tabernacle to the ground.*

Again, the translations make this "They have profaned the dwelling place of your name to the ground," not knowing what to make of a reference to a Tabernacle at the time of the destruction. But the book of Lamentations (2:6–7) also refers to the destruction of the Tabernacle at that time:

> And he has dealt violently with his pavilion as with a garden;
> He has destroyed his [Tent of] Meeting.
> Yahweh has caused holiday and Sabbath to be forgotten in Zion,
> And he has spurned in his angry indignation king and priest.
> The Lord has cast off his altar, abhorred his Temple.
> He has closed up the walls of her palaces in the enemy's hand.
> They have made noise in Yahweh's House as on a holiday.

It would be hard to claim that the reference to the pavilion here is merely figurative. Every other item in the passage is literal and real: holiday, Sabbath, king, priest, altar, Temple, walls.

Also, the Tabernacle's presence in the Temple is mentioned in nonfigurative prose parts of the Bible as well. The book of Chronicles refers to the Temple as

> the House of Yahweh, the House of the Tent.[5]

In another passage it refers to the Levites as serving before

> the Tabernacle of the House of God.[6]

In another passage it quotes a speech by King Hezekiah in which the king says, in the context of remarks about the Temple, that past generations

> turned their faces from Yahweh's Tabernacle and turned their backs.[7]

And, finally, in the Priestly source itself, in the list of covenant blessings on the land, one of the blessings is:

> And I shall put my Tabernacle in your midst.[8]

Leviticus, Chronicles, Lamentations, Psalms, Kings, the Talmud, and Josephus all offer evidence that the Tabernacle was understood to be in the Temple. And the architecture of the Tabernacle and the Temple indicates the same thing. The Tabernacle was not a symbol of the second Temple. It was not merely a symbol at all. It was real. And it was housed in the first Temple.

A tent inside a building is not so strange as it might seem. If ancient Israel had a Tabernacle that was its sacred shrine for years and was traditionally associated with Moses, they could hardly just discard it once a Temple was built. What do you do with a structure that is valued in your tradition and regarded as the proper place for religious ceremonies? A fairly close analogy might be the case of the bridal canopy used in Jewish weddings. The bride and groom stand under a canopy during the ceremony. Presumably this custom began when weddings were performed out of doors, as they are in Israel to this day. In the United States, however, weddings are performed in synagogues; nonetheless, a canopy is still set up inside the synagogue in accordance with tradition and law. Try to do without the canopy inside the building, and there will surely be an angry grandmother insisting that she was married under a canopy, and her mother was married under a canopy, and her granddaughter will most certainly be married under a canopy. To make the analogy even a bit closer, imagine that it is a particular canopy that has been used in the same family for two hundred years. So it was with the Tabernacle. And, even more than in the case of the bridal canopy, the Tabernacle was regarded as the only one of its kind, connected with Moses himself.

This is perhaps the reason why the place where the ark was kept in Shiloh in the days of Samuel is referred to in the Bible both as a Temple and as a Tabernacle.[9] The Tabernacle probably was housed in the Shiloh structure. And then it was housed in the first Temple until the Temple was burned down.

What does all of this have to do with finding the author of P? I think that it proves that P had to be written before the first Temple was destroyed. Laws all through P say that sacrifices and other ceremonies must take place at the entrance to the Tabernacle and no-where else—and that this is the law *forever*. How could anyone have written that after the Tabernacle was destroyed? Why would a priest write a law code that said that sacrifices can only be offered at a place that did not exist anymore? This is not pious fraud. That is destroying his own livelihood. If the United States Capitol burned down, the Congress would not pass a law the following year saying that citizens could pay their taxes only at the Capitol Building. And it is not as if another Tabernacle could have been built. The Tabernacle was a one-time creation, sacred because of its history and traditions.

The Tabernacle evidence pointed to the same conclusion as the linguistic evidence, namely that investigators since Reuss had been looking for the author of P in the right place but in the wrong time. The place was Judah, probably Jerusalem, but the time in which they were looking was *at least* a century and a half too late. The person who wrote P placed the Tabernacle at the center of Israel's religious life, back as far as Moses, and forever into the future. This person had to be living and writing before

> They cast your Temple into the fire;
> They profaned your name's Tabernacle to the ground.

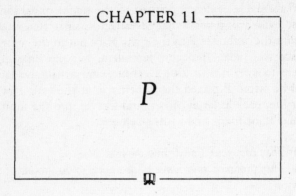

CHAPTER 11

P

Who Wrote P?

WHAT can we say so far about the author of the largest source of the Five Books of Moses? The person was an Aaronid priest, or at least someone who was representing the Aaronid priests' interests. The person was therefore probably male. He was from Judah, almost certainly from Jerusalem. It was someone who was quite familiar with the Jerusalem priestly practices and who probably had access to documents, since there is detailed description of sacrificial practice, incense burning, priestly garments and the Tabernacle and its accouterments. It was someone who was alive and writing before the fall of Jerusalem to the Babylonians in 587 B.C.

One more thing: it was someone who knew the JE text, in its combined form, intimately. An investigator in Norway in 1964 showed that P was not just similar to JE, and it did not just have an awfully high number of doublets of stories in JE. It was *following* JE. It was telling the same or similar stories, and in almost the same order.

Not only did P open with a creation story and a flood story like

JE, and then go on to the major matters of Abraham's covenant, the exodus from Egypt, and the covenant at Sinai. It referred to all kinds of specific matters, small and large, that appeared in the JE text. JE tells about Abraham's nephew Lot; P tells about Lot. JE tells a story about Moses striking a rock that produces water in the wilderness; P tells a story about Moses striking a rock that produces water in the wilderness. JE tells about an apostasy at Peor; P does the same. JE tells a story about a rebellion after a group of spies report to Moses; so does P. There are more than twenty-five cases of these parallel accounts. That is too many to explain as merely the result of P's being generally interested in the same things as JE. The similarities are blatant. The differences are fascinating.

The Norwegian investigator, Sigmund Mowinckel, was right about P's having some kind of connection with JE—I shall show you the evidence—but he had only touched the tip of the iceberg.

Mowinckel was very cautious in his conclusion. He said only that P depended on JE "directly or indirectly." That is a responsible conclusion, but a little frustrating. What it does tell us is that the author of P wrote after the fall of the northern kingdom of Israel in 722 B.C., when E had already come south and been combined with J. What it does not tell us is what is going on here. Why did this person get his hands on a copy of the JE narrative, follow it on some points, and make changes on other points? If he was satisfied with JE, why bother to write another version of the same stories? If he was dissatisfied, why not start over with a whole new historical account? That was the mystery to be solved: what was the connection between JE and P?

A *Torah* of Their Own

Imagine being a Jerusalem priest in the years following the fall of the northern kingdom. You have enjoyed a position of authority and distinction. You are a religious leader with special privileges of access to the Temple. You trace your ancestry to Aaron, the first high priest of Israel.

With the arrival of refugees from the fallen northern kingdom, your constituency grows dramatically. The new arrivals' religion is in most ways compatible with your own. They believe in the same God. They cherish traditions of the patriarchs, the exodus, the revelation at Sinai. On the other hand, they include members of rival priesthoods, notably some who trace their ancestry to Moses himself. They come carrying documents, including the text of E, the sacred story of your people's origin. It conflicts with J, the Judean version of that sacred story, but somehow the two come to be combined. Perhaps their combination is a literary compromise. Perhaps it is a political reconciliation. But, whatever the reason for their union, they are now a known text.

What does this known text say? It says that Aaron, your ancestor, made the golden calf.

What else? It says that Aaron and his sister Miriam criticized Moses on account of Moses' wife. It says that God personally chastised them for this. It has Aaron humbly address Moses as "my lord" on both these occasions. Aaron's role in this text generally is minimal. Meanwhile it aggrandizes Moses, the great ancestor of the rival priesthood. It does not emphasize sacrifice—which is your livelihood—and it does not suggest that sacrifice is solely the province of priests. The key person in the JE *torah* is the prophet, not the priest.

Most of this would be unwelcome. The part about the golden calf would be intolerable. What were the Aaronid priests to do?

They wrote a *torah* of their own.

An Alternative Version

P was written as an alternative to JE. The JE stories regularly said: "And Yahweh said unto Moses. . . ."[1] But the author of P often made it: "And Yahweh said unto Moses *and unto Aaron*. . . ."[2] In JE, miracles are performed in Egypt using Moses' staff.[3] But the author of P made it *Aaron's* staff.[4] In JE, Aaron is introduced as Moses' "Levite brother."[5] This would only mean that the two are fellow members of the tribe of Levi, not that they are literally brothers. But the author of P states categorically that Aaron and Moses were brothers, sons of the same mother and father, and that *Aaron was the firstborn.* [6] In a P genealogy of the Levites, Aaron's family is given but not Moses'. [7]

In P, there are no sacrifices in any of the stories until the last chapter of Exodus. There, the first sacrifice in P is the story of the sacrifice on the day that Aaron is consecrated as High Priest. [8] After all, all sacrifices in P are performed by Aaron or by his sons. The author of P, it seems, did not want to promote the idea that there was a precedent for anyone besides an Aaronid priest to offer a sacrifice. In JE, there are stories that involve sacrifices by Cain, Abel, Noah, Abraham, Isaac, and Jacob, among others. But the author of P either left the sacrifice out of the story or, in some cases, left the story out altogether.

Recall that in the twin stories of the flood that I separated in Chapter 2, the J version said that Noah took seven pairs of all the clean (i.e., fit for sacrifice) animals and one pair of the unclean animals on the ark. But P just said that it was two of every kind of animal. Why? Because, in J, at the end of the story Noah offers a sacrifice. He therefore needs more than two of each of the clean animals or his sacrifice would wipe out a species. In P's perspective, however, two sheep and two cows are enough because there will be no portrayals of sacrifices until the consecration of Aaron.

The issue is not just sacrifice. For the author of P, it is the larger principle that the consecrated priests are the only intermediaries between humans and God. In the P versions of the stories, there are no angels. There are no talking animals. There are no dreams. Even the word "prophet" does not occur in P except once, and there it refers to Aaron. [9] In·P there are no blatant anthropomorphisms. In JE, God walks in the garden of Eden, God personally makes Adam's and Eve's clothes, personally closes Noah's ark, smells Noah's sacrifice, wrestles with Jacob, and speaks to Moses out of the burning bush. None of these things are in P. In JE, God personally speaks the Ten Commandments out loud from the heavens over Sinai. In P he does not. P depicts Yahweh as more cosmic, less personal, than in JE. Perhaps it is only coincidental, but it is interesting to note that the JE creation story begins:

In the day that Yahweh God made *earth and heavens* . . . [10]

While the P creation story begins:

In the beginning of God's creating *the heavens and the earth*...[11]

JE's story starts with the earth; P's starts with the heavens. Whether the switch was intended or not, it correctly reflects the different perspectives of the two.

Likewise in the flood stories, as separated in Chapter 2, the P story is about a cosmic crisis. The windows of the heavens and the fountains of the deep are breaking up, and the waters that surround our habitable bubble are pouring in. In JE, it rains.

And so throughout P we read about the cosmic God of a great, ordered universe. The way to communicate with this God is through the formal, ordered structures that he has provided as the only channels to him. It is not through talking snakes or talking asses; not through meetings with angels; not through dreams or prophets. It is through prescribed sacrifices at prescribed times, performed by a prescribed priesthood in a prescribed manner.

Thus P has a story that two of Aaron's sons, Nadab and Abihu, make an offering that God did not prescribe. The result is that "fire went out from before Yahweh and consumed them, and they died...."[12]

Rebellion in the Wilderness.

Even more revealing is the way that the author of P transformed a JE story of a rebellion in the wilderness. The two are wound around each other in the Bible now like the two flood stories. I will unwind them again with different kinds of type. The JE story is in regular type, P is in boldface capitals. Read the JE story first, and then go back and see how a rebellion story appears when the author of P fashions it.

The Rebellion, Numbers 16

(Priestly text in boldface capitals; J text in regular type)

1 AND KORAH SON OF IZHAR SON OF KOHATH SON OF LEVI And Dathan and Abiram, sons of Eliab, and On son of Peleth, sons of Reuben,

2 rose up before Moses. AND TWO HUNDRED FIFTY PEOPLE FROM THE CHILDREN OF ISRAEL, PRINCES OF THE CONGREGATION, KNOWN IN ASSEMBLY, PEOPLE OF STATURE

3 ASSEMBLED AGAINST MOSES AND AGAINST AARON AND SAID TO THEM: "YOU HAVE A GREAT DEAL! FOR ALL OF THE CONGREGATION, ALL OF THEM ARE HOLY—AND YAHWEH IS IN THEIR MIDST. AND WHY DO YOU LIFT YOURSELVES UP OVER YAHWEH'S COMMUNITY?"

4 AND MOSES LISTENED, AND HE FELL ON HIS FACE.

5 AND HE SPOKE TO KORAH AND TO ALL OF HIS CONGREGATION, SAYING, "IN THE MORNING YAHWEH WILL MAKE KNOWN WHO IS HIS AND WHO IS HOLY AND WHOM HE WILL BRING CLOSE TO HIM. HE WILL BRING CLOSE TO HIM THE ONE WHOM HE CHOOSES.

6 DO THIS: TAKE YOURSELVES INCENSE BURNERS, KORAH AND HIS CONGREGATION,

7 AND PUT FIRE IN THEM, AND SET INCENSE ON THEM BEFORE YAHWEH TOMORROW. AND IT WILL BE THAT THE MAN WHOM YAHWEH WILL CHOOSE, HE WILL BE THE HOLY. YOU HAVE A GREAT DEAL, SONS OF LEVI!"

8 AND MOSES SAID TO KORAH, "LISTEN, SONS OF LEVI,

9 IS IT TOO SMALL A THING FOR YOU THAT THE GOD OF ISRAEL HAS SEPARATED YOU FROM THE CONGREGATION TO BRING YOU CLOSE TO HIM, TO DO THE SERVICE OF THE TABERNACLE OF YAHWEH AND TO STAND BEFORE THE CONGREGATION TO SERVE THEM,

10 AND THAT HE HAS BROUGHT YOU AND ALL YOUR BROTHERS

THE SONS OF LEVI WITH YOU CLOSE TO HIM? AND YOU SEEK THE PRIESTHOOD AS WELL?!

11 THEREFORE YOU AND ALL YOUR CONGREGATION WHO ARE GATHERING ARE AGAINST YAHWEH. AND AARON, WHAT IS HE THAT YOU COMPLAIN AGAINST HIM?"

12 And Moses sent to call Dathan and Abiram, sons of Eliab, and they said, "We will not come up.

13 Is it a small thing that you brought us up from a land flowing with milk and honey to kill us in the wilderness, that you lord it over us as well?

14 Besides, you have not brought us to a land flowing with milk and honey or given us possession of field or vineyard. Will you put out those people's eyes? We will not come up."

15 And Moses was very angry, and he said to Yahweh, "Do not incline to their offering. Not one ass of theirs have I taken away, and I have not wronged one of them."

16 AND MOSES SAID TO KORAH, "YOU AND ALL YOUR CONGREGATION, BE BEFORE YAHWEH—YOU AND THEY AND AARON—TOMORROW.

17 AND EACH MAN TAKE HIS INCENSE BURNER, AND PUT INCENSE ON THEM, AND EACH MAN BRING HIS INCENSE BURNER CLOSE BEFORE YAHWEH, TWO HUNDRED FIFTY INCENSE BURNERS, AND YOU AND AARON, EACH MAN, HIS INCENSE BURNER."

18 AND EACH MAN TOOK HIS INCENSE BURNER, AND THEY PUT FIRE ON THEM AND SET INCENSE ON THEM, AND THEY STOOD AT THE ENTRANCE OF THE TENT OF MEETING, AND MOSES AND AARON.

19 AND KORAH ASSEMBLED ALL THE CONGREGATION AGAINST THEM, TO THE ENTRANCE OF THE TENT OF MEETING. AND THE GLORY OF YAHWEH APPEARED TO THE WHOLE CONGREGATION.

20 AND YAHWEH SPOKE TO MOSES AND TO AARON, SAYING,

21 "SEPARATE FROM THE MIDST OF THIS CONGREGATION, AND I SHALL CONSUME THEM IN AN INSTANT."

22 AND THEY FELL ON THEIR FACES, AND THEY SAID, "GOD, THE GOD OF THE SPIRITS OF ALL FLESH, WILL ONE MAN SIN AND YOU BE FURIOUS AT THE WHOLE CONGREGATION?"

23 AND YAHWEH SPOKE TO MOSES, SAYING,

24 "SPEAK TO THE CONGREGATION, SAYING, 'GET UP FROM AROUND THE TABERNACLE OF KORAH[,Dathan, and Abiram[13]].'"

25 And Moses rose and went to Dathan and Abiram, and the elders of Israel went after him.

26 AND HE SPOKE TO THE CONGREGATION, SAYING, "TURN AWAY FROM THE TENTS OF THESE WICKED MEN AND DO NOT TOUCH ANY-THING THAT IS THEIRS, LEST YOU BE DESTROYED IN ALL THEIR SINS."

27 AND THEY GOT UP FROM AROUND THE TABERNACLE OF KORAH[, DATHAN, AND ABIRAM]. And Dathan and Abiram went out, standing at the entrance of their tents, and their wives and their sons and their infants.

28 And Moses said, "By this you will know that Yahweh sent me to do all these things, for it is not from my own heart.

29 If these die like the death of every human, and the event of every human happens to them, then Yahweh has not sent me.

30 But if Yahweh will create something, and the ground opens its mouth and swallows them and all that is theirs, and they go down alive to sheol,[14] then you will know that these men have provoked Yahweh."

31 And it was as he was finishing to speak all these things; and the ground under them was split.

32 And the earth opened its mouth and swallowed them and their houses. AND ALL THE PEOPLE WHO WERE WITH KORAH, AND ALL THE PROPERTY.

33 And they and all they had went down alive to sheol. And the earth covered them over, and they perished from the midst of the community.

34 And all Israel that was around them fled at the sound of them; for they said, "Lest the earth swallow us."

35 AND FIRE WENT OUT FROM YAHWEH AND CONSUMED THE TWO HUNDRED FIFTY PEOPLE OFFERING THE INCENSE.

For two thousand years people read this as one story, and it was confusing. It seemed to be taking place at two different locations at the same time. At some points it was at the tents of the rebels. At other points it was at the Tent of Meeting. At some points the rebels were just Dathan and Abiram. At other points it was Korah and his company. Separating the two stories solves these things and reveals a great deal.

The first story, from JE, is about the rebellion of Dathan and Abiram (and On), from the tribe of Reuben. They challenge Moses' leadership. In one of the great acts of ingratitude of all time, they complain that he has taken them *out* of a land flowing with milk and honey—meaning Egypt! Moses pleads that he has wronged no one and that he has done only what God told him to do, not what he planned himself. He is vindicated when an earthquake swallows the challengers.

In the second story, from P, the challengers are a group of *Levites*, backed by people of stature in the community. Their leader is Korah. Who is Korah? According to a P genealogy, he is Moses' and Aaron's cousin.[15] His challenge is not against Moses' leadership. It is against Aaron's exclusive hold on the priesthood: why cannot anyone else practice priestly functions, since *all* the people are holy? Moses defends Aaron. He sets up a test of just who is holy. The test is the offering of incense. Elsewhere in P it is forbidden for anyone but a priest to burn incense. When the challengers try to do it, therefore, they are stepping beyond the prescribed bounds. Their fate is the same as that of Aaron's sons who crossed those bounds in the other story: "fire went out from Yahweh and consumed them."

The JE story of the rebellion was a justification of Moses. But the Priestly version is a justification of Aaron. It conveys the message that other Levites' claims to having the right to be priests are false —even if supported by people of stature. The priesthood of the nation is the priesthood of Aaron.

Concepts of God

Over and over, P develops this point that the Aaronid priest at the sacrificial altar is the people's proper channel to the deity. If you have sinned and want to be forgiven, the thing to do is bring a sacrifice to a priest at the Tabernacle. In the P text, there is not a single reference to God as *merciful*. The very words "mercy," "grace," "faithfulness," and "repent" never occur. The point, apparently, is to develop the idea that forgiveness cannot be had just because one is sorry. One can be sorry without turning to a priest—and without bringing the priest an offering. Rather, in P, God is *just*. He has established a set of rules by which one can acquire forgiveness, and the rules must be followed. This is in stark contrast to the JE picture of God as

> merciful and gracious, long-forebearing and full of faithfulness and truth, storing faithfulness for thousands, bearing transgression and offense and sin. . . .[16]

The person who wrote P was not just changing details of stories. He was developing a concept of God. His work was literary, but his motivation was not only artistic, but also theological, political, and economic. He had to deal with challenges from other priests and other religious centers. He had to defend his group's legitimacy and to protect their authority. And he had to ensure their livelihood.

He also had to fight the insult to his ancestor Aaron. It is no great surprise that P does not include the stories of the golden calf or of snow-white Miriam. But this writer apparently also felt that the best defense is a good offense. They had challenged his ancestor, Aaron. He challenged their ancestor, Moses.

Diminishing Moses

Perhaps the most extraordinary thing about P is the way its author deals with Moses. This author was in an extremely sensitive position. The rival priesthood, who were quite possibly descendants of Moses, brought a *torah* which made Aaron look bad. This writer could not so easily respond by writing a work that made Moses a heretic or an unjust accuser. It was Moses, after all. Moses was the national hero and founder, who led the liberation from slavery and mediated the covenant at Sinai. It was one thing to say that Aaron was Moses' older brother. That was not offensive in itself. After all, Jacob and Joseph were not firstborn sons either. It was another thing to try to make up a story in which Moses was denigrated.

Besides, this author was not in the business of making up totally new stories out of thin air anyway, as we have seen. He was rather fashioning his own version of a sequence of known stories. He was engaged in something that was art, but not exactly fiction. It was also history. He had to be concerned with successful promulgation; that is, with his audience's willingness to accept this work as a believable account of their past. His art involved a constant balance between tradition and creativity. Therefore, for the most part, he respected the place of Moses in the tradition. Moses remains important in P. But he developed Moses' personality far less than in JE, and in a couple of instances he actually dared to refashion stories to Moses' discredit.[17]

The most impressive example is the story of water from a rock. In two different places there is a story of Moses' striking a rock with a stick and getting water from it. One is in Exodus, and one is in Numbers. In the continuity of the story in the Bible as it stands now, the two similar events happen years and miles apart. Yet both happen at a place with the same name: Meribah. Each story is only a few verses long, so it is worth looking at both. First, here is the story that the author of P read in the JE text:

Water from the Rock, Exodus 17:2–7

(E text in italics)

2   *And the people quarreled with Moses, and they said, "Give us water and let us drink." And Moses said to them, "Why do you quarrel with me? Why do you test Yahweh?"*
3   *And the people thirsted there for water, and the people complained against Moses and said, "Why did you bring us up from Egypt—to kill me and my children and my livestock with thirst?"*
4   *And Moses cried out to Yahweh, saying, "What shall I do with this people? A little more and they will stone me."*

5   *And Yahweh said to Moses, "Pass in front of the people, and take
some of the elders of Israel with you. And take in your hand the staff with
which you struck the river, and go.*
6   *Here I shall be standing in front of you there on the rock in Horeb.
And you shall strike the rock, and water will go out from it, and the
people will drink." And Moses did so in the sight of the elders of Israel.*
7   *And he called the name of the place Massah and Meribah on account
of the children of Israel's quarrel and on account of their testing Yahweh,
saying, "Is Yahweh in our midst or not?"*

There is no water for the people in the wilderness. They quarrel.
Yahweh stands on a rock (meaning a crag of a mountain, not a
stone). Moses hits the rock with his staff, and water comes out.
That was the story that the author of P read. Now here is how it
came out in his version:

Water from the Rock, Numbers 20:2–13

(Priestly text in boldface capitals.)

2   **AND THERE WAS NOT WATER FOR THE CONGREGATION, AND
THEY ASSEMBLED AGAINST MOSES AND AGAINST AARON.**

3   **AND THE PEOPLE QUARRELED WITH MOSES, AND THEY SAID,
"AND WOULD THAT WE HAD EXPIRED WHEN OUR BROTHERS EX-
PIRED BEFORE YAHWEH.**

4   **AND WHY DID YOU BRING YAHWEH'S COMMUNITY TO THIS WIL-
DERNESS TO DIE THERE, WE AND OUR CATTLE?**

5   **AND WHY DID YOU BRING US UP FROM EGYPT TO BRING US TO
THIS BAD PLACE? IT IS NOT A PLACE OF SEED AND FIG AND VINE AND
POMEGRANATE, AND THERE IS NO WATER TO DRINK."**

6   **AND MOSES AND AARON CAME BEFORE THE COMMUNITY TO THE
ENTRANCE OF THE TENT OF MEETING, AND THEY FELL ON THEIR
FACES. AND THE GLORY OF YAHWEH APPEARED TO THEM.**

7   **AND YAHWEH SPOKE TO MOSES, SAYING.**

8   **"TAKE THE STAFF, AND ASSEMBLE THE CONGREGATION, YOU**

AND AARON YOUR BROTHER. AND YOU SHALL SPEAK TO THE ROCK IN THEIR SIGHT, AND IT WILL GIVE ITS WATER. AND YOU SHALL BRING WATER OUT OF THE ROCK FOR THEM. AND YOU SHALL GIVE DRINK TO THE CONGREGATION AND THEIR CATTLE."

9   AND MOSES TOOK THE STAFF FROM BEFORE YAHWEH AS HE COMMANDED HIM.

10   AND MOSES AND AARON ASSEMBLED THE COMMUNITY OPPOSITE THE ROCK. AND HE SAID TO THEM, "LISTEN, REBELS, SHALL WE BRING WATER OUT OF THIS ROCK FOR YOU?"

11   AND MOSES LIFTED HIS HAND, AND HE STRUCK THE ROCK WITH HIS STAFF TWICE. AND MUCH WATER WENT OUT. AND THE CONGREGATION AND THEIR CATTLE DRANK.

12   AND YAHWEH SAID TO MOSES AND TO AARON, "BECAUSE YOU DID NOT TRUST IN ME, TO MAKE ME HOLY IN THE CHILDREN OF ISRAEL'S SIGHT, THEREFORE YOU SHALL NOT BRING THIS COMMUNITY TO THE LAND THAT I HAVE SET FOR THEM."

13   THEY ARE THE WATERS OF MERIBAH, OVER WHICH THE CHILDREN OF ISRAEL QUARRELED WITH YAHWEH, AND HE WAS MADE HOLY AMONG THEM.

The language here has so much in common with the P language in the Korah story that the similarity should be apparent even in translation and even to those who have never known about biblical sources before. It refers to the *congregation* and to the *community*. It has Yahweh speak to Moses *and to Aaron*. It says that the *glory of Yahweh appeared*. As a sign of distress, it says *they fell on their faces*. It takes place in front of the *Tent of Meeting*. It is concerned with signs of *holiness*. Also, it uses the word "expire" in reference to death, which I noted in the P version of the flood story in Chapter 2. Indeed, the language of P is so characteristic that undergraduate students can generally identify a P passage in the Bible on sight within weeks after being introduced to this study. The point is that we can observe the Priestly writer at work here. We can see what he kept of the story, we can see how he put it into his own language, and we can see what he changed.

The main thing is that hitting the rock was good in Exodus, and it is bad in Numbers. It was an act of obedience in Exodus. It is ultimate disobedience in Numbers. It is Moses' worst offense. His punishment is presumably the worst thing that could be done to him: he is not to live to bring the people into the land. And Aaron, who does not seem to have done anything wrong himself, suffers the same penalty on account of what Moses has done. The punishments are carried out later in the P narrative: Aaron and Moses both die shortly before the people enter the promised land.

Theological interpreters have pondered this passage for centuries, trying to understand just what the nature of Moses' offense was. Was it that he struck the rock instead of talking to it? Was it that he called the people "rebels"? Was it that he said, "Shall *we* bring out water from this rock?" instead of "Shall *God*...."? But whatever the offense was, the important point for our present purposes is: it was not in the earlier version of the story. The P author has gone out of his way to introduce it into the story. (And he refers to it again later on in his narrative.[18]) And he has portrayed Aaron as innocent and suffering for Moses' sin.

The Veil of Moses

The author of P also told a version of the story of the revelation at Mount Sinai. In many ways it was similar to the JE version. The mountain is fiery. Moses goes up alone. But the Priestly writer added a detail concerning Moses at the end of the story. He wrote that there is something unusual about Moses' face when he comes down from the mountain. When the people see him they are afraid to come near him. Moses therefore wears a veil from then on whenever he speaks to the people.[19] That is, according to the P source, whenever we think of Moses during the last forty years of his life, we are supposed to imagine him with a veil over his face.

What is it about Moses' face in the Priestly source? The meaning of the Hebrew term in the text is uncertain. For a long time people understood it to mean that Moses has horns. This gave rise to hundreds of depictions of a horned Moses in art, the most famous of which is the Moses of Michelangelo. Then the term was understood to mean that Moses' skin somehow beams light. Recently an American biblical scholar, William Propp, has assembled evidence that the term probably means that Moses' face is disfigured. This makes sense in the P context because Moses has just stepped out of the cloud surrounding the "glory of Yahweh." The last P narrative before this in the text informs us that the appearance of this "glory of Yahweh" is "like a consuming fire."[20] Moses has been in a fiery zone that is otherwise forbidden to humans. The result is some frightening effect on his skin that people cannot bear to see. In P, Moses is perhaps too ugly to be seen. At minimum, he is not to be pictured. That is not exactly a denigration of Moses. But it is not exactly attractive either.

Seduction and Worship

Let me give one more example of how this writer moved from the JE stories to his own. It is a story that involves sex and violence in both the JE and the P renditions. Women from another nation attract the Israelite men, first sexually and then to their pagan worship. In both sources, strong steps are taken in response to the heresy. The combined story, as it appears in the Bible now, splits right in the middle into JE and P, thus:

The Heresy of Peor, Numbers 25

(Priestly text in boldface capitals; J text in regular type)

1   And Israel abode in Shittim. And the people began to whore with the daughters of Moab.

2   And they called the people to their gods' sacrifices. And the people ate and prostrated themselves to their gods.

3   And Israel was joined to Baal Peor. And Yahweh's anger burned against Israel.

4   And Yahweh said to Moses, "Take all the heads of the people,

and hang them up to Yahweh opposite the sun, and the burning of Yahweh's anger will turn back from Israel."

5   And Moses said to Israel's judges, "Each man, kill his men who were joined to Baal Peor."

6   AND HERE WAS A MAN FROM THE CHILDREN OF ISRAEL, AND HE BROUGHT A MIDIANITESS CLOSE TO HIS BROTHERS IN THE SIGHT OF MOSES AND IN THE SIGHT OF ALL THE CONGREGATION OF THE CHILDREN OF ISRAEL. AND THEY WERE WEEPING AT THE ENTRANCE OF THE TENT OF MEETING.

7   AND PHINEHAS, THE SON OF ELEAZAR, THE SON OF AARON THE PRIEST, SAW, AND HE ROSE FROM THE MIDST OF THE CONGREGATION, AND HE TOOK A SPEAR IN HIS HAND.

8   AND HE CAME AFTER THE ISRAELITE MAN TO THE TENT-CHAMBER, AND HE THRUST THROUGH THE TWO OF THEM, THE ISRAELITE MAN AND THE WOMAN, TO HER STOMACH. AND THE PLAGUE WAS HALTED FROM THE CHILDREN OF ISRAEL.

9   AND THOSE WHO DIED IN THE PLAGUE WERE TWENTY-FOUR THOUSAND.

10   AND YAHWEH SPOKE TO MOSES, SAYING,

11   "PHINEHAS, THE SON OF ELEAZAR, THE SON OF AARON THE PRIEST, HAS TURNED BACK MY WRATH FROM THE CHILDREN OF ISRAEL, BY CARRYING OUT MY JEALOUSY IN THEIR MIDST. AND SO I DID NOT DESTROY THE CHILDREN OF ISRAEL IN MY JEALOUSY.

12   THEREFORE, SAY, 'HERE I AM GIVING HIM MY COVENANT OF PEACE.

13   AND HE AND HIS SEED AFTER HIM WILL HAVE IT, A COVENANT OF ETERNAL PRIESTHOOD, BECAUSE HE WAS JEALOUS FOR HIS GOD AND MADE ATONEMENT FOR THE CHILDREN OF ISRAEL.' "

14   AND YAHWEH SPOKE TO MOSES, SAYING,

15   "TROUBLE THE MIDIANITES, AND STRIKE THEM.

16   FOR THEY TROUBLED YOU WITH THEIR ENTICEMENTS BY WHICH THEY ENTICED YOU OVER THE MATTER OF PEOR. . . ."

This text is particularly strange because the two halves are both incomplete. The first half, which is JE, involves the Israelite men's attraction to Moabite women—and then to these women's god. Moses orders the "hanging up" of the people's heads. Then the story breaks off, and we do not hear about the execution of the order. Instead, familiar P language breaks in: "bring close," "congregation," "Tent of Meeting," "Aaron." And the women who were Moabite in the first part have now become Midianite. The second part of the story ends in the halting of a plague—but no plague had been mentioned up to that point.

Aaron himself has died in the preceding P story (which is why the people are weeping at the Tent of Meeting),[21] but now his grandson Phinehas is the hero. An Israelite man and a Midianite woman have gone into the Tent of Meeting "in the sight of Moses," but it is not Moses who acts, but Phinehas. He follows the man and woman inside the Tent. They are engaged in an activity whose arrangement makes it possible to thrust a spear through both the man and the woman, ending in the woman's abdomen. The execution without a trial is possible because death is the unquestionable fate of anyone entering the Tabernacle who is not a priest. Phinehas' reward is an *eternal* covenant of priesthood. This Priestly story, therefore, says that the priesthood belongs to the Aaronids forever.

It is difficult to say to what degree the story demeans Moses for not acting. All we can say is that the Priestly writer especially remarked that the blasphemy took place in Moses' sight, and that it was Phinehas who acted. And it is interesting to note that this writer went to the trouble of changing the Moabite women to Midianites. *Moses' wife is Midianite.*

Additions and Subtractions

We learn about the writer of P not only from the way he retold old stories, but also from looking at what he minimized or left out altogether. Notably, he cut the stories of Genesis down to a critical minimum. Stories that take pages or even chapters in JE come out as verses in P. The story of Joseph, for example, is about ten chapters long in JE but just a few sentences in P.[22]

We can explain this partly in recognizing that the person who fashioned P rejected the angels, dreams, talking animals, and anthropomorphisms of JE. And so he eliminated most of the Joseph story, which involves six dreams in the JE version. He did not include the story of Adam and Eve and the talking snake in Eden. He did not include the story of the angels who visit the cities of Sodom and Gomorrah before God destroys them. And he certainly did not tell the story of Jacob's wrestling with God face to face at Penuel— just as he did not have God standing on the rock that Moses strikes at Meribah. Also, since he would not tell any stories of sacrifices before the consecration of Aaron, he did not include the famous story of Abraham's near-sacrifice of his son Isaac, which takes place some four hundred years before Aaron.

But there is something more to P's reductions and its silences. This writer was not only eliminating items that he specifically rejected on theological or political grounds. He was eliminating the long, anecdotal tales of the older text. To extract the P stories from Genesis and then read them, one gets the impression of a writer who means to get down to business. And that means the age of Aaron. This writer does not show any interest in the lesser characters of Genesis or in the literary constructions based on clever puns and intricately designed ironies. In all of Genesis there are only four P stories of any length: the creation, the flood culminating in the covenant with Noah, the covenant with Abraham, and one other story (see below). Apparently he was in a hurry to get to Sinai.

Besides this writer's changes and his silences, one more element of his work provides knowledge of him: his additions. Most obvious is his enormous emphasis on law. It overwhelms the rest in quantity: half of Exodus, half of Numbers, nearly all of Leviticus. But he also was capable of adding a character to a story, and, rarely, he even introduced an entirely new story with no parallel at all in JE.

The P story of the death of Aaron's sons Nadab and Abihu is such a story. It is quintessentially a Priestly story. Its message is that offerings must be performed only as commanded by God. No one is free to institute any service that is not commanded in the Priestly law.

An example of this author's adding a whole new character is his spy story. I mentioned the JE version of this story in Chapter 2. In that earlier version, Moses sends a group of spies from the wilderness to report on the land. All but one of them says that the land is impregnable. The one exception is Caleb, who urges the people on.[23] But the people listen to the other spies, and they rebel. Yahweh responds by condemning the entire people to wander in the wilderness until they all die and a new generation grows up to inherit the land—forty years. The one exception to the condemnation is

Caleb, the one faithful spy.[24] He will live to arrive in the land.

Now, in the P version, the story is basically the same, except that now there are two faithful spies who urge the people on: Caleb and Joshua.[25] Why Joshua? This was the P writer's solution to a rather delicate problem. He knew that Joshua was the person who succeeded Moses as the people's leader. That was established tradition, and he was not in a position to change it. But what was Joshua's special merit? What enabled him to be the only Israelite adult besides Caleb to be born in Egypt and live to arrive in the promised land? According to JE, Joshua was the one Israelite who did not participate in the golden calf heresy. He was up on the mountain waiting for Moses. But the P writer could not tell the golden calf story, because Aaron was the villain! Also in JE, Joshua was Moses' faithful assistant who used to stand guard in the Tabernacle.[26] But the P writer could not tell that either, because according to P only a priest can enter the Tabernacle. By P's rules, Joshua would be executed for being in there. This writer had to find some other way to explain Joshua's merit. Adding Joshua to the spy story solved the dilemma.

I alluded above to one other full-length P story in Genesis. It is another example of a whole new story in P that has no equivalent in JE. It is the story of the cave of Machpelah.[27] It gives a lengthy description of the negotiations between Abraham and a Hittite over a piece of land with a cave on it, which Abraham buys as the family burial plot. Why does P, a source that leaves out so many interesting and important JE stories in Genesis, bother to tell a long, mundane account about buying this cave? Because the land and cave that Abraham buys are in Hebron. The story establishes a claim to a legal holding in that territory. And Hebron was an Aaronid priestly city.[28]

The point of this is that we can see in P—just as in J, E, and D—the relationship between the biblical text and the events of the author's world. Every biblical story reflects something that *mattered* to its author. Whenever we figure out what it was and why it mattered, we move a step closer to knowing who wrote a part of the Bible. And when we can assemble the pieces and see how they connect to one another, we move closer still.

Now we have enough evidence from P to locate its author in the biblical world.

CHAPTER 12

In the Court of King Hezekiah

Quoting JE

NOW we know that the collection of Priestly laws and stories was conceived and written as an alternative to JE. JE's stories offended the Priestly writer's ancestor Aaron. They did not emphasize law. They did not emphasize priests. They contained elements that the Priestly writer rejected: angels and anthropomorphisms, dreams and talking animals. The Priestly writer was not happy with JE—to put it mildly.

Is that what we should automatically expect a priest to feel about such stories? The Deuteronomistic writer was a priest, too, and he liked the old JE stories—to put it mildly. He quoted JE left and right. The opening chapters of Deuteronomy are filled with allusions to the JE stories. Deuteronomy is Moses' farewell address, and he refers to many of the events of his forty years with the people. His reminiscences—all but one—are to events from JE stories, not to P stories. When he refers to the great rebellion, he mentions Dathan and Abiram, the villains of the JE version, but he does not mention Korah, P's villain.[1] When he refers to the spy story, he mentions

Caleb as the exceptional faithful spy, not Joshua, P's extra hero.[2] He
refers to the golden calf and to snow-white Miriam.[3]

In fact, the author of Deuteronomy refers to these things as well-
known stories. For example, when he is giving instruction on what
to do in a case of leprosy, he stops and says:

Remember what Yahweh your God did to Miriam on the way when
you were leaving from Egypt.[4]

The writer assumes the readers' acquaintance with the story of
Miriam—that she was stricken with leprosy. If this kind of allusion
was possible in Deuteronomy, it means that the JE stories were well
known by this time. Or, it means that the JE stories were right there
on the scroll. That is, the Deuteronomistic writer may have set a
copy of the JE stories at the beginning of his own history.

One can learn a good deal about a person from seeing whom he or
she quotes. The Deuteronomistic writer, whom I identify as Jeremiah, accepted JE and was fond of quoting it. But he was not fond of
quoting P. Why not?

Is it that he did not know P? Were the P stories not written yet?
Or were they written, but he had never read them?

No. He knew the Priestly texts well enough.

Quoting P

P had to have been written by the time of the Deuteronomistic
writer. And the Deuteronomistic writer had to have been familiar
with it.

I said above that all but one of Moses' references in Deuteronomy
are to stories in JE. The one exception is to a story from P: the story
of the spies. The author of this part of Deuteronomy (Dtr[1]) had to
have known P, because he quotes the P spy story word for word.

In the P version of that story, the spies come back with their
discouraging report on the land. The people complain and say that
they would be better off to return to Egypt. Among their complaints
about the promised land, they say, "Our babies will become a prey."[5]

Yahweh's response to their complaint is his customary punishment to fit the crime: the entire older generation will die in the wilderness, but "your babies, which you said would become a prey, I shall bring *them*, and *they* will know the land that *you* rejected."[6]

Now, in Moses' reminiscence of the spy story in Deuteronomy, Moses quotes these exact words. He says that the older generation will not see the land, but "your babies, which you said would become a prey" will possess it.[7] Too close for coincidence — the Deuteronomist knew P.

But, if Jeremiah (or his scribe, Baruch) was the Deuteronomist, this should come as no surprise. We have already seen quotations of P in the book of Jeremiah itself.[8] Jeremiah plays upon P expressions, reverses the language of the P creation story, denies that God emphasized matters of sacrifices in the day that Israel left Egypt. Jeremiah knew the Priestly laws and stories. He did not like them, but he knew them.

How hostile he was to them can be seen in an extraordinary passage in the book of Jeremiah. Jeremiah says to the people:

How do you say, "We are wise, and Yahweh's *torah* is with us"? In fact, here, it was made for a lie, the lying pen of scribes.[9]

The lying pen of scribes! Jeremiah uses even tougher language than the modern Bible critics ("pious fraud"). Jeremiah says that a *torah* that the people have comes from a lying pen. What *torah* is that? Most investigators have claimed that it was Deuteronomy. They assumed that it had to be Deuteronomy because they accepted the Wellhausen hypothesis that P was not yet written in Jeremiah's days. But this meant seeing Jeremiah as attacking a book written in the same style as his own book. It meant seeing Jeremiah attacking a book with which he agreed on virtually every major point. And, to my mind, it meant seeing Jeremiah as attacking a book that he (or his scribe) wrote. All because they thought that P was not written yet. But it was.

It is not surprising to find Jeremiah so hostile to the Priestly *torah*. The Priestly stories attacked his hero, Moses. The Priestly laws excluded him and his family from the priesthood. What we have in Deuteronomy is just what we might expect: a hint that its author was acquainted with P, but no sign of acceptance of P as a source of law or history.

Conclusion: the P stories and laws were present in Judah by the time of Jeremiah and Dtr[1]; that is, before the death of King Josiah in 609 B.C.

In the Court of King Hezekiah

P was produced after 722 and before 609 B.C. How much more specific can we get? Can we say in which king's reign it was? I think we can. The evidence points to Josiah's great-grandfather, King Hezekiah.

P emphasizes centralization of religion: one center, one altar, one Tabernacle, one place of sacrifice. Who was the king who began centralization? King Hezekiah. Both the books of Kings and Chronicles attest that there was no effective centralization before him.

P is a work of the Aaronid priesthood. They are the priests in authority at the central altar—not Moses, not Korah, not any other Levites. Only those who are descended from Aaron can be priests. All other Levites are second-level clergy. Only P among the biblical sources sees "priests" as something distinct from "Levites." D speaks of priests generally as "the Levite priests."[10] But P always speaks of two distinct groups, the priests and the Levites. Who was the king who formalized the divisions of priests and Levites? King Hezekiah. Chronicles reports explicitly:

> And Hezekiah established the divisions of the priests and the Levites, according to their divisions, every man according to his task, for the priests and for the Levites.[11]

The Aaronid priesthood that produced P had opponents, Levites who saw Moses and not Aaron as their model. What was the most blatant reminder of Moses' power that was visible in Judah? The bronze serpent, "Nehushtan." According to tradition, stated explicitly in E, Moses himself had made it.[12] It had had the power to save people from death by snakebite. Who was the king who smashed Nehushtan? King Hezekiah.[13]

King Hezekiah was the best thing that ever happened to the Aaronid priests. Until his time, their greatest supporter among the kings had been King Solomon. Solomon had removed the Shiloh priest Abiathar from Jerusalem and had given the authority in the Temple entirely to the Aaronid priest Zadok. Hezekiah followed Solomon's priestly preferences.

In fact, it is extremely interesting to recall that Solomon had built various altars besides the Temple altar in Jerusalem. But, despite Hezekiah's interest in centralization, Hezekiah left Solomon's altars alone. What happened to those altars? *Josiah* defiled them.[14]

Josiah, the darling of the Shiloh priests, destroyed the altars of Solomon. Hezekiah, the darling of the Aaronid priests, destroyed Nehushtan.

The ties between the two most favored kings and the two great priesthood documents, D and P, are fascinating. There were two kings who established religious centralization, and there were two works that articulated centralization. The laws and stories of P reflect the interests, the actions, the politics, and the spirit of the age of Hezekiah the way that D reflects the age of Josiah.

The Chronicles Connection

The Bible contains two works that tell the history of the people in their land. The first is the Deuteronomistic history, and the second is the books of 1 and 2 Chronicles. The Deuteronomistic history came from the circle of the priests of Shiloh. The Chronicles history also came from a priestly circle: the Aaronid priests. Like P, it distinguishes between priests and Levites.[15] Like P, it recognizes only descendants of Aaron as legitimate priests. Like P, it is concerned with the priestly duties, the sacred places and objects, sacrifices, worship, and so on. We are not certain of the exact relationship between the books of Chronicles and P, but we can be certain that both are inextricably tied to the Aaronid priesthood.

And the Chronicles history makes a hero of Hezekiah.

Chronicles describes King Hezekiah's religious reform, just as the Deuteronomistic history does. But the book of 2 Chronicles adds about eighty verses of description of his great deeds that do not appear in the version in the book of Kings.[16] The Chronicles addition concludes with unqualified praise:

> He did what was good, right, and true before Yahweh his God. And in every deed that he began—in the work of the House of God and in the *torah* and in the commandment, to enquire of his God—he did it with all his heart; and he was successful.[17]

The Chronicles history does not agree with the Deuteronomistic history about who was the greatest king. Josiah still comes out favorably, but two other kings stand out as foremost: Solomon and Hezekiah—the two kings who did the most for the Aaronids.

The Deuteronomistic history has an entire chapter on Solomon's sins, and it blames the division of the kingdom on him.[18] Chronicles leaves this out.

The Deuteronomistic history tells a story in which the great prophet Isaiah chastises King Hezekiah. Isaiah tells Hezekiah that because of something that the king has done, Hezekiah's sons will be eunuchs in Babylon.[19] Chronicles leaves this story out. It makes a one-verse allusion to it, without any criticism, saying only that God was testing Hezekiah.[20]

In short, Chronicles omits the negative portions of the treatment of Solomon and Hezekiah.[21]

Also, Baruch Halpern has collected evidence that there was an ancient work that told the history of the kings of Judah from Solomon to Hezekiah.[22] The Deuteronomist made some use of this work. Chronicles used it far more. The important thing about all of this for our present interest is that Solomon-to-Hezekiah was a sensible, attractive historical unit to the Aaronid priests and their supporters. Indeed, the way that Chronicles describes the people's response to Hezekiah's religious leadership is:

> And there was great joy in Jerusalem; there had been nothing like it in Jerusalem *since the days of King Solomon*. . . .[23]

The books of Chronicles reflect the language and interests of the same circle as P, and they extol Hezekiah. In this Aaronid-circle work, Hezekiah is rated the greatest king of the years in which P was produced. The Aaronid priests had a special connection with Hezekiah. And Chronicles, an Aaronid work, holds him in special esteem.

The idea that P was written in a time when the Aaronid priests were on particularly good terms with the royal house also fits with the picture in the Priestly text. The P text mentions that Aaron's wife is the sister of Nachshon ben Amminadab.[24] Nachshon is the prince of the tribe of Judah and is also the ancestor of David.[25] That is, the writer of P informs his readers that there are ties of marriage between the royal family and the priestly family.

Hezekiah's Time

Admittedly, the evidence that I have mentioned so far does not amount to absolute proof that P had to be written in King Hezekiah's time. It rather is an indicator that that particular time fits and that it is the most likely place to look. Hezekiah's reign began around the time of the fall of the northern kingdom of Israel. It was the time when there was a flow of new population into Jerusalem, when the northern Levites were a new presence on the scene, when E arrived, and most probably when J and E were combined. It was when the Aaronid priesthood of Jerusalem faced its greatest challenge since the days of Solomon.

King Hezekiah gave the Aaronids their victory. He established priestly divisions in which they were favored, he destroyed the bronze ensign of their rivals, and he destroyed all places of worship outside the Temple at which they officiated.

Hezekiah's reign also fits with the linguistic evidence and the historical evidence. P had to be written after the fall of Israel but before Jeremiah, Ezekiel, and the fall of Judah.

Hezekiah's reign is also known to have been a time of literary production in Judah. In that age, much of the books of Isaiah, Micah, Hosea, and Proverbs were produced, as well as the Solomon-to-Hezekiah historical work that later became part of Kings and Chronicles.

Perhaps most important of all is the fact that it was the age of centralization of religion. The books of Kings and Chronicles may differ in their perspectives, in their evaluations of kings, and occasionally in their facts; but they agree on this fact: Hezekiah brought about centralization. He eliminated places of worship outside of Jerusalem. On what grounds could he have justified destroying places of worship of Yahweh? Deuteronomy could not have provided the grounds, because it was not promulgated until Josiah. JE could not have served the purpose, because JE does not clearly call for centralizing religion. P, though, was perfect. It said over and over that the Tabernacle was the only place where one could sacrifice. It is hard to imagine a more ideal constitution and justification for Hezekiah's reform.

About the Author

The identification of the author of P, like those of the authors of J and E, is without a name. But, as with J and E, we have information that is probably more important. Through clues from language, architecture, archeology, other literature, and, as usual, the Bible itself, we have traced the person who produced P to a particular group in a particular place at a particular time. The author's stories and much of his law reflect the concerns of that group in the political, religious, and social issues of that time.

This person was one of the Aaronid priesthood or their spokesman. He made the case for their theology and their status through stories and accompanying laws.

Was it one person or many? The P *stories* certainly seem to be by one person. They are united around a very consistent bank of ideas and interests, their language is consistent throughout, and they stand in a specific relationship to the JE stories. When they are separated from J and E they form a continuous, flowing narrative with very few breaks.

The P *laws*, on the other hand, may well have come from a variety of collections of laws. The Holiness Code mentioned earlier, for example, might originally have been a separate Aaronid document. This writer added laws of his own day and gathered all of the legal material together to form the definitive law code. He embedded the law code in the P stories. This gave it historical context, and thus historical authority. No one had to ask from where these laws came. The text was explicit: they came from God through Moses—and Aaron.

It may seem strange to us to mix stories and law codes under the same cover. I think that this is only because of our notion of categorizing things. We should remember that our inclination toward categories is something that we inherited from the Greeks, but P (and J, E, and D) was written centuries before the great Greek philosophers were born. Prose, poetry, and law, prophecy, philosophy, and lists of begats could all meet in the Bible, and it does not seem to have bothered anybody. It is currently in vogue to debate whether the Bible is more a work of literature or a work of history. I think that the ancient Israelites, including the writer of P, would have found this a pointless question. There are no words for "history" or "literature" in biblical Hebrew. To them it was: a book.

Was P an old set of stories, told orally for a long time, that the P writer merely collected and set down? Some biblical scholars believe that much of the Bible was originally oral composition. I see no evidence at all for this in the case of P. In fact, given the way that P is constructed as an alternative to JE, oral composition seems impossible. P appeared not long after JE. There were no generations between them in which oral composition could have taken place. On the contrary, P is a carefully formulated, step-by-step construction. The writer had to have composed it with JE on the table in front of him, or else knowing JE by heart. The similarities are too many and too close, the differences are too designed.

It is customary to say that P is inferior to J and E as literature. It is true that the P writer used fewer puns and literary ironies. It is also true that many details of ages, dates, and cubits are tedious to many modern readers. Perhaps ancient readers found them tedious as well. Still, we should not be too quick to berate this man's artistry. Precisely because he portrayed a more imperfect Moses than J or E did, he produced a psychologically rich portrait. He could not deny Moses' singular place as Israel's greatest leader and prophet, but he still sought to lower the image of Moses somewhat. His intent may have been to diminish Moses, but the effect was to give us a more complex, more interesting, and more *human* Moses. His picturing Moses as striking the rock and saying "Shall *we* fetch you water" made the hero more fallible. His picturing Moses always with a veil made him more mysterious.

Besides, who is to say that the P creation story in the first chapter of the Bible is not artistically as good as anything in J or E?

The story has an ironic finish. This writer had produced his work deliberately as an alternative to the JE work. And then someone *combined* them!

CHAPTER 13

The Great Irony

THE combination of P with J, E, and D was even more extraordinary than the combination of J and E with each other had been centuries earlier. P was *polemic*—it was an answer-*torah* to J and E. JE denigrated Aaron. P denigrated Moses. JE assumed that any Levite could be a priest. P said that only men who were descendants of Aaron could be priests. JE said that there were angels, that animals occasionally could talk, and that God could be found standing on a rock or walking through the garden of Eden. P would have none of that.

D, meanwhile, came from a circle of people who were as hostile to P as the P-circle were to JE. These two priestly groups had struggled, over centuries, for priestly prerogatives, authority, income, and legitimacy.

And now someone was putting all of these works together.

Someone was combining JE with the work that was written as an alternative to it. And this person was not merely combining them side by side, as parallel stories. He or she was cutting and intersecting them intricately. And at the end of this combined, interwoven collection of the laws and stories of J, E, and P, this person set Deuteronomy, the farewell speech of Moses, as a conclusion. Someone was merging the four different, often opposing sources so artfully that it would take millennia to figure it out.

This was the person who created the Torah, the Five Books of Moses that we have read for over two thousand years. Who was this person? Why did he or she do it?

This was the first question of this book: if Moses did not produce these books, who did?

I think that it was Ezra.

An Aaronid Priest

The person who assembled the four sources into the Five Books of Moses is known as the redactor. The redactor is harder to trace than any of the authors of the sources. For the most part, the redactor was arranging texts that already existed, not writing very much of his or her own, and so there is little evidence to shed light on who he was. We do not have whole stories or long groups of laws to examine in order to deduce where he came from, what his interests were, or whom he opposed.

Still, we do know a few things about this person. To start with, the redactor came from the circle of Aaronid priests. Either he was a priest himself, or he was aligned with them and was committed to their interests. There are several reasons for this conclusion.

In the first place, he began the major sections of his work with P stories or laws, never with J or E. What are now the books of Genesis, Exodus, Leviticus, and Numbers all begin with Priestly texts.[1]

Second, he used Priestly documents as the framework for the work. The first document he used was the Book of Generations, better known as the list of "begats" to readers of the Bible, most of whom find it one of the most tedious things in the Bible. It begins:

This is the Book of Generations of humans.[2]

Then it lists the generations of humans from Adam to Jacob, telling who begat whom and giving the ages of the people on the list.

Frank Moore Cross demonstrated that the Book of Generations was originally a separate document. The person who assembled the Torah cut it into several parts and then interspersed the parts through the book of Genesis.[3] This arrangement gave the stories from the different writers organization and continuity. The redactor took the part of the document that covered the ten generations from Adam to Noah and placed it between the Adam story and the Noah story, then he took the part that covered the ten generations from Noah to Abraham and placed it between the Noah story and the Abraham stories, and so on. This gave the stories of Genesis a sensible framework, setting all of them into a flow of history.[4]

The Book of Generations was a Priestly document. Like the P stories in Genesis, the Book of Generations refers to God as Elohim, not as Yahweh. Like the P creation story, the Book of Generations says that humans are created in God's image.[5] Like many P stories and laws, the Book of Generations is concerned with repetitious details of names and dates.

That is, the redactor used a Priestly document as the structuring text of the book of Genesis.

The redactor also used a Priestly text as the structure for the next fifteen chapters of the Bible—the stories of the enslavement of the Israelites and the exodus from Egypt. The text he used was the P version of the plagues that Yahweh inflicted upon the Egyptians. Simply put, he used the language of the P version to give unity to the different sources. In the P version, each of the plagues on the Egyptians was followed by the words:

But Pharaoh's heart was strengthened, and he did not listen to them, as Yahweh had spoken.[6]

The redactor inserted words similar to these following plagues in the JE stories as well.[7] Then, when he combined the P plague stories and the JE plague stories, the common endings gave the whole combined story a unity. The point is that the redactor was using *Priestly* documents as the governing structure of the work.

Third, he added texts of his own, and these new texts were in the typical language and interests of P. I shall refer to some of these texts below, and I have listed all of them in the Appendix. For now, let it suffice to say that they are so much like the P texts in their language that for a long time investigators thought that they were part of P itself.

Professor Cross went even further. He concluded that P and R (redactor) were virtually the same thing. He argued that there were major gaps in the flow of the P story. Since the P story was incomplete, and the structure of the work came from Priestly documents, Cross concluded that there never was a separate P source. Rather, he said, a single person (or circle) wrote the P portions of the Pentateuch around the JE portions in the first place. This same person fashioned the framework that held all the stories together. The redaction and the Priestly writing were all one process.

On this point I have disagreed with my teacher. As indicated in the preceding chapters, the P narrative appears to me to be a continuous, consistent story. If J and E are separated from it, we can read this story with hardly a gap. Where the gaps do occur, they are explainable in terms of the priestly author's interests, as I described in the last chapter. If we look at the biblical flood story with the two sources separated, we can see that each story is complete. Likewise with the rebellion story (Korah, Dathan, Abiram). Likewise with the two stories of the splitting of the Red Sea, and with the two stories of the event at Mount Sinai. In each case, the Priestly story is not written around the J or E story. It rather appears to be an originally separate, continuous, consistent story, which someone else has combined with the earlier version. Also, there is the matter of the P stories being *alternative* versions of the J and E stories. What would have been the point of the P author's writing these alternative presentations of the stories if he was combining them with the very texts to which they were alternative?

Still, even though I was persuaded by the evidence that the Priestly writer and the redactor were two different persons, I was also persuaded by Professor Cross that the redactor was himself from the Aaronid priestly family, using priestly documents and priestly terminology.

There is a way of distinguishing the original P texts from the Priestly redactor's insertions, which I shall discuss below. But, again, the point for now is that the redactor came from the same group as the P writer. His work explicitly expressed a priest's concerns and interests, he used P language, he started each major section of his work with a P text, and he framed the work with priestly documents.

It is not really surprising to find that the redactor was a priest. The majority of the stories and all of the law that we have looked at so far have turned out to be by priests (E, P, and D). Priests had access to documents and the religious authority to promulgate the documents. Part of the priests' official function was to teach law and tradition.[8] It is only natural that the priests who produced P and the Deuteronomistic history (which probably included JE) should have passed their works along to other priests, and that these documents should have been preserved in priestly circles. Then a moment in history came when a priest saw value in putting them together.

In the Days of the Second Temple

That moment had to be in the days of the second Temple. The sources—J, E, P, and D (Dtr[1] and Dtr[2])—were not all completed until shortly before that time. Also, if we look at what this priest added to these sources, we can see clues pointing even more specifically to the moment of creation of the final work.

For example, he added chapter 15 of the book of Numbers. It is a chapter of laws that is separated from all the other priestly laws. For some reason it was inserted between chapters that contain stories, rather than among the other laws. It is in between the spy story and the rebellion story. It is written in typical priestly language, and it is about a typical priestly concern: sacrifice.

It is too typical. It deals with regular sacrifice, holiday sacrifice, sacrifices of vows, and individual sacrifices for sin through error. These are all things that were dealt with already in P.[9] This chapter is largely a doublet, repeating things that have already been said, while adding some offerings to the list.

But there is one striking difference: Numbers 15 never mentions the Tabernacle.

The absence of any mention of the Tabernacle in a text that

duplicates priestly laws of sacrifice is no coincidence. Elsewhere in P
it is emphasized over and over that the Tabernacle is crucial to sacrifice. There cannot *be* any sacrifice except at the entrance of the
Tabernacle. This other text, Numbers 15, appears to come from a
time when priests could no longer insist on the presence of the Tabernacle for sacrifice. It fits the days of the second Temple, when the
Tabernacle no longer existed.

The second Temple had no Tabernacle, no cherubs, and no ark.
Yet sacrifices were made there. Numbers 15 appears to be the text
that created a link between the old days and the new, between the
first Temple and the second. It had to be written either in Jerusalem
as a second Temple law, or while still in Babylonian exile, as a
program for the future.

There is another insertion that is more revealing. The P source
gives laws about holidays in Leviticus 23. The text there lists the
three main holidays—the feast of Passover, the feast of Weeks, and
the feast of Booths—and also the new year and Day of Atonement
holidays. This holiday list is plainly marked. It begins (verse 4) and
ends (verse 37) with the words "These are the holidays of Yahweh."
But then, two verses after the end of the list (verse 39), suddenly
there is another law about one of the holidays: the feast of Booths.
This additional law, which is disconnected from all the other holiday
laws, says that on this holiday which is called "Booths" (Hebrew:
Sukkot) the people are actually supposed to build booths (i.e., huts
or tents) and live in them for a week. The text says that this practice
is to remind the people that their ancestors lived in temporary structures in the wilderness after they left Egypt. The text lists species of
trees that are to be used on this holiday. [10]

What is this all about? Why does this one law about one particular practice on one holiday appear separately, after the end of the
holiday section? The answer lies in the days of the second Temple.
According to the book of Nehemiah, when Ezra gathered the people
at the water gate to read the Torah to them, they found something
in the Torah that apparently was brand-new to them: a law that
prescribed actually living in booths on the feast of Booths. The text
is explicit that this law had never before been observed in the entire
history of the country. It says:

The children of Israel had not done so from the days of Joshua son
of Nun until that day. [11]

Now, this event in the days of Ezra refers to the passage in Leviticus about the booths. It even mentions the same species of trees that are listed in Leviticus. And so we have an oddly placed law in Leviticus, and we have a report that this oddly placed law was never part of the people's life or tradition until the days of the second Temple. This fits with the other evidence that the final stage of the formation of the Five Books of Moses was in the days of the second Temple.

This makes perfect sense. The second Temple days were the time when the Aaronid priests were in authority. There were no more kings. Rival priesthoods had been superseded. It is really no surprise that an Aaronid priest of the second Temple days should have been the redactor of the final work. This was the time, as never before, that the priests had the authority to promulgate the work—and to enforce it.

Ezra

One Aaronid priest in particular had all this power: Ezra. He had the backing of the emperor. He had enforcement powers. Even though he was not the High Priest, he had enormous authority. And his authority was directly linked to a scroll that he brought to Judah, a scroll that is identified as "the Torah of Moses which Yahweh God of Israel gave."[12]

As I said in Chapter 8, in the entire Bible only two men are known as lawgivers: Moses and Ezra. Ezra was a priest, a lawgiver, and a *scribe*. He had access to documents. And the biblical biography of Ezra is explicit about which documents interested him. It says:

Ezra had set his heart on seeking out Yahweh's Torah. . . .[13]

It also says:

He was a ready scribe in the Torah of Moses.[14]

It also reports that the emperor authorized him to teach and enforce

the law of your God which is in your hand.[15]

The first time that we find the full Torah of Moses in Judah, it is
in Ezra's possession. He sought it out, he was a scribe who worked
with it, he personally carried it to Jerusalem, and he personally gave
it its first public reading. And when he read it to the people, they
heard things that they had never heard before.

This does not prove that it absolutely had to be Ezra who fashioned the Five Books of Moses. But he was in the right priestly
family, in the right profession, in the right place, in the right time,
with the authority, and with the first known copy of the book in his
hand. If it was not Ezra himself who composed the work, then it was
someone close to him—a relative, a colleague in the priesthood, a
fellow scribe—because it could not have been produced very long
before he arrived with it in Judah. The Temple had been standing
for only about one generation when he came to Jerusalem.

In light of all this, it is fascinating that there actually was an
ancient tradition about Ezra and the Torah of Moses. The tradition
says that the original scroll of the Torah (and other books of the
Bible) was burned up in the fire that destroyed the Temple in 587
B.C. but that Ezra was able to restore it by a revelation. This tradition is preserved in a work called the Fourth Book of Ezra. This book
is not part of the Bible. It is rather part of the collection known as
the Pseudepigrapha, which are works written by Christians and Jews
between 200 B.C. and 200 A.D. The Fourth Book of Ezra comes
from around 100 A.D. In it, God speaks to Ezra from a *bush*. Ezra
says:

The world lies in darkness, and its inhabitants are without light.
For your law has been burned, and so no one knows the things
which have been done or will be done by you. If then I have found
favor before you, send the Holy Spirit to me, and I will write
everything that has happened in the world from the beginning, the
things which were written in your Law.[16]

Ezra then recites the lost texts for forty days.

Not to overstate the importance of this relatively late text, the
point of this is simply that already in early times Ezra was associated

with the production of the sacred text. Even Jerome, in the fourth century A.D., said:

> ... whether you choose to call Moses the author of the Pentateuch or Ezra the renewer of the same work, I raise no objection.[17]

Modern investigators, too, have occasionally expressed the suspicion that Ezra was the man who fashioned the Five Books of Moses. In the present state of our knowledge, the evidence seems to me to point with high likelihood to Ezra, the priest, scribe, and lawgiver who came to the land with the Torah of Moses in his hand.

The Combination

And so the nineteenth-century investigators who said that the Priestly writer came from second Temple days were partly right. The *final* Priestly hand on these texts was from those days. His Priestly *source* (P) was from earlier (Hezekiah) days.

Why did he do it? Why commit this extraordinary irony, combining texts that were diametrically opposed to each other?

He did it, presumably, for the same reasons that J and E had been combined about 250 years earlier. By this time, all of his source texts were famous. J and E had been around for centuries and were quoted in D. P had been around since Hezekiah's days, it had been associated with a national reform, and it had the support of the priesthood that was in power. D had been read publicly in the days of Josiah, and it contained a law requiring that it be read again publicly every seven years.[18] How could the redactor have left any of these out? The issue again was successful promulgation. Who would have believed that it was the Torah of Moses if it did not include the famous stories of Adam and Eve (J), the golden calf (E), Phinehas (P), and Moses' farewell speech (D)?

Besides, there were groups who supported these various texts. The Shiloh Levite priests who had produced E and D may not have been in priestly power in the second Temple days, but that did not mean that they did not exist. They could still raise their voices and protest the authenticity of a Torah that did not include their texts. Indeed, the combination of all the sources in this period may have been precisely as a compromise among various factions of Israelite-Judean society.

The question still remains as to why the redactor had to mix them all together. Why not just preserve them all side by side like the four Gospels of the New Testament? The difference was that by Ezra's time all of the sources apparently had come to be attributed to Moses. What was the redactor to do? He could not have two or three different texts all be by Moses, especially when they sometimes contradicted each other. And so he took on the enormous, intricate, and ironic task of combining these alternative versions of the same stories into one work.

Method

How does one set out on a task like that? It could not be done according to any existing guidelines, because it was a one-time effort, unique, a response to a very specific need at a particular moment in history. It could not be done in any systematic way, because the source texts were so diverse. They were in prose and poetry. They included stories, laws, lists, and architectural instructions. The person who set out to assemble them had to have exceptional literary sensitivity and exceptional skills. He had to have a sense of which contradictions were tolerable to readers and which were not. He had to make the jagged edges smooth, to make pieces of stories that were never meant to go together flow comfortably.

His only guideline seems to have been to retain as much of the original texts as possible without intolerable contradictions. The evidence of this is that when we separate JE from P in Genesis, Exodus, Leviticus, and Numbers, each flows sensibly on its own with very few gaps in its story. There are few signs of the redactor's having cut anything.

He had to solve problems involving different sorts of contradictions and repetitions at each new turn. He could not start with a single overarching decision of method. There was no one critical decision to be made. He had to make hundreds of correct decisions in order to turn his diverse sources into a flowing, sensible narrative.

His first decision was what to do with two creation stories. He chose to keep them both, back to back. The first one, Genesis 1 (P), had a broader, more cosmic perspective, and the second one (J) had a more earthly, human-centered perspective. Placed beside each other, they simply appeared to be a broad presentation of the major acts of the creation followed by a more specific focus on particular aspects of it. The fact that the order of events changed and that the name of the deity changed apparently did not trouble him. That is not an indictment of his logic or of his skill. He simply was able to live with these sorts of developments, as were his readers for the next two millennia.

Next came the J stories of Adam and Eve and of Cain and Abel. These stories involved close personal contacts with the deity, plus cherubs (real ones, not statues),[19] powerful plants (tree of life, tree of knowledge of good and bad), and a talking snake. P had no equivalents of such stories, and so the redactor was free simply to place the J texts after the two creation stories.

Then he inserted the first ten begats from the Book of Generations, which ended with Noah.

At that point, the redactor came to the first real challenge of his unique task. He had two flood stories. They were both complete. They had definite similarities and blatant differences. The J flood story was about forty days of rain. The P flood story was about a year-long cosmic crisis. The J story had fourteen of the clean animals and two of the unclean. The P story had two of each. The J story had Noah sending out three doves (or one dove three times) at the end. The P story had one raven.

There was no way that the redactor could place these two back to back as he had done with the creation stories. But apparently he was not prepared to discard one or the other either. And so he attempted to combine them into one story that would still make sense—and still be a good story. His final product was the first text I used in this book (Chapter 2, pages 54–59).

He cut the two stories up and wove the corresponding pieces together perfectly. Now the rain in J appeared to be nothing more than another reference to the waters that were spilling through the cosmic firmament of P. Now the "two-of-each" animals in P were understood to mean that the fourteen of each of J's clean animals came to the ark "two by two." Now the raven from P was understood to have flown away from the ark and not returned, so that Noah had to send out doves to see if the floodwaters had subsided. It was a brilliant synthesis of the two stories, all apparently without deleting a word of either of the original texts. And it worked for two and a half millennia.

This method of segmenting the stories and weaving the corresponding parts together worked so well that the redactor used it to assemble the P story of Korah with the JE story of Dathan and Abiram. He also used it to fashion the spy story, the story of the plagues in Egypt, and the story of the splitting of the Red Sea.

But he was not bound to this method. In some cases he chose to cut the P story into several small pieces and distribute these pieces through several JE stories. In this manner, he scattered the P components of the Jacob-and-Esau story through the much longer JE account of the twin brothers. He did the same with the short P record of the migration to Egypt, spreading its pieces through fourteen chapters of the JE story of Joseph.

In the case of the story of the rebellion at Peor, as we saw, he cut off the beginning of the P story and the end of the JE story to create the continuity he sought. Did it bother him that the seductive women were Moabite in the first half of the story and Midianite in the second half? Apparently not.

In other cases, he chose to separate the two versions of doublet stories, thus depicting them as separate events. For example, he placed the JE story of the covenant with Abraham at Genesis 15 and the P story of this covenant at Genesis 17, with another story in between the two. And so now the two versions of the Abrahamic covenant appeared to be picturing two separate meetings between God and Abraham. Even more dramatic was the redactor's separation of the two stories of Moses' getting water from the rock. The JE version now is located at Exodus 17. The P version comes two books later, in Numbers 20. Separated, they appear to tell about two different incidents, separated by years and distance, even though they both occur at places with the same name.

Thus some repetitions and contradictions were tolerable to him, and some were not. He was not prepared to have two floods that each destroy all the world except for a man named Noah. But he was willing to have Moses strike two rocks at two places called Meribah. He was willing to have Moses repeat the Ten Commandments in his farewell address in Deuteronomy 5, even though they came out differently there from the way they appeared in Exodus 20. In Exodus 20, the fourth commandment is:

> Remember the sabbath day to sanctify it . . . *because in six days Yahweh made the heavens and the earth, the sea and all that is in them, and he rested on the seventh day. Therefore Yahweh blessed the sabbath day and sanctified it.* [20]

But in Deuteronomy, when Moses repeats the commandment, he says that it was:

> Keep the sabbath day to sanctify it . . . *and you shall remember that you were a slave in the land of Egypt, and Yahweh your God brought you out from there with a strong hand and an outstretched arm. Therefore Yahweh your God commanded you to observe the sabbath day.* [21]

The first version is from P, and it quotes the P creation story for its reason for keeping the sabbath: because God rested on the seventh day. The second version is from D, and it gives a common D reason for keeping commandments: because God freed you from slavery. To the redactor, and to his readers, the two different wordings of the same commandment were compatible. (It is interesting to note that one of the Dead Sea Scrolls collapses these two texts and simply lists both reasons for keeping the sabbath side by side.) [22]

In all of this, no one method governs the process. The redactor's texts were diverse and complicated, and he was wise enough and skillful enough to handle each case according to his judgment of what it needed.

Continuity

The redactor still had to give the entire collection of pieces a meaningful organization. There had to be continuity. In part, the continuity was provided by the nature of the texts themselves. What made all of the stories naturally fit together was that they were all set in history. All of the texts pictured events in the order in which they were understood to have occurred in historical sequence.

That may seem so obvious as to be petty to us. But that is only because we live in a postbiblical (and post-Greek) world. *The Bible was the first attempt at writing history.* We may argue about whether it is good history-writing or bad—I would say that it is mostly very good—but the fact remains that it is the *first* history writing. The only things that come close to it in the ancient Near East are royal annals like the Sennacherib Prism Inscription, which record the kings' military campaigns, naming places conquered and spoils taken. But these are more like reports or lists than actual history. The first known extensive works of national history were precisely the sources that this redactor was assembling.

The redactor organized these sources into the flow of history by using three documents. The first was the Book of Generations. He cut up its long record of who begat whom, and then he distributed the pieces at the appropriate points in the stories from Adam to Jacob. By doing this, he gave a historical continuity to the entire book of Genesis.

The second document he used was the P plagues narrative. He used its language of "Pharaoh's heart was strengthened" as a framework that united the various JE and P stories of the exodus from Egypt. The structure covered the first twelve chapters of the book of Exodus, up to the moment of the people's departure from Egypt.[23]

His third document was a list of the stops that the Israelites made during their forty years in the wilderness. This itinerary list is now located in the book of Numbers, chapter 33. It begins with the explicit statement:

These are the journeys of the children of Israel who went out from the land of Egypt. . . .

Then it goes on to list each of the places they went, starting with the city of Rameses in Egypt, continuing through all their encampments in the wilderness, and ending with their arrival at the Jordan River, the doorstep of the promised land. Most biblical scholars had thought that this list was merely a summary of all of the places mentioned in the stories up to that point, but Frank Cross demonstrated that the list was originally an independent document like the Book of Generations. The redactor used this list as a framework for the wilderness stories, just as he had used the Book of Generations for the Genesis stories and the P plagues narrative for the Egypt stories. He distributed the pieces of the list of the people's journeys through the text, setting each of his stories in its appropriate place. This gave the same sort of continuity to the books of Exodus (starting at chapter 12), Leviticus, and Numbers that he had given to Genesis.[24]

Deuteronomy was already a continuous unit, depicting the last words and actions of Moses. All that the redactor had to do to fit it in was to move the JE and P stories of Moses' death to the end of Deuteronomy. The last chapter of Deuteronomy (chapter 34) is now a combination of all three versions of Moses' death (JE, P, and D).[25]

The redactor's contribution also included his adding occasional verses to enhance the transitions and combinations of his sources and to clarify or emphasize points that were especially important to him. He also added a few passages that were important in his own day, including the sacrificial laws in Numbers 15, the law about booths, a passage emphasizing the sabbath,[26] and a passage about returning from exile.[27]

This redactor was an Aaronid priest like the person who produced P. But, ironically, his task was the exact opposite of that earlier person's. The person who produced P was fashioning a work that was an alternative to earlier sources (JE). The redactor was fashioning a work that *reconciled* opposing sources. This was the key I found which, I believe, along with other supporting evidence, made it possible to separate P and the redactor's work from each other. The P texts struggled with the other sources. The redactor's text embraced them.

The First Bible

When the redactor included Deuteronomy among his sources, he achieved an additional effect which he may not even have intended. Deuteronomy was now both the last book of the Torah and the first book of the Deuteronomistic history. There was now a natural continuity from Genesis to the end of 2 Kings. The American biblical scholar David Noel Freedman has called this eleven-book continuous story the Primary History (Genesis, Exodus, Leviticus, Numbers, Deuteronomy, Joshua, Judges, 1 and 2 Samuel, 1 and 2 Kings). He has also referred to it as "The First Bible."

That really is a useful way to look at it. The Primary History formed the core around which the rest of the Bible was built. It told the stories of the events that set the stage for everything that was to happen later: the creation, the birth of the people, the settlement in the land, the establishment of the messianic line. It contained the four major covenants (Noah, Abraham, Sinai, David). The various prophets could be understood against the background of the history it told. Isaiah could be understood better when seen against the background of the reign of Hezekiah, in which he lived. Jeremiah could be understood better against the background of Josiah. The rest of the books of the Hebrew Bible (Old Testament) and the New Testament likewise came to be understood by the communities who preserved them in the context of the central events of the Primary History. That is why I chose to concentrate on these particular books here, and that is why the redactor's work was so important to the formation of the Bible.

Artistry Upon Artistry

The redactor, whom I identify as Ezra, has been the least appreciated of the contributors to the Five Books of Moses. Usually, more credit is given to the authors of the stories and the laws. That may be an error. The redactor was as much an artist, in his own way, as the authors of J, E, P, and D were in theirs. His contribution was certainly as significant as theirs. His task was not merely difficult, it was creative. It called for wisdom and literary sensitivity at each step, as well as a skill that is no less an art than storytelling. In the end, he was the one who created the work that we have read all these years. He assembled the final form of the stories and laws that, in thousands of ways, have influenced millions.

Is that *his* influence? Or is it the influence of the authors of the sources? Or would it be better to speak of a literary partnership of all these contributors, a partnership that most of them never even knew would take place? How many ironies are contained in this partnership that was spread over centuries? How many new developments and ideas resulted from the combination of all their contributions?

In short, the question for the last chapter of this book is: is the Bible more than the sum of its parts?

CHAPTER 14

The World
That the
Bible Produced

The Final Product

Is the Bible more than the sum of its parts?

Of course.

The mixing of the different stories, laws, poems, and points of view produced things that none of the authors dreamed of.

The author of E composed the story of Abraham's near-sacrifice of his son Isaac, one of the most famous, intriguing, and troubling stories in the Bible. It is the story of Abraham's being so committed to his God's will that he is even prepared to sacrifice his son. Divine intervention stops him and saves Isaac's life at the last instant.

The author of P, perhaps a hundred years later, composed the story of Abraham's buying the cave of Machpelah. Abraham buys the cave as a family burial plot because his wife Sarah has died.

The redactor, about two hundred years later, placed the story of Sarah's death and the purchase of the cave right after the story of the sacrifice of Isaac. The sacrifice of Isaac is in Genesis 22; the death of Sarah is in Genesis 23.

Interpreters ever since have suggested that perhaps the cause of

Sarah's death was that she saw her son being taken to be sacrificed, and she died of grief. That was not planned by the person who wrote E, nor by the person who wrote P. Even the redactor may not have intended it.[1] But it works. The mere juxtaposition of the two texts added another human element to the story. It added a new level psychologically. It opened up new possibilities of interpretation. It raised new questions and invited new answers.

There are hundreds, perhaps thousands, of examples of such new elements and ideas being born out of the mixing of the sources— new twists in the stories, new psychological levels, and new possibilities for interpretation. We still have barely begun to appreciate the impact of the Bible's extraordinary history on the way that the book came out.

Most remarkable of all, that history affected the Bible's picture of the relationship between God and humankind.

In the Image of God

In the story of creation in Genesis 1, God creates humans, male and female, in his image. The meaning of "in the image of God" is uncertain. Does it mean a physical image—that God has a face and body like ours? or a spiritual image? or an intellectual image? Whatever it means, though, we can say, at minimum, that the Bible pictures humans as participating in the divine in some way that an animal does not. There is something of God in humans, and this something is crucial to the events in Eden following the creation.

The humans are prohibited from eating the fruit of the tree of the knowledge of good and bad. The snake leads them to eat it anyway. What does the snake say that brings humans to do this? He tells the woman that if they eat from the tree, "you will be *like God. . . .*"[2] Now, in the Bible's terms, this argument would not have worked on a beast or a bird or a fish, because they do not participate in the divine. Only humans are created in God's image, and so only humans would aspire to the divine. The creation in the image of God in Genesis 1 is thus crucial to understanding what the humans do in Eden in Genesis 3.

But Genesis 1 and Genesis 3 are by two different people. The Eden story is from J, which never suggests that humans are created in God's image. The creation account is from P, which never includes powerful plants or talking snakes. And the redactor included both stories whole, so we cannot tell whether he was even aware of this exquisite coalescence of the two or not.

The combination of J and P here produced something that was more than the sum of the pieces. The story was now richer, with new interpretive possibilities. It set the humans' acts in Eden in a whole new light. God creates them in the divine image, and then he forbids them the fruit whose attraction is precisely to endow one with a divine power. He shares some divine quality with humans alone, and then he treats them as subordinates. He tells them to rule the other creatures, and then he communicates with them almost exclusively by commands. The scene is set so firmly for the humans to disobey that it probably has never come as a surprise to any reader when the humans are persuaded by the news that "When you eat from the tree you will be like God," and they eat the fruit.

As Mark Twain put it, "If the Lord didn't want them to be rebellious, why did he create them in his image?"

That is only one way of looking at the text. There are a hundred other possible interpretations, some more reverent and some cynical. And that is just the point. The mixing of the sources into one text enriched the interpretive possibilities of the Bible for all time.

Cosmic and Personal

The combination of the sources did more than just affect individual Bible stories. It had an impact on the biblical conception of God.

J, E, and D pictured God in very personal ways: moving around on the earth, taking visible forms, engaging in discussion and even debate with humans. P's conception was more of a cosmic, transcendent deity.

P's creation story begins with the creation of the cosmic structure: light and darkness, day and night, seas and dry land, the "firmament" and heavenly bodies. J's creation story is literally more down-to-earth. It begins with making vegetation possible, followed by the creation of humans, plants, and animals—without a single reference to light and darkness, the heavenly bodies, or even the seas.

In their own terms, P is the story of "heaven and earth," J is the story of "earth and heaven."

P's flood story is a cosmic crisis: the windows of the heavens and the fountains of the deep are broken up. The water that is above the firmament is spilling down. The water that is below the earth's surface is bursting up. The habitable part of the universe is a bubble of air surrounded by water, and the threatening waters are bursting in from above and below. J's flood story, meanwhile, is simply forty days and forty nights of rain.

In P's creation and flood stories, God remains above and beyond, commanding and controlling humans and nature. In J's story, Yahweh personally walks in the Garden of Eden, makes the humans' first clothes, closes the ark, and smells Noah's sacrifice.

In E's story of Moses' striking the rock at Meribah, God is standing on the rock. In P's version of the story, he is not.

In J's story of Mount Sinai, Yahweh personally descends on the mountain in fire.[3] In P he does not.[4]

In J and in E, Moses actually sees God.[5] In P he does not.

In J, Abraham pleads with God over the fate of the cities of Sodom and Gomorrah,[6] and Moses pleads with God over the fate of the people in the spy story.[7] In E, as well, Moses pleads over the people's fate in the golden calf story, and later he pleads passionately and eloquently with a God he has come to know "the way a man talks to a fellow man."[8] He can even say to God himself, "Why have you injured me?" and "If you treat me this way, then kill me."[9] In D, Moses pleads with God to let him live to arrive in the promised land, but God refuses.[10] P never has humans speaking to God with such intimacy.

In P, God is more transcendent, more distant. He gives commandments, and his will is done.[11]

In D, meanwhile, Moses tells the people:

This commandment that I command you today is not too awesome for you, and it is not distant.

It is not in the heavens, [that people would] say, "Who will go up to the heavens for us and take it for us and make it known to us so we will do it?"

> And it is not across the sea, [that people would] say, "Who will cross the sea for us and take it for us and make it known to us so we will do it?"
>
> But the word is very close to you, in your mouth, and in your heart, to do it.[12]

Not to overstate the case, God is sometimes pictured as personal in P, and he is sometimes pictured as transcendent in J, E, and D. But the difference overall is still blatant and profound. When the redactor combined all the sources, he mixed two different pictures of God.

By doing that, he formed a new balance between the personal and the transcendent qualities of the deity. It was a picture of God as both universal and intensely personal. Yahweh was the creator of the cosmos, but also "the God of your father." The fusion was artistically dramatic and theologically profound, but it was also filled with a new tension. It was now picturing human beings coming into close personal dialogue with the all-powerful master of the universe.

It was a balance that none of the individual authors had intended. But that balance, intended or not, came to be at the heart of Judaism and Christianity. Like Jacob at Peni-El, both religions have lived and struggled ever since with a cosmic yet personal deity. That applies to the most sophisticated theologian and to the simplest believer. Ultimate things are at stake, but every human being is told, "The master of the universe is concerned with you." An extraordinary idea. But, again, it was not planned by any of the authors. It was probably not even the redactor's design. It was so embedded in the texts that the redactor could not have helped but produce the new mixture as long as he was at all true to his sources.

Justice and Mercy

There was another, even more paradoxical result of the union of the sources. It created a new dynamic between Yahweh's justice and his mercy.

Recall that P never once uses the word "mercy." It also never uses the words "grace" or "repentance." It never refers to the faithfulness of Yahweh. The priest who wrote it rather emphasized the divine aspect of justice. That is, you get what you deserve. Obedience is rewarded. Transgression is punished. There is no throwing oneself on the mercy of the divine judge.

J and E are virtually the opposite. They emphasize the divine aspect of mercy. Transgression can be forgiven through repentance. God is gracious and generously faithful to his covenant. In J's depiction of the ultimate human experience of the divine, when Moses actually sees God on Sinai, Yahweh declares that he is

Yahweh, merciful and gracious God, long-forbearing, and abundant in faithfulness . . . [13]

The words that P never mentions occur about seventy times in J, E, and D.

It is not just a matter of vocabulary. J, E, and D also develop the idea of the deity as merciful through the stories they tell far more than P does. In the E story of the golden calf, Yahweh at first declares that he will destroy the entire people and start a new people descended from Moses instead. But Moses appeals to Yahweh's mercy, and the deity relents. [14] In the J spy story, the same thing happens. Yahweh says that he will destroy the nation and start over with Moses. Moses appeals again to his compassion, and again he relents. [15]

The author of P rejected this depiction of God. In his version of the spy story, Yahweh decides the people's fate, and there is no further plea from Moses.

Again, it would be a mistake to draw the line too absolutely between the sources. J, E, and D occasionally can picture God as acting strictly according to justice, and P can picture his mercy. But, on the whole, the distinction between them is apparent and dramatic. P's focus primarily is on divine justice. The other sources' focus is on divine mercy.

And the redactor combined them. When he did that, he created a new *formula*, in which justice and mercy stood in a balance in which they had never been before. They were more nearly equal than they had been in any of the source texts. God was both just and merciful, angry and compassionate, strict and forgiving. It became a powerful tension in the God of the Bible. It was a new and exceedingly complex formula. But that was the formula that became a crucial part of Judaism and of Christianity for two and a half millennia.

The justice-and-mercy balance is more charged—psychologically as well as theologically—than the cosmic-and-personal balance. There is a constant tension in Yahweh between his justice and his mercy. They are not easily reconcilable. When should one predominate, and when should the other?

Everyone who has ever been a parent—or a child—knows the problem. The parent says, "If you do that, then you're going to be punished." But the child does it. And then the parent must decide what to do. Justice says: punish. But then there is also compassion. What happens in most families is that a balance develops between the two, a balance in which sometimes discipline prevails and sometimes forgiving. Probably few parents could name all of the factors that make them decide this way on one occasion and that way on another. The conflicting factors include, not least of all, the emotions anger and love.

In the combined biblical text, God is as torn as any loving parent. He makes a covenant with humans, and the contract has terms. When they break the terms, his immediate just response could be anything from termination of the covenant to the arrival of any of the horrible entries on the covenant curse lists in Leviticus 26 and Deuteronomy 28. But his mercy nearly always delays and/or tempers his execution of justice.

The often-repeated image of the "Old Testament God of justice and anger" has always been only half of the real picture. It is as if those who say it have only read P and not the rest of the text. Ironically, this image appears to be based usually on the legal principle of "an eye for an eye and a tooth for a tooth."[16] But that principle applies to *human* justice. In the biblical accounts, the deity almost always acts more compassionately than that.

And so the two religions developed around a Bible that pictured God as a loving and faithful but sometimes angry parent. To whatever extent this picture makes the Bible more real for its readers, to that extent the redactor was more successful than perhaps he even intended to be. To whatever extent the tension between God's justice and mercy *itself* became an important factor in the Bible's story, to that extent the Bible is, once again, more than the sum of its parts.

In a very real way, the Bible is greater than the individuals who wrote it.

Synthesis

And so we have, in a sense, come a full cycle back to dealing with the Bible as a whole. That is perhaps what has been lacking in much of the research on the authors of the Bible thus far. It has often been a tearing-down without a putting-back-together. And that may be, in part, why this sort of analysis so offended the faithful of Christianity and Judaism. For a long time it appeared that the aim of the enterprise was to take the Bible apart and arrive at numerous pieces, none of which was the Bible any longer. Perhaps that was as far as the enterprise could go in its early stages. However, we are now at a point at which our discoveries concerning the Bible's origins can mean an enhanced understanding and appreciation of the Bible in its final, developed form.

We have come a considerable distance from the early hints of the medieval scholars. What began as an interest in some puzzling passages in the Five Books of Moses led to the suggestion that a few lines of those books were not by Moses himself. This was followed by the suggestion that larger portions of the text were by someone other than Moses. Then investigators isolated several separate, continuous works and identified them by characteristics of language and content. And then we began to refine our identification of each of these works and to observe the process of the formation of the Bible.

As the investigation was advancing in this way, new breakthroughs were being made in archeology and in our understanding of the social and political history of the biblical world. It is through the merger of what we have learned from these literary and historical enterprises that we have arrived at the picture presented here, a picture of the formation of the Bible that is inseparable from the history of its writers' world. It is in the context of a divided kingdom of Israel and Judah that we find two writers who fashioned two versions of their people's story, J and E. Each version was intimately associated with the life of the community from which it came—one from Israel by an advocate of the priestly family of Shiloh and possibly a descendant of Moses, and one from Judah by an advocate of the Davidic royal house. It is in the context of the fall of the Israelite kingdom and the reunion of the divided peoples that we find someone uniting the two versions, forging a single story that might serve the reunited community.

Similarly, I believe that we find the historical context of the Priestly work in the age of King Hezekiah. It was an age in which priestly divisions of status were established, with the Aaronid priesthood of Jerusalem enjoying a favored position. The Priestly work (P) was that priesthood's alternative to the JE work, which reflected a different, often hostile view of God, of history, and particularly of their ancestor Aaron.

Their opponents for priestly status, the Shilonite (possibly Mushite) priesthood, in turn, found their moment in the age of King Josiah. It was an age in which the law code which they had preserved was royally endorsed as the book of the Torah (D). An advocate of that priesthood, Jeremiah or possibly Baruch, fashioned a history that flowed from Moses and that law code to the writer's own historical moment (Dtr[1]). The death of Josiah and the fall of the kingdom moved the author to produce a new edition of the history, taking the new, catastrophic historical circumstances into account (Dtr[2]).

The joining of these parts into a continuous story, "the first Bible," is also to be found in historical context, reflecting the life of a community returning from exile, looking forward to rebuilding their country and their place and mode of worship. It was an age when all of the parts had become too well known to ignore. The scribe who was responsible for this redaction (R)—whom I identify as Ezra—was an advocate of the Aaronid priests who rose to leadership in this age. He was responsive to their concerns and to the situation of his people generally in that moment. He preserved their valued works in a form that could be accepted for millennia and that could be the context in which other sacred texts would be understood.

The Bible is thus a synthesis of history and literature, sometimes in harmony and sometimes in tension, but utterly inseparable. And, I believe, the recovery of much of this history and the appreciation of this synthesis are now, after centuries, finally within our sight.

Whence and Whither

What are we to do with this knowledge?

Until now, the search for who wrote the Bible has been mainly in the realm of the study of history. For the most part, the investigators were interested in the history of religion, the history of Israel, or the history of the formation of the Bible itself.

Those who write on the Bible as literature and those whose interest has been the religious study of the Bible—i.e., the Bible as *sacred* literature—have rarely put this knowledge to use. This was due in part to a perception that this kind of analysis would be threatening to religion. It was also due to the fact that the analysis was incomplete. There were large gaps in our knowledge about the authors: when they lived, why they wrote, the relationship between what they wrote and the events of their world.

But the situation has changed. The threat to religion never really materialized. Wellhausen said that he resigned from teaching this subject to theology students because he was "incapacitating them for their office." But the experience of subsequent generations has apparently proved him wrong. Many—probably most—Protestant, Catholic, and Jewish clergy have now been learning, and teaching, this subject for over a century and have managed to reconcile it with their beliefs and traditions.

The seeds of that reconciliation were present from the days of the earliest investigators. Simply put, the question all along was not "Who *inspired* the Bible?" or "Who *revealed* the Bible?" The question was only which human beings actually composed it. Whether they did so at divine direction, dictation, or inspiration was always a matter of faith. Joseph ben Eliezer Bonfils, perhaps the first Jewish scholar to say outright about a verse of the Torah, "Moses did not write this," made this point six hundred years ago. He said:

... insofar as we are to believe in the received words and in the words of prophecy, what is it to me if Moses wrote it or if another prophet wrote it, since the words of all of them are truth and through prophecy.[17]

The Christian writer Andreas von Maes suggested over four hundred years ago that an editor, perhaps Ezra, at least inserted explanatory words and phrases. But von Maes, too, said that for the faithful there was no need to quarrel over which human hands recorded the text:

But in truth there is no great need for contending concerning the writer, as long as we believe that God is the author, both of the events themselves and of the words wherewith they have been communicated to us. . . . [18]

The challenge that this investigation presents is not to the belief in the revealed or inspired character of the Bible, but to traditions about which humans actually wrote it on the parchment.

The incomplete state of the analysis also is not the problem it once was. Certainly there are still gaps—for example, the names of the authors of J and E. But, after all, it took nearly a thousand years to write the Hebrew Bible, and it took hundreds more before Christians added the New Testament to it. If it took that long to construct the mystery, it is not shocking that it should take about a thousand years (since the medieval investigators) to unravel it. The significant thing is that the discoveries of the last few years—literary, linguistic, and archeological discoveries—have brought us to a stage where this knowledge can now be useful.

Now we can study and appreciate the artistry that went into forming each part of the book. We can appreciate the variety of human experience over centuries that made it so complex and so rich. We can learn how responsive the parts of the book were to the real needs and real situations of life. If we say that the book is great, we can better understand what made it great.

Reading the Bible will never be quite the same. Aware of the Bible's extraordinary history and its resulting complexity, we can— and probably must—read the book with a new depth of appreciation. We can read a page of the Bible and know that three or even four persons, all artists, all writing from their own experience, in their own historical moments, separated by centuries, contributed to composing that page. And, *at the same time*, we can read the page as it is, to enjoy the story, to learn from it, to find out how others interpreted it over millennia.

For those of us who read the Bible as literature, this new knowledge should bring a new acquaintance with the individuals who wrote it, a new path to evaluating their artistry, and a new admiration for the book's final beauty and complexity.

For those of us who read it in search of history, this enterprise continually opens new channels to uncovering what was happening in various historical moments, and new sensitivity to how individuals in biblical society responded to those moments.

For those who hold the Bible as sacred, it can mean new possibilities of interpretation; and it can mean a new awe before the great chain of events, persons, and centuries that came together so intricately to produce an incomparable book of teachings.

And for all of us who live in this civilization that the Bible played so central a part in shaping, it can be a channel to put us more in touch with people and forces that affected our world.

The question, after all, is not only who wrote the Bible, but who reads it.

Appendix

Identification of the Authors of the Five Books of Moses

THE BOOK OF GENESIS

	J	E	P	R
Creation	2:4b–25		1:1–2:3	
Generations of heaven and earth				2:4a
Garden of Eden	3:1–24			
Cain and Abel	4:1–16			
Cain genealogy	4:17–26			
Generations of man	5:29			*5:1–28, 30–32
Sons of God and human women	6:1–4			
The flood	6:5–8; 7:1–5, 7, 10, 12, 16b–20, 22–23; 8:2b–3a, 6, 8–12, 13b, 20–22		6:9–22; 7:8–9, 11, 13–16a, 21, 24; 8:1–2a, 3b–5, 7, 13a, 14–19; 9:1–17	

*Entries marked with an asterisk, see Notes on Identification of Authors.

	J	E	P	R
Noah's drunkenness	9:18–27			
Noah's age				•7:6; 9:28–29
Generations of Noah's sons	10:8–19,21 24–30		10:1b–7, 20, 22–23, 31, 32	10:1a
The tower of Babel	11:1–9			
Generations of Shem				11:10a, •10b–26
Generations of Terah				11:27a, •32
Abraham's migration	12:1–4a		11:27b–31; 12:4b–5	
Promise to Abraham	12:6–9			
Wife/sister	12:10–20			
Abraham and Lot	13:1–5, 7–11a, 12b–18 [•14:1–24]		13:6, 11b–12a	
Abraham's covenant	•15:1–21		17:1–27	
Hagar and Ishmael	16:1–2, 4–14		16:3, 15–16	
The three visitors	18:1–33			
Sodom and Gomorrah	19:1–28, 30–38		19:29	
Wife/sister		20:1–18		
Birth of Isaac	21:1a, 2a, 7	21:6	21:1b, 2b–5	
Hagar and Ishmael		21:8–21		
Abraham and Abimelek		21:22–34		
The binding of Isaac		22:1–10, 16b–19		•22:11–16a

	J	E	P	R
Abraham's kin	22:20–24			
The cave of Machpelah			23:1–20	
Rebekah	24:1–67		25:20	
The sons of Keturah		25:1–4		25:5–6
The death of Abraham	25:8a		•25:7, 8b–11	
Generations of Ishmael			25:13–18	25:12
Generations of Isaac				25:19
Jacob and Esau	25:11b, 21–34; 27:1–45		26:34–35; 27:46; 28:1–9	
Wife/sister	26:1–11			
Isaac and Abimelek	26:12–33			
Jacob at Beth–El	28:10–11a, 13–16, 19	28:11b–12, 17–18, 20–22		
Jacob, Leah, and Rachel	29:1–30			
Jacob's children	29:31–35 30:1a, 4a, 24b	30:1b–3, 4b–24a	35:23–26	
Jacob and Laban	30:25–43; 31:49	31:1–2, 4–16, 19–48, 50–54 32:1–3		
Jacob's return	31:3, 17, 18a; •32:4–13;	32:14–24 33:1–17	31:18b; 35:27	
Jacob becomes Israel		32:25–33	35:9–15	
Shechem	34:1–31	33:18–20		•33:18
Return to Beth–El		35:1–8		
Rachel dies in childbirth		35:16–20		

	J	E	P	R
Reuben takes Jacob's concubine	35:21–22			
The death of Isaac			35:28–29	
Generations of Esau	36:31–43		•36:2–30	36:1
Joseph and his brothers	37:2b, 3b, 5–11, 19–20, 23, 25b–27, 28b, 31–35	37:3a, 4, 12–18, 21–22, 24, 25a, 28a, 29, 30, 36	37:1	37:2a
Judah and Tamar	38:1–30			
Joseph and Potiphar's wife	39:1–23			
The butler and the baker		40:1–23		
Joseph and the Pharaoh		41:1–45a, 46b–57	41:45b–46a	
Jacob's sons in Egypt	42:1–4, 8–20, 26–34, 38; 43:1–13, 15–17, 24–34; 44:1–34; 45:1–2, 4–28;	42:5–7, 21–25, 35–37; 43:14, 18–23; 45:3		
Jacob in Egypt	46:5b, 28–34; 47:1–6, 11–27a, 29–31; *49:1–27; 50:1–11, 14–23	46:1–5a; 47:7–10; 48:1–2, 8–22; 50:23–26	46:6–27; 47:27b, 28;48:3–6; 49:29–33; 50:12–13	•48:7; 49:28

THE BOOK OF EXODUS

	J	E	P	R
Those who come to Egypt				1:1–5
The new generation	1:6		1:7	
The enslavement		1:8–12	1:13–14	
Killing the male infants	1:22	1:15–21		
Moses' birth and youth	2:1–23a			
God hears Israel's cry			2:23b–25	
Yahweh summons Moses	3:2–4a, 5, 7–8, 19–22; 4:19–20a, 24–26	3:1, 4b, 6, 9–18; 4:1–18, 20b, 21a, 22–23, 27–31	6:2–12, 14–25;7:1–9	4:21b; 6:13, 26–30
Moses and Pharaoh	5:1–2	5:3–6:1; 7:14–18, 20b–21a, 23–29; 8:3b–11a, 16–28: 9:1–7, 13–34; 10:1–19, 21–26, 28–29; 11:1–8	7:10–13 19–20a, 21b, 22; 8:1–3a, 12–15; 9:8–12	8:11b; 9:35; 10:20, 27; 11:9–10
The Exodus	12:21–23	12:˙24–27, 29–36, 37b–39; ˙13:1–16	12:1–20, 28, 40–49	12:37a, 50–51

	J	E	P	R
The Red Sea	13:21–22; *14:5–7, 9a, 10b, 13–14, 19b, 20b, 21b, 24, 25b, 27b, 30–31; *15:1–18	13:17–19; 14: 11–12, 19a, 20a, 25a; 15:20–21	14:1–4, 8, 9b, 10a, 10c, 15–18, 21a, 21c, 22–23, 26–27a, 28–29	13:20; 15:19
Water in the wilderness	15:22b–25a			15:22a, 27
Commandments		15:25b–26		
Food in the wilderness	16:4–5, 35b		16:2–3, 6–35a, 36	16:1
Water in the wilderness		17:2–7		17:1
Amalek		17:8–16		
Jethro		18:1–27		
Horeb/Sinai	19:10–16a, 18, 20–25	19:2b–9, 16b–17, 19; 20:18–26	19:1	19:2a
The Ten Commandments			*20:1-17	
The Covenant Code		*21:1–27; 22:1–30; 23:1–33		
Horeb/Sinai (continued)		24:1–15a; 18b	24:15b–18	
Tabernacle instruction			25:1–31:11	
Sabbath command			31:12–17	
The tablets			31:18	
The golden calf		32:1–33:11		
Theophany to Moses	34:1a, 2–13	33:12–23		34:1b

	J	E	P	R
The Ten Commandments	34:14–28			
The skin of Moses' face			34:29–35	
Execution of the Tabernacle instruction			35–40	

THE BOOK OF LEVITICUS

	J	E	P	R
Entire book			1–27	
Except: Booths on Sukkot			23:39–43	
Restoration from exile			26:39–45	

THE BOOK OF NUMBERS

	J	E	P	R
The last days at Mt. Sinai			1:1–2:34; 3:2–9:14; 10:1–10	3:1; 9:15–23
Departure from Mt. Sinai	10:29–36		10:11–12, 14–27	10:13, 28
Taberah		11:1–3		
Food in the wilderness		11:4–35		
Moses' Cushite wife		12:1–16		

	J	E	P	R
The spies	13:17–20, 23–24, 27–31, 33; 14:1b, 4, 11–25, 39–45		13:1–16, 21–22, 25–26, 32; 14:1a, 2–3, 5–10, 26–39	
Additional sacrificial law				15:1–31
A sabbath violation			15:32–36	
Fringes on apparel			15:37–41	
Korah, Dathan, & Abiram	16:1b–2a, 12–14, 25, 27b–32a, 33–34		16:1a, 2b–11, 15–24, 26, 27a, 32b, 35	[*16:24, 27]
Aaronids and Levites			17:1–18:32	
The red heifer			19:1–22	
Water in the wilderness			20:1b–13	20:1a
Israel and Edom	20:14–21			*21:4a?
The death of Aaron			20:23–29	20:22
Israel and Arad	21:1–3			
The bronze serpent		21:4b–9		
Journeys				21:10–11, [*12–20]
Sihon and Og	21:21–35			
Balaam		22:2–24:25		22:1

	J	E	P	R
The heresy of Peor	25:1–5		25:6–19	
Census			26:1–8, 12–65	26:9–11
The daughters of Zelophehad			27:1–11	
The appointment of Joshua			27:12–23	
Additional sacrificial law				28:1–31; 29:1–39
Laws on annulling women's vows			30:1–17	
The defeat of the Midianites			31:1–54	
Tribal portions			•32:1–42; 33:50–56; 34:1–29; 35:1–34; 36:1–13	
The stations list			•33:1–49	

The Book of Deuteronomy

	DTR¹	DTR²	OTHER	E	P
Moses' introduction	1:1–4:24, 32–49; 5:1–8:18; 9:1–11:32	4:25–31; 8:19–20			

	DTR¹	DTR²	OTHER	E	P
Law code	26:16–19; 27:1–10		12:1–26:15		
Covenant ceremony	27:11–26				
Blessings and curses	28:1–35, 38–62	28:36–37, 63–68			
Moses' con-clusion	28:69; 29:1–20, 28; 30:11–13; 31:1–8	29:21–27; 30:1–10, 14–20			
The appoint-ment of Joshua			31:14–15, 23		
The *torah*	31:9–12, 24–27				
The Song of Moses		31:16–22, 28–30; 32:44	•32:1–43		
Moses' last words	32:45–47				
The Blessing of Moses			•33:2–27	33:1	
The death of Moses	34:10–12		•32:48–52 (R)	34:1–6	34:7–9

Notes on Identification of Authors

Gen 5:1–28,30–32; 7:6; 9:28–29; 11:10b–26,32

These passages are drawn from the "Book of Generations," which apparently was originally a separate document, containing terminology similar to that of P. The redactor cut it into segments and then distributed these segments through the book of Genesis. This unified the stories by setting them within a chronological flow of generations.

Gen 15:1–21

This chapter is thought by many scholars to be a composite of two sources because of various difficulties in the text. (For example, Abraham is shown the stars in v. 5, but according to v. 12 the sun had just begun to set.) It is marked here as J, but note should be taken of its complexity. Notably, the prediction of the Egyptian slavery in vv. 13–16 is curious. It combines elements of data or terminology that are otherwise characteristic uniquely of J, of E, or of P. And it is embedded in an epanalepsis (the resumptive repetition of the matter of the setting of the sun, vv. 12 and 17). The passage may have been written by the redactor himself. It would thus have served two purposes: (1) to enhance the connection between the patriarchal stories of Genesis and the slavery-exodus story in Exodus; and (2) to enhance the union of the sources themselves in Genesis.

Gen 22:11–16a

The story of the near-sacrifice of Isaac is traced to E. It refers to the deity as Elohim in vv. 1,3,8, and 9. But, just as Abraham's hand is raised with the knife to sacrifice Isaac, the text says that the angel of Yahweh stops him (v. 11). The verses in which Isaac is spared refer to the deity as Yahweh (vv. 11–14). These verses are followed by a report that the angel speaks a second time and says, ". . . because you *did not* withhold your son from me. . . . " Thus the four verses which report that Isaac was not sacrificed involve both a contradiction and a change of the name of the deity. As extraordinary as it may seem, it has been suggested that in the original version of this story Isaac was actually sacrificed, and that the intervening four verses were added subsequently, when the notion of human sacrifice was rejected (perhaps by the person who combined J and E). Of course, the words "you did not withhold your son" might mean only that Abraham had been *willing* to sacrifice his son. But still it must be noted that the text concludes (v. 19), "And *Abraham* returned to his servants." Isaac is not mentioned. Moreover, Isaac never again appears as a character in E. Interestingly, a later midrashic tradition developed this notion, that Isaac actually had been sacrificed. This tradition is discussed in S. Spiegel's *The Last Trial* (New York: Schocken, 1969; Hebrew edition 1950).

Gen 25:8

The first word of the verse ("And he expired") and the second half of the verse are P. The rest is J.

Gen 32:4–13

This passage is difficult to identify by author. It has affinities to both J and E material which surrounds it. The identification with J here is tentative.

Gen 33:18

The words "when he was coming from Paddan Aram" in the middle of this verse are curious. The context is E, but the name Paddan Aram is used elsewhere only in P. These words appear to be an addition by the redactor, perhaps to compensate for the fact that the combination of the sources made it appear that Jacob was taking an excessive amount of time to return to his father Isaac (in Gen 35:27).

Gen 36:2–30

These lists of Esau's family involve some contradictions with other P texts (Gen 26:34–35; 28:9). They may be originally independent documents which the redactor included here.

Gen 48:7

This verse does not connect easily with the text that precedes it (P) or with the text that follows it (E), and it combines allusions to earlier texts from P (Gen 35:9) and E (Gen 35:16–20). It therefore appears to be an addition by the redactor. This was perhaps for the purpose of softening the redundancy of the combined P and E texts in Genesis 48. In verse 5 (P), Jacob promotes Joseph's sons, Ephraim and Manasseh, to equal status with Jacob's own sons; but in verse 8 (E), Jacob looks at Ephraim and Manasseh and says, "Who are these?"

Gen 49:1–27

This song, known as the Blessing of Jacob, was probably not composed by the author of J, but was rather a source that this author used and then wove into the narrative.

Exod 14:5–7

Verses 5b and 7 may be E.

Exod 12:24–27; 13:1–16

These texts have some small similarities to Deuteronomistic texts, and so some scholars have suggested that a Deuteronomistic editor added these lines to the text of Exodus. This is possible; but (1) the similarities are slight, (2) it is not clear why these particular things should have been added out of all possibilities open to such an editor, and (3) D and E have many similarities and come from the same community anyway. I therefore think that it is at least as likely that these passages were in the E text in the first place.

Exod 15:1–18

This song, known as the Song of the Sea, like the blessing of Jacob, was probably not composed by the author of J, but was rather a source that this author used and then wove into the narrative.

Exod 20:1–17

The differences between the Ten Commandments as they appear here and in Deuteronomy 5 indicate that there was an original text of the Ten Commandments—which appears to have been a part of E originally—that was elaborated upon by the person who produced P in typical P terminology, and by the person who produced Dtr[1] in typical D terminology. Compare especially the Sabbath commandment in Exod 20:11 and Deut 5:15. The J text of the Ten Commandments meanwhile appears in Exodus 34:14–28.

Exod 21:1–27; 22:1–30; 23:1–33

The Covenant Code is a legal text that may not have been composed by the author of E, but was rather a source that this author wove into the narrative.

Num 16:24,27

The names Dathan and Abiram do not fit here. Only the Tabernacle of Korah is mentioned in these verses. Dathan and Abiram (and their own tents) are mentioned separately in verse 27b. The names Dathan and Abiram appear to have been added by the redactor as part of the process of combining the two originally separate stories.

Num 21:4a

This may be one of the redactor's notices of the stations of the journey through the wilderness, serving as editorial connections of the various texts that concern the years in the wilderness.

Num 21:12–20

These verses, which cite older texts, including "the book of the battles of Yahweh," are difficult to identify.

Num 32:1–42

This chapter appears to contain elements of J and P. Precise identification by verses is difficult.

Num 33:1–49

The stations list in Numbers 33, like the book of generations in Genesis, appears to have been a separate document originally, which the redactor used as a means of uniting the various texts with chronological continuity.

Deut 32:1–43

This song, known as the Song of Moses, was woven into the text here by the person who produced Dtr², as indicated by the fact that some themes and terms that are developed in Dtr² (e.g., "the hiding of the face") appear to derive from this song (v. 20).

Deut 33:2–27

This song, too, known as the Blessing of Moses, was probably originally a separate composition that was woven into the text.

Deut 32:48–52

These verses repeat the P text of Num 27:12–14. They are the redactor's epanalepsis, resuming the matter of Moses' death, which had been moved because of the addition of the text of Deuteronomy to the work.

Notes

Introduction

1.   There is an account in the book of Deuteronomy of Moses' writing a "scroll of the *torah*" before his death, which is kept with the golden box (the "ark") containing the two stone tablets of the Ten Commandments, but the account in Deuteronomy does not claim that this scroll contained the entire text of all five books on it (Deut 31:9,24–26). The word "*torah*" here in Deuteronomy 31 does not necessarily mean the Torah, the name that later came to mean the entire Pentateuch. The word also can simply mean instruction in general.

2.   There are many persons who claim to be biblical scholars. I refer to scholars who have the necessary training in languages, biblical archeology, and literary and historical skills to work on the problem, and who meet, discuss, and debate their ideas and research with other scholars through scholarly journals, conferences, etc.

3.   The author was male, as we shall see.

Chapter 1

1.   Haddu and other male deities are often referred to in the Bible simply as the *ba'al* (plural: *b⁼'alim*), which means "lord."

2.   *Note on the translation of the name of God:* The name of God in the Bible is Yahweh. After the Bible was completed, the custom developed not to pronounce this name out loud. Most translations therefore write "the LORD" (in capital letters) whenever the name Yahweh appears in the Hebrew. For the purposes of this book, it will be better to follow the original.

3. For readers who are interested in more precise details, Samuel had died by this time, and Shiloh had fallen to the Philistines. The priests of Shiloh therefore were located at this time at the city of Nob.

Chapter 2

1. The first version of the creation story is Gen 1:1–2:3; the second version is Gen 2:4–24.

2. The flood story appears here on pp. 54–59 with the two versions separated.

3. Genesis 15 and Genesis 17.

4. The term "Higher Criticism" was used to distinguish this kind of work from textual study, which was referred to as "Lower Criticism." In textual study, a biblical scholar compares the various oldest surviving manuscripts of the Bible—the Masoretic Hebrew text, the Greek versions, the Vulgate (Latin), the Aramaic, and now the Qumran ("Dead Sea Scrolls") texts, among others. When the versions differ, the scholar tries to determine which is the original and which is the result of a scribal error or emendation. Often fascinating and important for biblical interpretation, this study of the words of the text itself was nonetheless regarded as "lower" (though not necessarily in a negative sense) than the study of content and history involved in study of the sources.

5. The names of God were the first, not the only, clue. For example, the E source speaks of the mountain of God at Horeb; the J source calls it Mount Sinai. E calls Moses' father-in-law Jethro; J calls him Reuel.

6. Gen 13:18; 18:1.

7. Gen 15:18.

8. Gen 32:25–31; 1 Kings 12:25.

9. J = Gen 28:11a,13–16,19. E = Gen 28:11b,12,17–18,20–23; 35:1–7.

10. Genesis 34.

11. Gen 33:19.

12. The birth of Benjamin is described in Gen 35:16–20, usually regarded as E. For the technical discussion of this matter, see my article

"The Recession of Biblical Source Criticism" in *The Future of Biblical Studies*.

13. Gen 30:1–24a.

14. Gen 29:32–35.

15. Gen 49:3–4.

16. Gen 49:5–7.

17. Gen 49:8.

18. Gen 48:8–20.

19. 1 Kings 12:25.

20. Isa 7:17; Jer 7:15.

21. Gen 37:21–22.

22. Gen 37:26–27.

23. Gen 48:22.

24. Gen 13:17; 19:2; 26:22; 34:21; Exod 3:8; 34:24.

25. Gen 50:24–26.

26. Exod 13:19.

27. Josh 24:32.

28. Exod 1:11.

29. 1 Kings 11:1.

30. Exod 17:8–13; 24:13; 32:15–17; 33:11; Num 11:24–29.

31. Num 13:8; Josh 24:1,30.

32. Num 13:17–20,22–24,27–31.

33. Josh 14:13.

34. Gen 25:23.

35. Gen 25:29–34.

36. Gen 27:1–40.

37. 2 Kings 8:16,20–23.

Chapter 3

1. Note that the name Yahweh occurs here in an E story. I shall explain this later on.

2. Exodus 32.

3. 1 Kings 12:28.

4. According to a J account:

And Yahweh said to Moses, "Carve for yourself two stone tablets [like the first ones], and I shall write on the tablets [the words that were on the first ones, which you smashed]."

Since the J source contains no reference to the golden calf story, the references in this verse to the first set of smashed tablets—i.e., the words in brackets—were presumably added by the redactor who combined J and E.

5. 1 Sam 1:1.

6. The marriage connection appears to be reflected in the Priestly tradition that Aaron married the sister of Nachshon ben Amminadab, the prince of the tribe of Judah; Exod 6:23; Num 2:3.

7. Exod 34:17.

8. Exod 20:23.

9. The description of their departure is identifiable as J because it refers to Moses' father-in-law by the name Reuel, not by the E name Jethro.

10. Num 14:44.

11. Exod 33:7–11.

12. Gen 3:24.

13. Note that the name Yahweh occurs here in an E story. I shall explain this later on.

14. Num 11:11–15.

15. Exod 3:8.

16. Exod 3:10.

17. Individual persons in J stories use the word Elohim, but the *narrator* does not.

18. Exod 3:13.

19. Exod 3:15.

20. Exodus 21–23. This legal corpus is referred to as the Covenant Code.

21. Jo Ann Hackett discusses this phenomenon in "Women's Studies and the Hebrew Bible," in R. E. Friedman and H. G. M. Williamson, eds., *The Future of Biblical Studies*.

22. 2 Kings 8:16,20–22.

23. Research that I am presently doing indicates that E was written during the last twenty-five years before the fall of the kingdom of Israel in 722.

Chapter 4

1. Num 21:5–9.

2. 2 Kings 18:4.

3. 2 Kings 18:13–19:37; Isaiah 36–37; 2 Chr 32:1–23.

4. 2 Kings 19:35.

5. I have translated the relevant portion here. The text of the entire Prism Inscription can be found in *Ancient Near Eastern Texts*, James Pritchard, ed.

6. 2 Kings 18:14–15.

7. 2 Chr 32:3–4.

8. 2 Kings 22:8; 2 Chr 34:14–15.

9. Isa 2:4; Micah 4:3.

Chapter 5

1. 2 Sam 7:16.

2. 1 Kings 11:35–36.

3.   1 Kings 15:3–4.

4.   2 Kings 8:18–19.

5.   Cross' book, *Canaanite Myth and Hebrew Epic*, and the works of other investigators who are referred to in this chapter are listed in the bibliography.

6.   Other examples of passages containing the words "to this day" are 1 Kings 9:21; 10:12; 12:19; 2 Kings 8:22; 10:27; 14:7; 16:6; 17:23.

7.   1 Kings 13:1–2.

8.   2 Kings 23:15–18.

9.   2 Kings 20:12–19.

10.   2 Kings 23–25.

11.   Deut 34:10.

12.   2 Kings 23:25.

13.   Deut 6:5.

14.   2 Kings 23:25.

15.   Deut 17:8–13.

16.   2 Kings 22:13.

17.   Deut 17:11.

18.   Deut 17:20.

19.   2 Kings 22:2.

20.   Deut 31:26; Josh 1:8; 8:31,34; 23:6; 2 Kings 22:8.

21.   Deut 31:11.

22.   2 Kings 23:2.

23.   Deut 9:21.

24.   2 Kings 23:6.

25.   2 Kings 23:12.

26.   Deut 12:3.

27.   Deut 5:8.

28. Deut 4:16,23,25;27:15.

29. Deut 7:25.

30. 2 Kings 21:17.

31. 2 Kings 18.

32. Deuteronomy 12.

33. Examples: King Asa, 1 Kings 15:11–14; King Jehoshaphat, 1 Kings 22:43–44.

34. Jer 17:3; Ezek 6:3,6.

35. 2 Kings 22:2.

36. 2 Kings 16:2; 18:3; 21:7.

Chapter 6

1. Deut 12:20.

2. Deut 17:14–20.

3. Deut 10:6.

4. Deut 9:20.

5. Deut 24:9.

6. 2 Kings 11:5–7.

7. 2 Kings 23:13.

8. 1 Kings 12–13; 2 Kings 23:15.

9. Jer 1:2.

10. 2 Chr 35:25.

11. Jer 29:1–3.

12. Jer 36:10.

13. Jer 26:24.

14. Jer 39:14; 40:6.

15. Jer 7:12,14; 26:6,9; cf. 41:5.

16. Jer 7:12.

17.   Josh 21:18–19.

18.   Jer 11:21–23.

19.   Jer 8:17–22.

20.   2 Kings 24:8.

21.   Jer 15:1.

22.   E = Exod 3:1; 17:6; 33:6. D = Deut 1:6,19; 4:10,15; 5:2; 9:8; 18:16; 28:69.

23.   E = Exod 20:24. D = Deut 12:5,11,21; 14:23,24; 16:2,6,11; 26:2.

24.   Deut 1–3; 4:1–24,32–49; 5–7; 8:1–18; 9–11; 26:16–19; 27; 28:1–35,38–62,69; 29:1–20,28;30:11–14; 31:1–13,24–27; 32:45–47; 34:10–12; 2 Kings 22:1–23:25.

25.   Josh 1:7–9; 8:30–35; 21:41–43; 22:5; 23:1–16.

26.   Judg 2:11–23; 3:1–11; 10:6–7,10–16.

27.   1 Sam 7:3–4; 8:8; 12:20–21,24–25.

28.   2 Sam 7:1b,13–16.

29.   1 Kings 16:29.

30.   1 Kings 22:41.

31.   1 Kings 22:39. The "Book of the Chronicles of the Kings of Israel" is not the same thing as the biblical book of Chronicles.

32.   1 Kings 11:38–39.

33.   Ps 89:21–38; 132:11–18. The covenant wording in 2 Samuel 7 appears to be based on the wording of Psalm 89.

Chapter 7

1.   The exiled writer's insertions are listed in the chart of sources, pp. 254–55. For those who are interested in the specific descriptions of the grammatical, syntactical, structural, and other evidence, see my article "From Egypt to Egypt: Dtr[1] and Dtr[2]," in J. Levenson and B. Halpern, eds., *Traditions in Transformation: Turning-Points in Biblical Faith*.

2. E = Exod 20:3; J = Exod 34:14.

3. Deut 4:25; 8:19–20; 29:25; 30:17; 31:16,18; Josh 23:16; 1 Kings 9:6,9; 2 Kings 17:35–39.

4. Deut 31:16–18.

5. 2 Kings 21:8–15.

6. 2 Kings 23:26.

7. 1 Kings 9:3.

8. 1 Kings 9:7.

9. Deut 28:68.

10. 2 Kings 25:26.

11. Deut 4:25–31.

12. Jeremiah 36.

13. Babylonian Talmud, Baba Batra 15a.

14. Since the first edition of this book I have treated this matter in greater detail in "The Deuteronomistic School," in A. Beck et al., eds., *Fortunate the Eyes That See: Essays in Honor of David Noel Freedman* (Grand Rapids, MI: Eerdmans, 1995), pp. 70–80.

15. Jer 32:12,13,16; 36:4,5,8,10,13,14,15,16,17,18,19,26,27,32; 43:3,6; 45:1,2.

Chapter 8

1. Zechariah 7–8.

2. Ezekiel 40–42.

3. Ezra 1:8,11; 2:2; 3:8; 4:2,3; 5:2,14,16; Neh 7:7; 12:1,47.

4. Hag 1:1,12,14; 2:2,4,21,23; Zech 4:6,7,9,10.

5. Jer 52:28ff.; 2 Kings 24:14.

6. Ezra 2:64.

7. Jer 52:11; 2 Chr 36:21,22; Ezra 1:1.

8. See especially Nehemiah 9, in which the reading of the Torah is followed by a recital that merges all of the sources. E. g., verses 7 and 8

recall Genesis 15 (J) and 17 (P); verse 13 recalls Exod 19:20 (J) and Exod 20:22 (E); verse 25 recalls Deut 6:11 (D).

Chapter 9

1. See R. J. Thompson, *Moses and the Law in a Century of Criticism Since Graf,* pp. 42f.

2. Ezek 44:15–16.

3. Gen 1:1–3.

4. Jer 4:23.

5. Gen 1:22,28; 17:20; 28:3; 35:11; 47:27; 48:4; cf. Exod 1:7; Lev 26:9.

6. E. g., Exodus 25.

7. Jer 3:16.

8. Lev 7:37f.

9. Jer 7:22.

10. Lev 26:3.

11. Lev 26:15.

12. Ezek 5:7.

13. Lev 26:29.

14. Ezek 5:10.

15. Lev 26:22,25.

16. Ezek 5:17.

17. Exod 6:8.

18. Ezek 20:28.

19. Listed in Friedman, *The Exile and Biblical Narrative,* p. 63.

20. Ezek 7:26; 22:26; see also 43:11;44:5,23.

21. Ezekiel 40–42; Exodus 26.

22. See the selected Bibliography.

23. Jacob Milgrom, Robert Polzin, Gary Rendsburg, Ziony Zevit, and A. R. Guenther; see the selected Bibliography.

24. Lev 17:3–4.

Chapter 10

1. 1 Kings 6:2.

2. 1 Kings 8:4; 2 Chr 5:5.

3. *Jewish Antiquities*, VIII: 101, 103.

4. Babylonian Talmud, Sotah 9a.

5. 1 Chr 9:23.

6. 1 Chr 6:33.

7. 2 Chr 29:6.

8. Lev 26:11. For more details of the architecture and measurements of the Tabernacle, and citation and discussion of additional biblical references to the Tabernacle in the Temple, see my article "The Tabernacle in the Temple."

9. 1 Sam 1:9,24; 3:3; Judges 18:31; Psalm 78:60.

Chapter 11

1. Exod 6:1; 7:14; 8:16; 10:1; Num 11:16,23; 14:11.

2. Exod 6:13; 7:8; 9:8; 12:1; Lev 11:1; 13:1; 14:33; 15:1.

3. Exod 7:15,17; 9:23; 10:13.

4. Exod 6:10–12; 7:19; 8:1,12–13.

5. Exod 4:14.

6. Exod 7:7.

7. Exod 6:20–25.

8. Exod 40:13,29–32.

9. Exod 7:1.

10. Gen 2:4b.

11. Gen 1:1.

12. Lev 10:1–2.

13. The names Dathan and Abiram had to be added here by the editor who was reconciling the two stories. The verse refers only to *one* tabernacle, not three; and Dathan and Abiram are mentioned without Korah again in the middle of v. 27.

14. The meaning of *sheol* in the Bible is uncertain. Some think that it refers to some kind of realm of the dead. Others think that it simply means the grave.

15. Exod 6:18–21.

16. Exod 34:6–7.

17. Frank Moore Cross analyzed these instances in connection with the rivalry between the priestly families in "The Priestly Houses of Early Israel," in *Canaanite Myth and Hebrew Epic*.

18. Num 20:23–24.

19. Exod 34:29–35.

20. Exod 24:16–18a.

21. Num 20:29.

22. See the identification of biblical passages by authors in the Appendix.

23. Num 13:30.

24. Num 14:24.

25. Num 14:6–9.

26. Exod 33:11.

27. Genesis 23.

28. Josh 21:13.

Chapter 12

1. Deut 11:6.

2. Deut 1:36. Note that Joshua is referred to two verses later; on this point, see opposite.

3. Deut 9:16; 24:9.

4. Deut 24:9.

5. Num 14:3.

6. Num 14:31.

7. Deut 1:39. Earlier investigators (Driver, Carpenter, and Harford-Battersby) thought that the verses in Numbers containing the expression "babies will become a prey" were JE. But assigning these verses to JE resulted in breaking the context and sense of both JE and P in Numbers. Later scholars (Martin Noth, Y. Kaufmann, and I) recognized them as P. For those who are interested in more detail on this point, see my *The Exile and Biblical Narrative*, pp. 68–69.

Note that Deut 1:36 says explicitly that only Caleb is excepted from the condemnation, yet two verses later (1:38) it says that Joshua is to be Moses' successor. This verse stands back-to-back with the "babies a prey" reference to P (1:39), and so it looks like an effort by the Deuteronomist to resolve the conflict between his sources editorially. In any case, it is further evidence of his familiarity with the P version.

8. See Chapter 9, pp. 167–68.

9. Jer 8:8.

10. Deut 17:9,18; 18:1; 24:8; 27:9.

11. 2 Chr 31:2.

12. Num 21:4b–9.

13. 2 Kings 18:4.

14. 2 Kings 23:13.

15. 1 Chr 13:2; 15:14; 23:2; 28:13; 2 Chr 8:15; 11:13; 13:9,10.

16. 2 Chr 29:3–36; 30:1–27; 31:1–21.

17. 2 Chr 31:20–21.

18. 1 Kings 11.

19. 2 Kings 20:12–19.

20. 2 Chr 32:31.

21.   Chronicles does criticize Hezekiah once for becoming haughty, but it adds immediately that he became humble and averted divine anger (2 Chr 32:25–26).

22.   B Halpern, "Sacred History and Ideology: Chronicles' Thematic Structure—Indications of an Earlier Source," in Richard Elliott Friedman, ed., *The Creation of Sacred Literature.*

23.   2 Chr 30:26.

24.   Exod 6:23.

25.   Num 2:3; Ruth 4:20–22.

Chapter 13

1.   Gen 1:1–2:4a; Exod 1:1–7; Leviticus (all); Num 1:1–10:29.

2.   Gen 5:1.

3.   Gen 5:1–28,30–32; 7:6; 9:28–29; 11:10–26,32.

4.   Cross, "The Priestly Work," in *Canaanite Myth and Hebrew Epic.*

5.   Gen 5:1.

6.   Exod 7:13,22; 8:15; 9:12.

7.   Exod 8:11b; 9:35; 10:20, 27.

8.   Lev 10:11.

9.   Leviticus 1–7.

10.   Lev 23:40.

11.   Neh 8:17.

12.   Ezra 7:6.

13.   Ezra 7:10.

14.   Ezra 7:6.

15.   Ezra 7:14.

16.   This translation is from B. M. Metzger, in J. H. Charlesworth, ed., *The Old Testament Pseudepigrapha,* I: 554.

17.   Quoted in E. M. Gray, *Old Testament Criticism.*

18. Deut 31:10–11.

19. Gen 3:24.

20. Exod 20:8,11.

21. Deut 5:12,15.

22. The All Souls Deuteronomy Scroll.

23. For those who are interested in the details of this structure, see my "Sacred Literature and Theology: The Redaction of Torah," in R.E. Friedman, ed., *The Creation of Sacred Literature.*

24. Cross, "The Priestly Work," in *Canaanite Myth and Hebrew Epic.*

25. Deut 34:1–6 is E; 7–9 is P; and 10–12 is Dtr[1].

26. Exod 31:12–17.

27. Lev 26:39–45.

Chapter 14

1. I have tried to uncover the redactor's motives in his decisions in my article "Sacred Literature and Theology: The Redaction of Torah," in R.E. Friedman, ed., *The Creation of Sacred Literature.*

2. Gen 3:5.

3. Exod 19:18.

4. Exod 24:16–17.

5. Exodus 33–34.

6. Gen 18:23–33.

7. Num 14:13–20.

8. Exod 32:7–14; 33:11.

9. Num 11:11,15.

10. Deut 3:23–26.

11. Gen 1:3,9; 6:22; Exod 7:6; 39:32.

12. Deut 30:11–14.

13.   Exod 34:6–7.

14.   Exod 32:7–14.

15.   Num 14:13–20.

16.   Exod 21:24; Lev 24:20; Deut 19:21.

17.   From Bonfils' comment on Gen 12:6.

18.   From Masius' *Commentariorum in Josuam Praefato* (1574), quoted in E. M. Gray, *Old Testament Criticism*, p. 58.

Selected Bibliography

Addis, W.E. *Documents of the Hexateuch*. London, 1892.

Aharoni, Yohonan. "The Solomonic Temple, the Tabernacle, and the Arad Sanctuary." In H. A. Hoffman, Jr., ed., *Orient and Occident, Cyrus Gordon Festschrift*. Neukirchen: Neukirchener, 1973.

Albright, William Foxwell. *The Biblical Period from Abraham to Ezra*. New York: Harper, 1963.

_____. *From the Stone Age to Christianity*. Garden City, N.Y.: Doubleday, 1946, 1957.

Alt, Albrecht. *Essays on Old Testament History and Religion*. Garden City, N.Y.: Doubleday, 1966. German edition, *Kleine Schriften zur Geschichte des Volkes Israel*, I, II, III, 1953.

Astruc, Jean. *Conjectures sur les mémoires originaux dont il parait que Moyse s'est servi, pour composer le livre de la Genèse 1753*.

Bacon, Benjamin W. *The Genesis of Genesis*. Hartford, 1892.

Baltzer, Klaus. *The Covenant Formulary*. Philadelphia: Fortress, 1971. German edition, 1964.

Bright, John. *A History of Israel*, 3rd ed. Philadelphia: Westminster, 1981.

Brown, Raymond E.; Fitzmeyer, J.A.; and Murphy, R.E., eds. *The Jerome Biblical Commentary*. Englewood Cliffs, N.J.: Prentice-Hall, 1968.

Busink, Th. A. *Der Tempel von Jerusalem*. Leiden: Brill, 1970.

Carpenter, J.E., and Harford-Battersby, G. *The Hexateuch*. London: Longmans, Green, 1902.

Cheyne, T.K. *Founders of Old Testament Criticism*. London: Methuen, 1893.

Clements, R.E. *Abraham and David*. London: SCM, 1967.

Cross, Frank Moore. *Canaanite Myth and Hebrew Epic.* Cambridge: Harvard, 1973.

––––––. "The Priestly Tabernacle." *Biblical Archeologist* 10 (1947): 45–68.

Driver, S.R. *Introduction to the Literature of the Old Testament.* Gloucester: Peter Smith, 1972. Original edition, 1891.

Duff, Archibald. *History of Old Testament Criticism.* London: Watts, 1910.

Eissfeldt, Otto. *The Old Testament, an Introduction.* P.R. Ackroyd, trans. Oxford: Basil Blackwell, 1965.

Emerton, J.A. "The Origin of the Promises to the Patriarchs in the Older Sources of the Book of Genesis." *Vetus Testamentum* 32:14–32.

Engnell, Ivan. *A Rigid Scrutiny.* Nashville: Vanderbilt University Press, 1969.

Fohrer, Georg. *Introduction to the Old Testament.* Nashville: Abingdon, 1968.

Frankfort, Henri; Frankfort, H.A.; Wilson, John; Jacobsen, Thorkild; and Irwin, W.A. *The Intellectual Adventure of Ancient Man.* Chicago: University of Chicago Press, 1946.

Freedman, David Noel. "Divine Commitment and Human Obligation." *Interpretation* 18 (1964): 419–431.

––––––. "Pentateuch." *Interpreter's Dictionary of the Bible.*

––––––. *Pottery, Poetry, and Prophecy.* Winona Lake, Ind.: Eisenbrauns, 1980.

Friedman, Richard Elliott, ed. *The Creation of Sacred Literature.* Berkeley: University of California Press, 1981.

––––––. *The Exile and Biblical Narrative.* Harvard Semitic Monographs. Decatur, Ga.: Scholars Press, 1981.

––––––, ed. *The Poet and the Historian.* Harvard Semitic Studies. Decatur, Ga.: Scholars Press, 1984.

––––––. "The Tabernacle in the Temple." *Biblical Archeologist* 43 (1980).

––––––, and Williamson, H.G.M., eds. *The Future of Biblical Studies: The Hebrew Scriptures.* Semeia Studies: Decatur, Ga.: Scholars Press, 1986.

Grant, Robert M. *A Short History of the Interpretation of the Bible.* New York: Macmillan, 1948.

Gray, Edward M. *Old Testament Criticism.* New York: Harper, 1923.

Habel, Norman. *Literary Criticism of the Old Testament.* Philadelphia: Fortress, 1971.

Hahn, E. *The Old Testament in Modern Research.* Philadelphia: Fortress, 1966.

Halpern, Baruch. *The Constitution of the Monarchy in Israel.* Harvard Semitic Monographs. Decatur, Ga.: Scholars Press, 1981.

_____. *The Emergence of Israel in Canaan.* Society of Biblical Literature Monographs. Decatur, Ga.: Scholars Press, 1983.

_____. "Sectionalism and the Schism." *Journal of Biblical Literature* 93 (1974): 519–32.

Hanson, Paul. "Song of Heshbon and David's NÎR." *Harvard Theological Review* 61 (1968): 297–320.

Haran, Menahem. "The Priestly Image of the Tabernacle." *Hebrew Union College Annual* 36 (1965): 191–226.

_____. "Shiloh and Jerusalem: The Origin of the Priestly Tradition in the Pentateuch." *Journal of Biblical Literature* 81 (1962): 14–24.

_____. *Temples and Temple Service in Ancient Israel.* New York: Oxford, 1978.

Herrmann, S. *A History of Israel in Old Testament Times.* Philadelphia: Fortress, 1975.

Hillers, Delbert. *Covenant: The History of a Biblical Idea.* Baltimore: Johns Hopkins, 1969.

Hobbes, Thomas. *Leviathan,* Part 3, Chapter 33. 1651.

Hurvitz, Avi. "The Evidence of Language in Dating the Priestly Code." *Revue Biblique* 81 (1974): 24–56.

_____. *A Linguistic Study of the Relationship Between the Priestly Source and the Book of Ezekiel.* Cahiers de la Revue Biblique. Paris: Gabalda, 1982.

Hyatt, J. P. "Torah in the Book of Jeremiah." *Journal of Biblical Literature* 60 (1941): 381–96.

Ishida, Tomoo, ed. *Studies in the Period of David and Solomon and Other Essays.* Tokyo: Yamakawa-Shuppansha, 1982.

Jenks, Alan W. *The Elohist and North Israelite Traditions*. Decatur, Ga.: Scholars Press, 1977.

Kapelrud, A. S. "The Date of the Priestly Code." *Annual of the Swedish Theological Institute* III (1964): 58–64.

Kaufmann, Yehezkel. *The Religion of Israel*. Trans. and ed. Moshe Greenberg. Chicago: University of Chicago Press, 1960. Hebrew edition, 1937.

Kennedy, A. R. S. "Tabernacle." *Hastings Dictionary of the Bible* IV: 653–68.

Knight, Douglas A. *Rediscovering the Traditions of Israel*. Society of Biblical Literature Dissertation Series. Decatur, Ga.: Scholars Press, 1973.

Levenson, Jon. "Who Inserted the Book of the Torah?" *Harvard Theological Review* 68 (1975): 203–33.

————, and Halpern, Baruch, eds. *Traditions in Transformation: Turning-Points in Biblical Faith*. Essays presented to Frank Moore Cross. Winona Lake, Ind.: Eisenbrauns, 1981.

Liver, Jacob. "Korah, Dathan, and Abiram." *Scripta Hierosolymitana* 8. Jerusalem: Hebrew University, 1961.

Lohfink, Norbert. "Auslegung deuteronomischer Texte, IV." *Bibel und Leben* 5 (1964).

Lundbom, Jack R. "The Lawbook of the Josianic Reform." *Catholic Biblical Quarterly* 38 (1976): 293–302.

Malamat, Abraham. "The Twilight of Judah: In the Egyptian-Babylonian Maelstrom." *Vetus Testamentum Supplements* 28 (1975): 123–145.

————. "Origins and the Formative Period." In H. H. Ben-Sasson, *A History of the Jewish People*, pp. 3–87. Cambridge, Mass.: Harvard University Press, 1976.

May, Herbert, ed. *Oxford Bible Atlas*, 3rd ed. New York: Oxford, 1981.

McBride, Samuel Dean. "The Deuteronomic Name Theology." Dissertation, Harvard University, 1969.

McCarthy, D.J. *Old Testament Covenant*. Richmond: John Knox, 1972.

————. *Treaty and Covenant*. Rome: Pontifical Biblical Institute, 1963.

McEvenue, Sean. *The Narrative Style of the Priestly Writer*. Rome: Pontifical Biblical Institute, 1971.

McKenzie, Steven L. *The Chronicler's Use of the Deuteronomistic History.* Harvard Semitic Monographs. Decatur, Ga.: Scholars Press, 1984.

Mendenhall, G.E. *Law and Covenant in Israel and the Ancient Near East.* Pittsburgh: Biblical Colloquium, 1955.

Milgrom, Jacob. *Cult and Conscience.* Leiden: Brill, 1976.

_____. *Studies in Levitical Terminology,* I. Berkeley: University of California Press, 1970.

Moran, W. L. "The Literary Connection Between Lev 11:13–19 and Deut 14:12–28." *Catholic Biblical Quarterly* 28 (1966): 271–277.

Mowinckel, S. *Erwägungen zur Pentateuch Quellenfrage.* Trondheim: Universitetsforlaget, 1964.

Myers, Jacob M. *Ezra/Nehemiah, The Anchor Bible.* Garden City, N.Y.: Doubleday, 1965.

Nelson, Richard. *The Double Redaction of the Deuteronomistic History.* JSOT Supplement Series. Sheffield, 1981.

Nicholson, E.W. *Deuteronomy and Tradition.* Philadelphia: Fortress, 1967.

_____. *Preaching to the Exiles.* Oxford: Blackwell, 1970.

Noth, Martin. *Exodus.* Philadelphia: Westminster, 1962.

_____. *A History of Pentateuchal Traditions.* Englewood Cliffs, N.J.: Prentice-Hall, 1972. German edition, 1948.

_____. *The History of Israel.* New York: Harper and Row, 1960. German edition, 1958.

_____. *The Laws in the Pentateuch.* Edinburgh: Oliver and Boyd, 1966.

_____. *Leviticus.* Philadelphia: Westminster, 1965.

_____. *Numbers.* Philadelphia: Westminster, 1968.

_____. *The Old Testament World.* Philadelphia: Fortress, 1966. German edition, 1964.

_____. *Uberlieferungsgeschichtliche Studien.* Tubingen: Max Niemeyer Verlag, 1957. Original edition, 1943. Pp. 1–110 in English translation as *The Deuteronomistic History.* JSOT Supplement Series. Sheffield, 1981.

Perdue, L.G., and Kovacs, B.W., eds. *A Prophet to the Nations: Essays in Jeremiah Studies.* Winona Lake, Ind.: Eisenbrauns, 1984.

Polzin, Robert, *Late Biblical Hebrew: Toward an Historical Typology of Biblical Hebrew Prose.* Decatur, Ga.: Scholars Press, 1976.

Pritchard, James B., ed. *Ancient Near Eastern Texts Relating to the Old Testament,* 3rd ed. Princeton, 1969.

Propp, William H. "The Skin of Moses' Face—Transfigured or Disfigured?" *Catholic Biblical Quarterly,* 1987.

von Rad, Gerhard. *Deuteronomy: A Commentary.* London: SCM, 1966.

————. *Genesis.* Philadelphia: Westminster, 1961.

————. *Der Priesterschrift im Hexateuch* (Berlin: W. Kohlhammer, 1934).

————. *The Problem of the Hexateuch.* New York: McGraw-Hill, 1966.

Rendsburg, G. "Late Biblical Hebrew and the Date of P." *Journal of the Ancient Near East Society* 12 (1980): 65–80.

Rendtorff, Rolf. *Das überlieferungsgeschichtliche Problem des Pentateuch (Beihefte zur Zeitschrift für die alttestamentliche Wissenschaft* 147. Berlin/New York: Walter de Gruyter, 1977.

Rogerson, John. *Old Testament Criticism in the Nineteenth Century: England and Germany.* London: SPCK, 1984.

Rowley, H.H. *The Old Testament and Modern Study.* New York: Oxford, 1951.

Sarna, Nahum. "Hebrew and Bible Studies in Medieval Spain." *The Sephardic Heritage,* vol. 1. London: Vallentine, Mitchell, 1971.

van Seters, J. *Abraham in History and Tradition.* New Haven: Yale University Press, 1975.

Shiloh, Yigal. *Excavations at the City of David,* vol. 1. Jerusalem: Institute of Archeology, Hebrew University, 1984.

Speiser, E.A. *Genesis, The Anchor Bible.* Garden City, N.Y.: Doubleday, 1964.

Spinoza, Benedict. *Tractatus theologico-politicus.* 1670.

Tadmor, Hayim. "The Period of the First Temple, the Babylonian Exile and the Restoration." In H. H. Ben-Sasson, *A History of the Jewish People,* pp. 91–182. Cambridge, Mass.: Harvard University Press, 1976.

Thompson, R.J. *Moses and the Law in a Century of Criticism Since Graf. Vetus Testamentum Supplements* 19. Leiden: Brill, 1970.

Tsevat, Matitiahu. "Studies in the Book of Samuel, III." *Hebrew Union College Annual* 34 (1963): 71–82.

de Vaux, Roland. *Ancient Israel.* New York: McGraw-Hill, 1961.

Weinfeld, Moshe. "The Covenant of Grant in the Old Testament and in the Ancient Near East." *Journal of the American Oriental Society* 90 (1970): 184–203.

_____. *Deuteronomy and the Deuteronomic School.* New York: Oxford University Press, 1972.

_____. "Getting at the Roots of Wellhausen's Understanding of the Law of Israel on the 100th Anniversary of the *Prolegomena*." Report No. 14/79. Jerusalem: Institute for Advanced Studies, Hebrew University, 1979.

_____. "Jeremiah and the Spiritual Metamorphosis of Israel." *Zeitschrift für die alttestamentliche Wissenschaft* 88 (1976): 17–56.

Wellhausen, Julius. *Prolegomena zur Geschichte Israels.* Edinburgh, 1885. Reprinted, Gloucester, Mass., Peter Smith, 1973. German edition, 1883.

de Wette, W.M.L. *Dissertatio critica qua a prioribus Deuteronomium Pentateuchi libris diversam, alius cuiusdam recentioris auctoris opus esse monstratur.* 1805. Reprinted in *Opuscula Theologica.* Berlin, 1830.

Williamson, H.G.M. *Israel in the Books of Chronicles.* Cambridge University Press, 1977.

Wolff, Hans Walter. "Das Kerygma des deuteronomistischen Geschichtswerks." *Zeitschrift für die alttestamentliche Wissenschaft* 73 (1961): 171–86.

Wright, George Ernest, ed. *The Bible and the Ancient Near East.* Garden City: N.Y.: Doubleday, 1961.

_____. *Biblical Archeology.* Philadelphia: Westminster Press, 1962.

_____, *The Book of Deuteronomy, The Interpreter's Bible,* II:311–537. New York: Abingdon, 1953.

_____, and Fuller, R.H. *The Book of the Acts of God.* Garden City, N.Y.: Doubleday, 1957.

_____. "The Lawsuit of God: A Form-Critical Study of Deuteronomy 32." In B. Anderson and W. Harrelson, eds., *Israel's Prophetic Heritage.* New York: Harper, 1962.

_____. *The Old Testament Against Its Environment.* London: SCM, 1950.

Zevit, Ziony. "Converging Lines of Evidence Bearing on the Date of P." *Zeitschrift für die alttestamentliche Wissenschraft* 94 (1982): 502–09.

_____, "The Priestly Redaction and Interpretation of the Plague Narrative in Exodus." *Jewish Quarterly Review* 66 (1976): 193–211.

Acknowledgments

My research for this book was supported by a fellowship from the American Council of Learned Societies, with funds from the National Endowment for the Humanities. I am grateful for their support.

I pursued a portion of the research and writing in Oxford during a stay as a visiting scholar at the Oxford Centre for Hebrew Studies. I appreciate the many kindnesses shown to me during that stay by the President, Dr. David Patterson, and the Fellows and staff of the Oxford Centre, particularly Ms. Sally Arkley.

I am also grateful to the University of California, San Diego, for grants in support of this research.

My interest in this question began during my graduate years in the Departments of Old Testament and Near Eastern Languages and Civilizations at Harvard University. The passage of time has not diminished the tremendous feeling of indebtedness that I feel to my teachers there, beginning with G. Ernest Wright, of blessed memory, and including Frank Moore Cross, Thomas O. Lambdin, William L. Moran, Thorkild Jacobsen, and Paul Hanson. I must particularly acknowledge my debt to Professor Cross, who supervised my education, whose scholarship continues to be a model for me, and who has done me more kindnesses than I can hope to repay.

I am grateful to the distinguished archeologist Professor Nachman Avigad of the Hebrew University of Jerusalem for graciously providing me with the photograph of the bulla of Baruch ben Neriyah the scribe which appears in this book.

One of the strokes of good fortune in my life was my meeting Professor David Noel Freedman, who has done many acts of hesed for me and who, through example and wise counsel, has taught me much. I hold the man and his scholarship in great respect.

My debt to Baruch Halpern should be clear from the references to him in this book. There is no scholar of my generation whom I respect more. I believe that his contributions that I cite here are of considerable importance to our field, and I have learned more about historical method from him than from anyone else.

My colleague at the University of California, William Propp, is the ideal colleague. He is congenial, independent, a careful, original scholar, and a friend. I owe him thanks for comments and criticism that improved the book on several points.

One of the fine things that came about through this project was my acquaintance with Joann Ellison Rodgers, who helped me learn a new kind of writing and who supported and encouraged me and became my friend.

As indicated in the Preface, I determined some time ago to attempt to relate these findings in a manner that would be accessible to the general public as well as to scholars. My literary agent, Elaine Markson, showed confidence in this book and in this aim. Her particular mixture of professionalism and humanity are admirable and sincerely appreciated.

Arthur H. Samuelson, this book's Redactor, at Harper & Row, is an editor in the tradition of the Deuteronomist. Readers of this book will know that that is high praise. He has my professional respect and my personal gratitude.

Richard Elliott Friedman
December 1986

INDEX

Aaron, 40, 42, 124
  golden calf and, 29–30, 70–74,
    76, 78–79, 113
  Miriam and, 76–79, 124, 128,
    190, 208
  Moses and, 29–30, 70–74, 76,
    78–79, 113, 190–91
  priests as descendants of, 74, 76,
    120–21, 122, 124, 126, 155,
    157–58, 166–67, 211–12
Abel, 191, 227
Abiathar, 40, 42
  banishment of, 42, 44, 47–48, 72,
    121, 125–26, 211
Abihu, 192, 205
Abijam, King, 106, 115
Abiram, 193–96, 207, 228, 259
Abraham, 22, 50, 67, 81, 82, 83, 88,
    191
  cave purchased by, 206, 234–35
  God's covenant with, 22, 51, 62,
    80, 105, 228
  Isaac and, 205, 234, 256–57
Absalom, 41
Adam and Eve, 76, 191, 205, 225,
    227
Adonijah, 41–42
Ahab, King, 132
Aharoni, Yohanan, 183
Ahaz, 115
Ahijah of Shiloh, 48, 72, 105–6, 134
Ahikam, 99, 125
Akkadian language, 93
Amalekites, 66
Ammon, 34, 40
Amnon, 41

Amon, King, 96
Amorites, 34
Amos, 36
Anathoth, 42, 125–26
animals, "two-by-two," 55–56, 227–
    228
Aphrodite, 152
Arad, 183
Aramaic language, 35
Ararat, 57
archeology, 150
  evidence uncovered by, 39, 87, 91,
    92, 93, 147–48, 183
  modern developments in, 32
  revolution in, 29, 34
"argument from silence," 115
ark, 47, 75, 86, 129
  carrying poles for, 107
  disappearance of, 99, 155–56
  Temple placement of, 42, 43, 74,
    112, 156
  Ten Commandments contained in,
    37, 43
Artaxerxes, 159
Asa, King, 132
Asher, tribe of, 63
Asherah, 113, 140
Ashtoreth, 124, 152
Assyria, 49, 86–87, 93–98
  Babylonian conquest of, 98
  decline of, 97–98
  Israel conquered by, 49, 86–87,
    89–90, 96, 99, 121, 123, 135
  Judah dominated by, 89–90, 96
Astruc, Jean, 23, 26, 52
Avigad, Nachman, 147–48

Baal-Haddad, 151
Baal Peor, 202–3
Babylon, 96, 97, 98
Babylonia, 89–90
  Assyria conquered by, 98
  Jews exiled in, 98, 99, 150–55,
    143, 157
  Judah conquered by, 98–99, 103,
    106, 146, 151, 155
  Persian conquest of, 155, 158
  religion in, 151–52
Babylonian Talmud, 183
Baruch son of Neriyah, 146, 147, 209
  clay stamp of, 148
Bathsheba, 41, 110
"begats," lists of, 215, 218–19, 227
Benjamin, tribe of, 39, 45, 63
Beth-El, 22, 62, 71, 74, 76, 114
  high places of, 46–48, 72, 97,
    109–10, 113
  priests of, 120, 121
Biblical Archeologist, 183
biblical scholars, 24–27, 50–52
  American, 43
  Catholic, 19–21, 28, 243
  Christian, 18–21, 27–28, 243
  clerical, 15, 19–21, 27, 50, 243
  "Deuteronomistic school" theory of,
    145–46
  eighteenth century, 23, 52, 60
  forced recantations of, 20, 21
  Jewish, 18–19, 28, 243–44
  medieval, 18–19
  mistakes by, 161–73
  modern, 43, 103–4, 164–65
  moral and theological questions of,
    30
  multi-author hypothesis of, 79
  nineteenth-century, 24–27
  persecution of, 20, 21, 27
  separate biblical versions discovered
    by, 51–53
  tools and methods of, 29, 115,
    170–71
Blessing of Jacob, 64–65, 85, 258
Blessing of Moses, 260
Bonfils, Joseph ben Eliezer, 19, 243

Bonfrere, Jacques, 20
Book of Generations, 218–19, 227,
  230–31, 256
Booths, feast of, 222–23
bridal canopy, 186
British Museum, 93
"Bull El," 81
bulls, 47, 81–82
burning bush, story of, 81
"By the rivers of Babylon," 152–53

Cain, 191, 227
Caleb, 67, 205–6
Calebites, 67
Canaan, 151–52
Canaanite (Ugaritic) language, 35
Canaanites, 34, 47
Carlstadt, 19
cedars of Lebanon, 44
Chemosh, 124
Cheretites, 40
cherubs, *see* golden cherubs
Christianity, 107
  cosmic but personal deity of, 238
  Hebrew Bible and, 15, 143
  justice and mercy in, 240
  messiah tradition in, 39, 134, 143
Chronicles, books of, 75, 91, 97,
  109, 125, 132, 156, 185–86,
  211–13
circumcision, 62
City of David excavations, 39, 87, 95
clay stamps, 35, 148
Colenso, John, 27
Court History of David, 39, 41, 69,
  103, 130
Covenant Code, 259
covenant lawsuits, 168–70
covenants, 104–7, 141–43
  four major, 232
  see also Abraham; David
creation, 162
  two versions of, 50–51, 227, 236–
    237
Cross, Frank Moore, 31, 107–11,
  219–20, 230–31

Cushan, 78
Cyrus the Great, 155, 159

D (source document):
  Deuteronomy as, 24, 53, 117–35
  E compared with, 128
  identification of, 25
  middle stage of religious
    development in, 25
  other source documents compared
    with, 53
  prophets in, 128
  spiritual/ethical religious stage in,
    26
Dan, 46–48, 72, 76, 109, 114, 124
Dan, tribe of, 63
Daniel, 150
Daniel, book of, 150
Dathan, 193–96, 207, 228, 259
David, King, 47, 62, 86, 102, 130
  army established by, 40, 41
  children of, 41–42
  fall of kingdom of, 98, 106–7, 108,
    111, 135–36, 156
  God's covenant with, 105–7, 108,
    111, 115, 131–35, 141–43
  Judah/Israel unification under, 38–
    41
  marriage of, 40, 41, 110
  military successes of, 40, 42, 68
  political ascendancy of, 38–39, 89
  Psalms traditionally authored by, 15
  ruling dynasty established by, 39,
    83, 90–98, 105–7, 132, 156
  source material on, 38–39
Day of Atonement, 166, 172, 222
Dead Sea, 33
Dead Sea Scrolls, 13, 129–30, 229
Deborah, 130
de la Peyrère, Isaac, 20
"Deuteronomistic history," 104–10
  centralization of religion emphasized
    in, 115, 118, 122
  collaboration in, 147
  conquest and exile in, 137–42
  creation of, 130–32
  definition of, 104

  events and tradition combined in,
    134–35, 139
  first and second editions of, 107–8,
    110–11, 117, 136–37, 145–46
  importance of covenants in, 104–7,
    141–43
  life of King David in, 115
  literary style and structure in,
    130–32, 137–38
  possible authorship of, 146–49
  seven books in, 103–4, 111, 116–
    117
  worship of alien gods in, 139–40,
    143
"Deuteronomistic school" theory,
  145–47
Deuteronomy, book of, 17, 20–21,
  53, 101–21, 129
  book of Jeremiah compared with,
    126–27
  curses in, 144
  dating of, 101–2, 107–10
  "discovery" of, 101–2, 108, 112
  as farewell speech of Moses, 103,
    123, 207, 225, 229
  kings rated in, 104, 132
  as last book of Torah, 231
  law code of, 26, 30, 101,
    102,103–5, 108, 112, 114,
    117–21, 123
  origins of, 101–4, 108
  prophecy in, 109–10, 114
  "scroll of the *torah*" and, 101–2,
    112, 123
  significance of King Josiah in,
    108–16, 129
  six books of Early Prophets and,
    103–4, 111, 116–17
De Wette, W. M. L., 23, 26, 101–2,
  108, 165
Dinah, 62
Divino Afflante Spiritu encyclical,
  27–28
Documentary Hypothesis, 26–28, 60
doublets, 26, 162
  defined, 22
  examples of, 50–51, 188–89

E (source document):
  covenants in, 105
  D compared with, 128
  early religious development in, 25,
    162
  Exodus story in, 66, 79–80
  in first four books of Pentateuch, 53
  God/Elohim references in, 24,
    50–52, 81–82
  golden calf story in, 70–74, 82
  historical age of, 25, 163
  Israel central to, 61–63, 65, 67,
    162
  J combined with, 87–88
  Moses as hero in, 71–74, 79–80,
    128
  nature/fertility religious stage in, 26
  prophets in, 128
  religious practice criticized in,
    74–75
  Shechem acquisition in, 62–67
  Shiloh priest as author of, 79
  similarity of J to, 83–85
  Snow White Miriam story in,
    76–79
  Ten Commandments in, 139
  Tent of Meeting in, 75
Early Prophets, 103–4
Edom, 34, 40, 49, 87
  Babylonia allied with, 151, 153
  David's defeat of, 68
  Esau and, 68–69
  independence of, 68
  kings of, 18–19, 20
Egypt, 34, 44, 49, 89, 90, 98
  Assyria allied with, 98
  Babylonian invasion of, 153
  Israelites in, 35, 45, 46, 66, 82
  Judeans in, 99, 152–53
  land of milk and honey as, 196
  Persian conquest of, 155
  plagues inflicted upon, 219, 228,
    231
  slave labor in, 45, 66, 82
Eichhorn, Johann Gottfried, 23, 26,
  52

El, 35, 47
  see also Elohim
Elasah, 125
Eleazar, 203
Elephantine, 153, 154
Eliab, 193–94
Elohim, 24, 52, 61, 62–63, 81–82,
  219
Encyclopedia Britannica, 27
Ephraim, 63
Ephraim, territory of, 66, 73
Ephraim, tribe of, 63, 65, 66, 71, 74
Esau, 67–69, 87, 228
Ethiopia, 78
Exodus, 46, 66, 79–82, 103, 104,
  219, 230, 259
Exodus, book of, 17, 29, 45, 53, 73,
  81, 162, 164, 198–99
Ezekiel, 36, 100, 115, 154, 158
  covenant lawsuit of, 168–70
  prophecies of, 166–67, 168–70
Ezekiel, book of, 109, 152, 166–71
Ezra, 158–60, 218
  as redactor, 223–25, 232, 244
Ezra, book of, 156, 157, 159

Fall New Year, 166
fast days, 152
"First Bible, The," 231–32, 242
Five Books of Moses, see Pentateuch
flood, 51
  two versions of, 54–60, 191, 227,
    237
Fourth Book of Ezra, 224–25
Free Church of Scotland College, 27
Freedman, David Noel, 232

Gad, tribe of, 63
Garden of Eden, 76, 191, 217,
  235–36, 237
Gedaliah, 99, 125, 143
Gemariah, 125
Genesis, book of, 17, 76, 85, 86
  creation of the world in, 50–51
  great flood in, 54–60
  kings listed in, 18–19, 20

sources of, 53
writing styles in, 23–24
Gideon, 130
Girgashites, 34
God:
Abraham's covenant with, 22, 51,
62, 80, 105, 228
attributes of, 59–60, 196–97
biblical concepts of, 236–41
David's covenant with, 105–7,
108, 111, 115, 131–35, 141–43
"hiding the face" of, 139–40
humans created in image of,
235–36
names of, 22, 47, 50–51, 52,
61–62, 81–83
people's covenants with, 104–7,
141–43
golden calf, story of, 29–30, 70–74,
76, 78–79, 88, 113
golden calves, 47–48, 73–76, 97,
109, 113, 114, 124
golden cherubs, 43, 47, 73, 75, 76,
156, 163, 181–82
Gomorrah, 205, 237
Gospels, 53, 226
Graf, Karl Heinrich, 24–25, 26,
163–64, 165, 170, 173–75, 176
Gray, Edward M., 21
Greece, 151–52
guilt offering, 166, 172

Haddu, 35
Haggai, 156–57
Halpern, Baruch, 43, 44, 119,
120–21, 122–23, 126–28, 183,
212
Ham, 54, 56
Hamor, 62–63
Hampden, John, 21
Harvard Divinity School, 28
Harvard University, 31, 43, 107, 111,
119
Hebrew Bible, 18, 32, 38
as divinely inspired, 21, 243
editing and combining in, 19–20,

21, 23–24, 51, 87–88, 103,
160, 190, 216–18, 225–31
as history of people of Israel, 15,
103, 106
Judaism and, 15, 143
lawgivers in, 159, 223
literary merit of, 15, 215–16, 245
New Testament compared with, 53
oral composition theory of, 215
Hebrew language, 35, 87, 148
biblical, 29, 171, 215
written, 148
Hebrew Union College, 28
Hebrew University, 171
Hebron, 39, 40, 42, 62, 67, 83, 88,
206
Hezekiah, King, 91–98, 100, 108,
110, 115, 207–16
Assyrian domination resisted by,
91, 93
descendants of, 96–98, 140
relic destroyed by, 92, 126, 210
religious and political reform by,
91–92, 113, 114, 140, 210–11
water tunnel built by, 95
"Higher Criticism," 60
high places:
building of, 96, 98, 109, 114–15,
124, 140
definition of, 91
destruction of, 91, 97, 109–10,
113, 140
High Priests, 72, 121
as regents, 97
sacred objects used by, 157
Hilkiah:
Jeremiah as possible son of,
125–26, 146
"scroll of the *torah*" found by, 97,
99, 101–2, 108, 112, 123
Hiram of Tyre, King, 44, 47
Hittites, 34, 40
Hivites, 34
Hobbes, Thomas, 20, 26, 101, 108
holidays, religious, 26, 46, 166, 228
Holiness Code, 172, 214–15

Holy of Holies, 43, 76, 156, 181–82
Holy Scriptures, *see* Hebrew Bible
Horeb, 75, 80, 105, 128
Hosea, book of, 213
Hurvitz, Avi, 170–71

ibn Ezra, Abraham, 19
ibn Yashush, Isaac, 18–19
incense burning, 92, 109, 196
Index of Prohibited Books (Catholic), 20, 21
Isaac, 22, 67–68, 81, 82, 191
    near-sacrifice of, 205, 234, 256–57
Isaiah, 29, 100, 110
Isaiah, book of, 29, 91, 152, 213
Ishbaal, 38, 105
Ishtar, 151
Israel (modern), 40
Israel, kingdom of, 67
    Assyrian conquest of, 49, 86–87, 89–90, 96, 99, 121, 123, 135
    daily life in, 35
    Ephraim as name for, 65
    first king of, 37–38, 39
    history of kings of, 132
    Judah compared with, 89–90
    monarchic period in, 37
    political structure of, 37–38
    required labor in, 45, 66, 71
    tribes of, 36–41, 44–45, 49, 63–66
    women in, 86
Israelite religion, 35
    attempts to reconstruct, 25
    development of, 25, 26, 46–48
    judges in, 36–37
    nature and fertility in, 25
    politics and, 37–38, 46
    priests in, 36, 46–47
    symbols of faith in, 74–76
Israelites, 34–36
    Assyrian deportation of, 49, 86, 157
    daily life of, 35
    Egyptian captivity of, 35, 45, 46, 66, 82
    Exodus of, 46, 66, 79–82, 103,
        104, 219, 230, 259
    Judeans as kin to, 87
    political life of, 36
    prehistory of, 35
    return to Egypt of, 143–44
Israel Museum, 93, 148
Issachar, tribe of, 63
Izhar, 193

J (source document):
    anthropomorphic quality of, 59–60, 204–5
    conditions of period reflected in, 70
    covenants in, 105
    early religious development in, 25, 162
    E combined with, 87–88
    E compared with, 83–85
    Egyptian captivity of Israelites in, 66
    Esau/Edom story in, 68–69
    in first four books of Pentateuch, 53
    historical age of, 25, 163
    Judah central to, 61–63, 65, 67, 162
    nature/fertility religious stage in, 26
    Noah story in, 54–60
    patriarchs depicted in, 72
    rebellion story in, 193–96
    Shechem acquisition in, 62–67
    Ten Commandments in, 139
    Yahweh/Jehovah references in, 24, 51–52, 81–82
Jacob, 22, 50, 81, 82, 191
    deathbed blessing of, 64–65, 85, 258
    descendants of, 62–65
    Esau and, 67–69, 87, 228
Japheth, 54, 56
Jebusites, 34, 39
Jehoahaz, King, 98, 155
Jehoiachin, King, 98, 155
Jehoiakim, King, 98
Jehoram, King, 68, 87, 115
Jehoshaphat, King, 132
Jehovah, *see* Yahweh

Jeremiah, 100, 115
  character of, 149
  as Deuteronomist, 146–49,
    208–10
  difficulties of mission of, 149
  Egyptian exile of, 147, 158
  Lamentations traditionally authored
    by, 15
  as pro-Babylonian, 99, 158
  prophecies of, 146, 149, 167–69
Jeremiah, book of, 99, 109, 125
  authorship of, 147
  deportation of Jews in, 157
  Deuteronomy compared with,
    126–27
Jericho, 130
Jeroboam, King, 66, 81–82, 105–6,
    134
  golden calves of, 47, 97, 113, 114
  Israel ruled by, 45
  new religious centers established by,
    46, 109
  priests appointed by, 47–48,
    120–21
  Shechem built by, 62, 65, 71
Jerome, Saint, 101, 225
Jerome Biblical Commentary, 27–28
Jerusalem:
  Assyrian assault on, 93–96
  Babylonian destruction of, 98, 99,
    159
  David's capture of, 39–40
  dynastic succession of rulers in,
    91–98, 106, 133–34
  excavations in, 39, 87, 95
  Jebusite rule of, 39
  population growth in, 96
  rebuilding of, 159
  religion and politics centered in,
    40–41, 42, 46
  religious conflict in, 90
Jethro, 92
Jewish Theological Seminary, 28
Jews:
  Babylonian exile of, 150–55
  Egyptian exile of, 150–51, 153–54
  Israelites assimilated with, 87

  see also Judah, kingdom of
Joab, 42
Joash, King, 97
John, gospel of, 53
Jordan River, 20, 33
Joseph, 65, 73
  tomb of, 66, 71
Josephus, 183
Joshua, 19, 73, 130, 139
  death of, 131
  Moses assisted and succeeded by,
    66, 71, 103, 131
Joshua, book of, 66, 103, 112, 123,
    130–31
Josiah, King, 96–98, 100, 101–2,
    117, 123, 130
  Davidic covenant culminated in,
    135–36
  death of, 98, 125, 135–36
  importance of, 111–12, 114, 129
  kings of Israel and Judah compared
    with, 110, 114, 141
  Moses compared with, 111–14
  prophesied existence of, 109–10,
    114
  religious reform by, 97, 102,
    109–10, 113, 124
Judah, 63–65
Judah, kingdom of, 44–48, 49, 62,
    65–67
  Assyrian domination of, 89–90, 96
  Babylonian conquest of, 98–99,
    103, 106, 146, 155
  history of kings of, 132, 155
  Israel compared with, 89–90
  Israelites assimilated into, 87
  Persian conquest of, 155
  pro-Babylonian party in, 99, 158
  reign of King Hezekiah in, 91–97
  return of Jews to, 155–58
  size of, 89
Judah, tribe of, 38, 39, 40, 42, 44,
    63–64, 105, 133
Judaism, 21, 107
  cosmic but personal deity of, 238
  Hebrew Bible and, 15, 143
  justice and mercy in, 240

Judaism (cont.)
　messiah tradition in, 39, 134, 143
　weddings in, 186
judges, 73
　functions of, 36
Judges, book of, 103, 123, 130–31

Kennedy, John F., 136–37
Kings, books of, 75, 96, 102, 113,
　　131–32, 135, 156
　first book of, 73, 103, 107, 109,
　　115, 130
　second book of, 91, 92, 95, 99,
　　103, 108, 109, 113, 115, 130,
　　155
Kohath, 193
Korah, 193–96, 207, 210, 228, 259

Lachish, 93
Lamentations, book of, 152, 185–86
　Jeremiah as traditional author of,
　　15
languages:
　analysis of, 29, 170–71
　Semitic, 35
　written, 35, 148
　see also specific languages
Last Trial, The (Spiegel), 257
Law of the King, 112, 118, 119
laws:
　Deuteronomic, 26, 30, 101, 102,
　　103–5, 108, 112, 114, 117–21,
　　123
　dietary, 91–92, 118
　Ezra and Moses as givers of, 159
　sacrificial, 91–92, 118
　war, 30, 119–20
　on women, 30, 119
lentil stew, red, 67–68
leprosy, 77–78, 208
Levi, 36, 62–64, 128, 193
Levites, 47–48, 71–73, 118, 122,
　　123
　Egyptian names of, 82
　as official priests, 36, 82, 85–86,
　　120–21
　secondary position of, 128, 158

Leviticus, book of, 17, 53, 162, 171,
　　185–86
linguistic analysis, 29, 170–71
Lot, 189
Luke, gospel of, 53
Luther, Martin, 19

Machpelah, 206, 234
Manasseh, 63, 65
Manasseh, King, 96, 113, 115,
　　140–41, 143
Marduk, 151
Mark, gospel of, 53
Masada, 93
Matthew, gospel of, 53
Megiddo, 98
Meribah, 198, 205, 228, 237
Mesopotamia, 22, 34, 89, 157
messiah, 39, 134, 143
Micah, book of, 213
Michelangelo, 201
Midian, 78, 92
Midianites, 17–18, 78, 92, 203–4,
　　228
Milcom, 124
Miriam, 76–79, 124, 128, 190, 208
missîm, 45, 66, 71
Moab, 34, 40, 49, 105
Moabite language, 35
Moabites, 17, 228
monotheism, 152, 160
　guilt and, 154
Moses:
　Aaron and, 29–30, 70–74, 76,
　　78–79, 113, 190–91
　bronze snake and, 92, 126, 211
　burning bush and, 81
　Cushite wife of, 76–78
　death of, 18, 20, 103, 123, 139,
　　231
　descendants of, 37, 40, 42, 48,
　　129, 155
　farewell addresss of, 103, 123, 207,
　　225, 229
　golden calf destroyed by, 29–30,
　　76, 82
　horns of, 201–2

humility of, 18, 20–21
King Josiah compared with, 111–14
leadership of, 71–72, 79–80, 103
name of Yahweh revealed to, 81–82
Pentateuch traditionally authored by, 15, 17–22, 53, 60, 101–3
personality of, 79–80, 128
as prophet, 18, 21, 78, 111
rebellion against, 192–96
Tabernacle built by, 18, 163, 164
tablets of Ten Commandments smashed by, 29, 71, 73–74
Ten Commandments given to, 29, 70
third-person accounts of, 19, 20
torah of, 131, 159–60, 167
veil of, 201–2, 216
water produced from rock by, 189, 198–201, 205, 228, 237
Mount Ebal, 131
Mount Sinai, 74, 105, 128, 164, 174–75, 190, 201, 220, 237
Mowinckel, Sigmund, 189
Mushites, 155

nābî', 36
Nachmanides, 18
Nachshon ben Amminadab, 213
Nadab, 192, 205
Naphtali, tribe of, 63
Nathan, 41
Near Eastern Languages and Civilization Department (Harvard), 31, 111, 119
Nebat, 109
Nebuchadnezzar, King, 98–99, 125
Negev desert, 67
Nehemiah, 159
Nehemiah, book of, 156, 159, 222
Nehushta, 126
Nehushtan, 126, 210–11
New Testament, 53, 226, 232
Nineveh, 34, 93–94
Noah, 53, 191

ark of, 51, 54–60, 191
two versions of story of, 54–60
Noth, Martin, 103–4, 106
Numbers, book of, 17, 53, 75, 76–78, 79, 162, 171, 199–201

Obadiah, book of, 29
Old Testament, *see* Hebrew Bible
Origen, 18

P (source document), 162–73
as alternative to earlier versions, 190–92, 215–16, 220
authorship of, 188–89, 206–16
blessings and curses in, 168–69
creation story in, 162
in first four books of Pentateuch, 53
Moses diminished in, 197–98, 209, 215
Noah story in, 54–60, 162
priestly and legal references of, 24, 52–53, 162
rebellion story in, 193–96, 220
relative size of, 162
spy story in, 205–8
Tabernacle described in, 163–64
Paddan Aram, 257
pagan religions, 34–35
compatibility of, 151–52
gods and goddesses of, 35, 113, 124, 140, 151–52
nature and fertility in, 35
prohibitions against, 118, 139–40
statues in, 35, 96, 113, 140
papyrus scrolls, 35, 148
Passover, 222
Peleth, 193
Peletites, 40
Peni-El, 62
Pentateuch:
combinations in, 87–88, 160
conclusions denying Mosaic authorship of, 19–21, 23, 25, 60, 101, 102, 241
contradictions in, 17–18, 19–21, 23, 51, 53, 107

Pentateuch *(cont.)*
  editing of, 19–20, 21, 23–24, 51,
    87–88, 103
  Ezra and, 159–60
  laws of, 21, 24, 25
  as link with past, 160
  Moses as traditional author of, 15,
    17–22, 53, 60, 103
  sources of, 22–25, 52–53
  stages in investigation of, 18–21,
    23–24, 50–53
  writing styles in, 19, 23, 52–53,
    113, 137–38
Penuel, 71, 74, 205
Peor, 202–3, 228
Pereira, Benedict, 20
Perizzites, 34
Persian empire, 155, 158, 159
Pharaoh, 80, 219, 230
Philistines, 34, 37, 38, 91
Phinehas, 203–4, 225
Phoenicia, 40, 49
Phoenician language, 35
Phoenicians, 34, 44, 72
"pious fraud" cases, 102, 119, 134,
    164, 175, 209
Pius XII, Pope, 27–28
poisonous snakes, 92
priests, 36–37, 40, 47–48, 52–53
  Aaronid, 74, 76, 120–21, 122,
    124, 126, 155, 157–58, 166–67,
    211–12
  chief, 40, 46
  Levite, 36, 82, 85–86, 118,
    120–22, 128, 158
  Midianite, 92
  modern rabbis compared with, 40
  Mushite, 129, 155, 157–58
  political authority of, 37, 40, 159–
    160
  rival, 155, 158, 197
  sacrifices performed by, 36, 196–97
  Shiloh, 38, 40, 47–48, 72, 74,
    120, 122–24, 129–30
  Temple, 42, 97, 102, 121, 157–58
  see also High Priests
Primary History, 232

Princeton Theological Seminary, 28
Prism Inscription of Sennacherib,
    93–95
promised land, 75, 157–58
prophets, 128
  biblical scribes as, 21
  community functions of, 36
  decline of age of, 156–57
  definition of, 36
  false, 118
  kings designated by, 37, 118
  poetry and prose messages of, 36
  scribes as, 21
Propp, William H., 201–2
Protestantism, 21
Proverbs, book of, 213
Psalm 27, 184
Psalm 137, 152–53, 154
Psalms:
  David as traditional author of, 15
  Davidic covenant tradition in, 134
Pseudepigrapha, 224
Pythagoreans, 145–46

Qumran archives, 129–30

Rameses, 230
Rashi, 18
ravens, 227, 228
Rebekah, 67–68
redactor, 60–61, 218–19, 229–31,
    232–33, 234–35
Red Sea, parting of, 220
Rehoboam, King, 45–46, 105–6, 115
Reuben, 63–65, 193, 196
Reuss, Eduard, 162–63, 165, 167,
    170, 173
Roman Catholic Church:
  biblical investigation encouraged
    by, 27
  biblical investigation repressed by,
    20–21, 27

Sabbath observance, 159, 229
sacrifice, 221–23
  animals as, 91, 118
  at decentralized altars, 91, 102

laws concerning, 91–92, 118
Temple, 46, 91–92, 97, 102, 135
tithing of, 82, 92, 120
Samaritans, 151
Samson, 130
Samuel, 74, 102, 103, 122
as priest, prophet and judge, 37, 47, 126
Saul and, 37–38, 47
speeches of, 131
Samuel, books of, 102, 103, 113, 115
first book of, 38, 130–31
second book of, 39, 105, 130–31, 133
Sarah, 22, 234–35
Saul, 47, 102, 105, 130
David as rival of, 38
as first king of Israel, 37–38, 39
priests massacred by, 38, 40
scribes, 21, 86, 129, 147–48, 223
"scroll of the *torah*," 97, 99, 101–2, 108, 112, 123, 125
Sea of Galilee, 33
šekem, 65–66
Sennacherib, 93–95
Shaphan, 97, 99, 125
Shechem, 62–63
Shechem (city), 45, 71, 73, 74
as capital of Israel, 46, 62–63, 65, 66
origin of name of, 65–66
people massacred in, 63, 64, 128
two versions of acquisition of, 62–67
Shem, 54, 56
Sheshbazzar, 156, 158
Shiloh, 37, 75, 79, 120
priests expelled from, 47–48, 72
priests massacred in, 38, 40
as religious center, 122
Simeon, 62–65
Simeon, tribe of, 63, 86
Simon, Richard, 21, 22
Sinai wilderness, 35, 46, 75, 82, 83, 88, 128
sin offering, 166, 172
Smith, William Robertson, 27

Snow White Miriam, 76–79, 124, 128, 190, 208
Sodom, 205, 237
Solomon, King, 102, 121, 125
ascendancy of, 41–42
building projects of, 42–44, 82
David and Bathsheba as parents of, 41
death of, 45
marriages of, 42, 66
northern tribes alienated by, 44
offenses of, 105, 124, 135
priests expelled by, 47–48, 72
reign of, 43, 47–48, 66, 72, 86, 89, 115
Temple built by, 42–44, 75, 139, 142, 156
territorial redistribution by, 44–45
wealth of, 42
wisdom of, 42
source documents:
combinations of, 53, 87–88, 190, 216–18, 225–31
final work assembled from, 221–45
groups vs. individuals as authors of, 85
history tied to, 26
similarities in, 83–85
time dating of, 86–87
see also D; E; J; P
Spiegel, S., 257
Spinoza, Benedict, 19–20, 26
Judaic excommunication of, 21
statues:
laws against making of, 74–75, 113
molten, 47, 72–76, 87, 113
pagan, 96, 113
Sukkot, 222–23
Syria, 34, 40, 44, 49

Tabernacle, 47, 163–66
Arad temple and, 183
ark contained in, 37, 75, 163, 164, 175
Moses as builder of, 18, 163, 164
proportions of, 164, 175–81

Tabernacle *(cont.)*
  second Temple compared with, 175–87
  as symbol of second Temple, 164–66, 187
Talmud, 147, 185–86
Tamar, 41, 86
Temple (Elephantine), 154, 160
Temple (second), 221–23
  Aaronid priesthood in, 157–58
  ark missing from, 155–56, 157
  building of, 155–57
  description of, 157
  religion centralized in, 160
  religious implements in, 156
Temple of Solomon, 46, 74
  ark as central object in, 43, 75, 107
  Babylonian destruction of, 99, 107, 154
  cherubs in, 43, 76, 181–82
  descriptions of, 42–43, 181–82
  pagan statues in, 96, 113, 140
  religion centralized in, 91–92, 97, 102, 121, 135
  religious implements in, 121
  sacrificial ritual in, 43, 46, 91–92, 97, 102, 135
  Solomon's construction of, 42–44, 75, 139, 142, 156
  Tabernacle contained in, 182–87
  two rooms of, 43, 181–82
Temple Scroll, 130
Ten Commandments, 43, 156
  conflicting versions of, 53, 228–29, 258–59
  first of, 139
  Moses and, 29, 70–71, 73–74, 113, 228
ten lost tribes of Israel, 49
Tent of Meeting, 66, 75, 171, 183
  see also Tabernacle
Thummin, 157, 163, 175
Torah, *see* Pentateuch
torah of Moses, 131, 159–60, 167
Tostatus, 19
trade routes, 89

travel routes, 34
tree of knowledge, 235
tribes, 36
  leaders of, 37
  lost, 49
  merged, 63
  northern, 44–45
  origins of, 63–65
  political aspects of, 37
  rulers' and prophets' relations with, 37–38
  thirteen, 36–37, 39–40
  troops mustered by, 37, 40, 41
  unification of, 40
triplets, 23
Twain, Mark, 236

Ugarit, 34
Urim, 157, 163, 175

van Maes, Andreas, 19–20, 244
Vatke, Wilhelm, 25–26

Wadi Eshkol, 67
Warren's Shaft, 39
Washington, George, 136
Weeks, feast of, 222
Wellhausen, Julius, 25–27, 29, 170–77, 209, 243
  model of study created by, 26–27
  scholarship components synthesized by, 26, 164–67
Witter, Henning Bernhard, 23, 52
women:
  laws concerning, 30, 119
  Moabite, 202–4
  noble class of, 86
  prophets as, 36
  seduction by, 202–4, 228
Wright, G. Ernest, 111

Yadin, Yigael, 130
Yahweh:
  anger of, 77–78, 139–40

attributes of, 35, 152, 154, 191,
236–41
El and, 47, 61–62, 81–82
mercy of, 144–45
name of, 22, 51, 52, 59, 61–62,
63, 81–83
throne of, 43, 47, 81, 82
"Yahweh's House," 184
Yale Divinity School, 28

Zadok, 40–41, 42, 62, 72, 121, 166,
211
Zebulon, tribe of, 63
Zechariah, 156–57
Zedekiah, King, 98, 106, 155
Zerubbabel, 156–57, 158
Zeus, 151
Zipporah, 78, 92

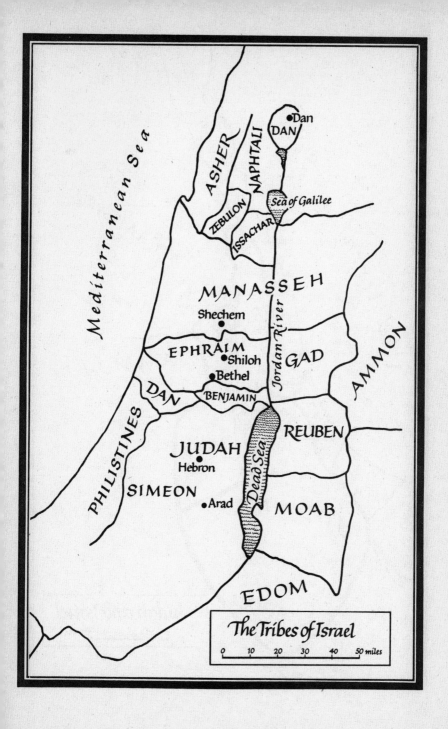

The Tribes of Israel

0 10 20 30 40 50 miles

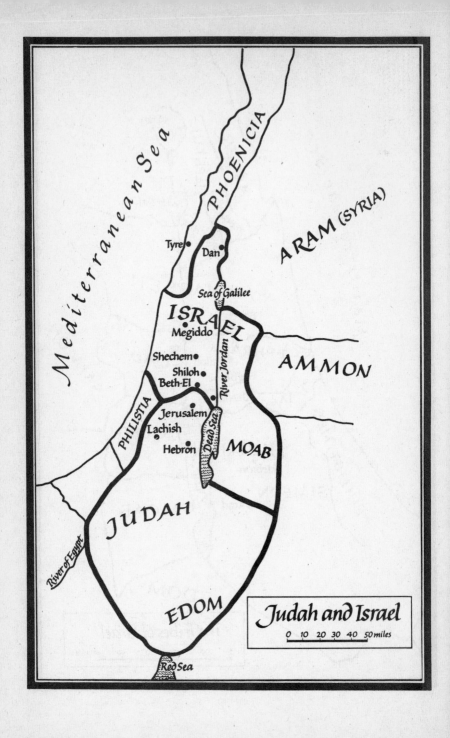

Judah and Israel

0 10 20 30 40 50 miles

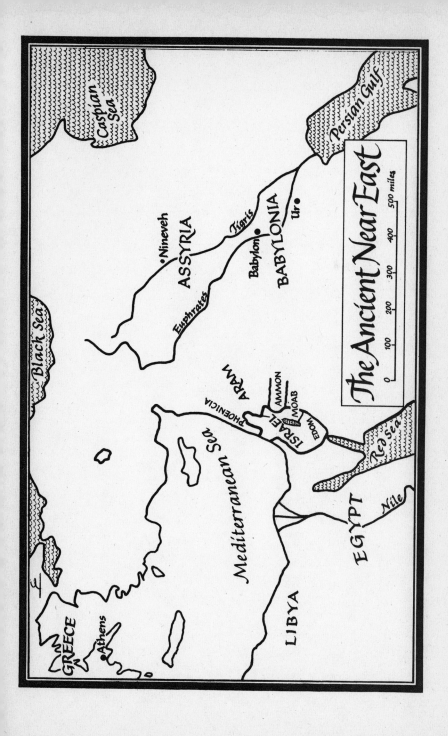

The Ancient Near East

0   100   200   300   400   500 miles

Caspian Sea

Persian Gulf

Black Sea

•Nineveh

ASSYRIA

Tigris

Babylon•

BABYLONIA

Ur•

Euphrates

ARAM

PHOENICIA

ISRAEL

AMMON

MOAB

EDOM

Red Sea

Mediterranean Sea

EGYPT

Nile

LIBYA

GREECE

•Athens